Mi Mathematics
Numerical synchronicities from my Entity experience

Larry Dale

Mi Mathematics
Numerical Synchronicities from my Entity Experience

Copyright © 2008 Larry Dale

Type Font: Times New Roman size 12
Language – English (U.S.A)
Printed and bound in the United Sates of America by
BookSurge, Publishing, ☎ 1-866-308-6235

ISBN 10: 1-4196-8017-X
ISBN 13: 9781419680175

To order additional copies visit
www.booksuge.com
amazon.com, amazon.co.uk

Cover design by Larry Dale

Previous title by Larry Dale
Mi: My Entity experience

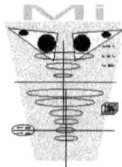

ISBN 1-4196-4484-X

A Future title 'GeoMitry' will complete the trilogy

Not knowing how close the truth is we often search for it far from home.

Let the mind be still and calm – the light of truth will come to you.

I dedicate this book to all those witnesses of strange phenomena, for whom life has been changed forever. To those who search for the truth.

Contents

I

Contents

Contents

Mi Mathematics
Preface

In the first book, Mi, about my entity experience I omitted many of the numerically related details because a mixed work might not appeal to the 'general public'. It was suggested to me that such a book would 'fall between two camps' and therefore might be ignored by both. Since my main aim was to make the 'general public' aware of my experience I opted for the alternative to omit all but the most essential numerical material. For example, the simultaneous equations given to Mi were, to my mind, an important part of the experience. Mi's answer to these gave some idea of the way in which the entity did calculations – bearing in mind my limited ability to interpret such methods. I also believed it was essential to inform the reader about the various directions that Norman Oliver and I had taken during our researches. Hence, in the form of just basic arithmetic, I felt some numerical examples were necessary. However, ideas relating to deeper mathematical analysis were omitted. Therefore this volume is not self-contained and reading the Mi book is a prerequisite.

The Mi book was best described in Norman Oliver's 'Foreword' as being about Synchronicity, though I maintained the use of the word 'coincidence' throughout. In the early parts of this volume the term 'coincidence' might still be more appropriate, but when the number of these colligations increases page by page, the term 'coincidence' does not really relate to the way in which this volume is written. In addition, most of the latter parts of this volume relate to temporal, spatial and electromagnetic ideas and as such qualify as being synchronicities. Using both 'coincidence' and 'synchronicity', alternating between one and the other, I thought would be confusing and so in this work I use the term 'synchronicity', only using 'coincidence' where grammar dictates.

This volume is aimed at the 'mathematically inclined layperson', though having said that, it is not aimed at the mathematician. Apart from one or two occasions, there are no rigorous derivations or 'proofs'. Throughout this work the idea has been to *use* mathematical procedures on the ideas given in the Mi book, thereby revealing a deeper synchronistic structure.

i

Mi Mathematics
Preface

Mi Mathematics is composed of six parts without chapters, with each Part containing sections. Parts 1 and 2 are really the 'preliminaries' because they describe the early synchronicities and their source.

Early in Part 1 for example, there is a brief inclusion of a Fibonacci sequence that was not mentioned, specifically, in the Mi book. What I had tried to convey there was that a sequence of some kind is present in the material, hoping that the reader would be prompted to perform some investigation of their own. Indeed, Norman himself suggests such an idea at the end of his Chapter 5 "....AND A FEW MORE....".

Considerable work includes name counts, whereby the synchronicities appear in such numbers that not all of them are in the main text – some are just listed in "NOTES". In finding the repeated synchronicities I was sure to follow a certain path leading to the conclusions of Part 5.

Parts 3, 4 and 5 focus on forming a framework based on the synchronicities, thereby providing an interpretation of Mi's ideas about Time – hence my GATE equations.

Norman's introduction of Enki turned out to be so involved with the synchronicities that I thought to include further items of an historical nature at the end of Part 1. Even here there are some *peculiar* synchronicities and I felt inclined to consider going to one of the actual ancient sites of interest. However, current problems in the Middle East make such a journey unlikely and in any case some sites have probably been demolished. One interesting thought arises from this idea. Apparently in the Philadelphia Museum, USA, there are many pieces from ancient Sumer, Philadelphia being the area of concern during experiments aboard the USS Eldridge, so perhaps I should go there instead. (What did I just say about the number of synchronicities? I think that I have just found another one!) Be that as it may, for the present this historical addition does raise an important question, one that you may have already considered.

Mi Mathematics
Preface

The title 'Mi Mathematics' is intended to be what it seems – a contradiction – because Mi stated that Mi life did not use numbers. 'Geo-Mi-try' might be another description, which would be more about shapes than numbers and represents another approach. Therefore, this book is neither exhaustive in content or approach and indeed, there are some synchronicities that are not presented here because they represent other such approaches.

A little by way of explanation about the cover design. On the bottom left of the front cover there are some musical signs that represent Norman's Chimes experience. The musical clef is there to represent the drawing that I made and the shirt design as mentioned in my first book, Mi. My symbol for the resulting Chimes Expression, ^eC, can been seen in the background. On the bottom right is a diagrammatic representation of both early (top) and later (bottom) Sumerian numerals, both of these being equal to Tridel 1, $^{\equiv}\partial$, which is pictured in the background. The color of the front cover, fire-like red and yellow, has a couple of meanings for me but perhaps the important one here is that 'fire and Sun' represent the desire to make progress, representing my need to understand the meaning of the Mi encounter. The back cover color simply represents darkness receding as light begins to shine through and is related to the words on the Dedication page. Other items are examples from the main text.

The writing of any book requires a motivation of some kind, whether it is artistic, biographical, study etc. and usually fulfils an expression. My motivation is twofold. Firstly, and perhaps obvious, this present volume is as an extension of the first book, which I personally thought of as being incomplete. Secondly, and more importantly, I do feel very much for those people who have had an experience that has affected and changed their lives. Such explanations as '...a weather balloon...', '...a trick of the light...' and so on might apply to many 'sightings' but these are unlikely to affect one's life in the extreme: others create such mental turmoil that hospital treatment becomes necessary. Incidents producing the latter cannot be explained easily, if at all, and the witness (victim if you prefer) is left with a 'blank' in their life. Researchers of the paranormal then become the only people who may provide some answers, and some comfort. This book is about *my* search for those answers – and why I am spending my time searching. Whatever one's opinion about my experience, the synchronicities in this book require an answer to the question as to why they are there in the first place.

In conclusion, this book is my attempt to interpret the ideas of Mi, although as Norman Oliver quite rightly pointed out in the Mi book, we should not consider Mi as being any less fallible than ourselves or any other species. This makes any interpretation by me at least equally fallible. In the end it is the synchronicities themselves that, existing in their own right, really require an interpretation as to what *they mean*. Indeed, on some occasions I give more than one possible interpretation myself but overall one can see my general trend. It is my opinion that the equations herein represent some kind of 'parallel' to actual situations that may be far more complicated in reality. My claim, If I were asked, would be no more substantial than this.

I would like to take this opportunity to thank the staff at BookSurge, Kelly Martin and Lindsey Usher in particular, for their help and encouragement in my 'self publishing' venture.

I especially want to thank Norman Oliver for allowing me to use material from his own studies, including personal details. Norman also read an early manuscript and offered advice regarding various items but, although the basic structure remains the same, the final manuscript differs from the one that he read due to additions and alterations. Thanks also to my wife, Ratanaporn, for her assistance with the Spinorial Object photographs.

Then, of course, there is the Mi entity; Mi, you will remain in my thoughts every day for the rest of my life.

L. Dale F.R.A.S.
April 2008

Mi Mathematics
Prologue

This is not a book about mathematics and as such has some important consequences.

There is no need for a strict logical layout concerning the level of mathematics used at any given point and that 'studying' one part does not mean its repetition is unnecessary later. Indeed, in several instances, certain computations are repeated avoiding the need to refer to previous pages. However, this cannot be maintained throughout and there are some back-references. This format of repeated computations may seem a little tedious but I feel there is enough inherent mystery already without my adding some inconvenience.

However, the presentation does have a basic structure, passing from the simple synchronicities to the more detailed investigation of how the synchronicities might be used and what they could mean. In short, the 'original' synchronicities → 'ordinary' synchronicities → 'mathematical' synchronicities: from the 'original' and 'ordinary' synchronicities → Interpretation.

Interpretations, such as they are, bring me to an important point. Much of mathematical physics require dimensions of length, speed etc. and most scientists today use the SI system, or Metric System, of measurement – meter-kilogram-second (m.k.s.) or derivatives thereof (cm.g.s.). However, we could not say that the Imperial System of measurement, feet-pounds-second system, has been completely replaced by the Metric System – it hasn't, as people living in the United Kingdom and the United States of America well know. Certain numbers being synchronistic with one system of measurement might not be so with the other.

Let me illustrate my point with an example. Some time ago I looked at one researcher's figures concerning musical notes, geometrical figures and various land features. The researcher claims synchronicities are present while using one system of measurement for one item but a different system for another item. For example, a frequency in Hertz compared to the number of feet in a mile is not really consistent. Hertz is a SI unit of measurement; the Mile an Imperial unit. A skeptic would criticize synchronicities based on this inconsistency thereby refuting any theory produced from the mixed systems. As for the 'Mi experience study', 5280 feet divided by 180° is exactly 8 × Tridel 1, but the answer for 1609 meters is 8.938888. This number is not coincidental in this work and so not a true synchronicity as far as Tridel is concerned. Therefore, in this study I have avoided such 'half' or 'pseudo-synchronicities' and any that I have found have not been included. Having said that, the units of Earth Years, Days, Hours, Minutes and Seconds are used throughout, being *our* universal notation for both the scientific and lay communities. There is one set of derivations that become dependent on the number 343 which does have the dimensions of meters in the source formula, but applied substitution then deletes the dimensions of meters.

The main base numbers in this study may give rise to a frown or two – letter count numbers, which might have the dimensions of the English alphabet. However, an integer is convertible into a letter of the alphabet, but numbers involving fractions generally, are not. Therefore, many numbers in this book are construed as being synchronistic with the line of investigation being pursued without reference to dimensions. The universal constant, π, results in a important synchronicity in this regard and is considered in the appropriate section, while the question of name counts is revisited in the final part.

Up to and including Part 2 much of the mathematics is straightforward and uncomplicated. The second set of three simultaneous equations given to Mi are solved by various methods simply because if the reader is not acquainted with one method, then one of the others might be more familiar. In short, I have assumed that, like me, you are not a mathematician but an interested layperson. If you are mathematically qualified then you will probably find the repetition unnecessary.

In Part 3 however, the mathematics become a little more sophisticated, or perhaps unfamiliar, though not complicated. One of the problems in learning mathematics, particularly in England, is that the subject was divided into two types, 'Traditional' and

Mi Mathematics
Prologue

'Modern'. Up to around the late 1950's, pupils studied what was known as the three R's, 'Reading' '(W)Riting' and '(A)Rithmetic'. The third of these usually consisted of basic Algebra, Geometry and a little Trigonometry. If you were lucky (as I was) you might have been taken aside and given a very (very) brief introduction to Finite Increments as a prelude to very basic operations of Calculus.

After this time the 'Modern' variety was introduced and one could choose which type to study. Modern Mathematics, as it was called, differed in many ways. Some topics that were previously taught at more advanced levels, such as Elementary Logic, Set theory and an introduction to 2×2 Matrix theory, replaced certain topics in the Traditional mathematics and were taught at the Secondary level. At some point later the two would join. How many parents of my generation scratched their heads when their children said, "I'm confused about the difference between $A \subseteq B$ and $a \in B$?" Fortunately, I had already studied these topics, but I am sure that many of us actually ended up sitting down with our children and learning something new from the children's homework material.

Matrix theory proved to be such a powerful mathematical tool that it is now taught extensively, and the language of Set Theory is used to define what and where, in a previously defined number category, a particular item is. If you are unacquainted with Set Theory, why not take a trip to your local library where you will probably find a large selection of books on the subject.

Simplification of mathematical expressions has not been rigorously followed in this book. For example, expressions such as $(^{(124+90)}\!/_2)^{-1} \times 24 \times 60$ (see page 72) should conventionally be written as $(^2\!/_{124+90}) \times 24 \times 60$, eliminating negatives when it is possible to do so. Another example concerns equations with the radical sign and the radicand with exponents >1. Among the rules for simplifying this type of equation is that the exponents of the radicand should have no factors in common with the index of the radical sign and that exponents should be reduced to lower values where possible. The example below (from page 175) is simplified showing the various steps to complete simplification. The final figure of $e^{1.3}$ gives no hint of its derivation: -

$$\sqrt[4]{e^{22+(-2.8\times6)}} = \sqrt[4]{\left(e^{16}\right)}\sqrt[4]{e^{6}}\sqrt[4]{e^{(-2.8\times6)}} = e^{4}\sqrt[4]{\left(e^{3}\right)^{2}}\sqrt[4]{e^{(-2.8\times6)}}$$

$$= e^{4}\sqrt{e^{3}}\sqrt[4]{e^{(-2.8\times6)}} = e^{5.5}\sqrt[4]{\left(e^{(-2.8)}\right)^{6}} = e^{5.5}\sqrt{\left(e^{(-2.8)}\right)^{3}}$$

$$= e^{5.5}e^{-4.2} = e^{1.3} = 3.669296668 \approx {}^{\equiv}\partial$$

Throughout I have tried to preserve the origin of the numbers.

The mathematical topics used in this book include Algebra, Linear Algebra and Matrix calculations, and to a much lesser extent, Calculus, Tensors and Spinors, none of which are at an advanced level. Any standard formulae used are mentioned by name so that the reader can check in standard texts. However, no deliberate attempt has been made to form a structured mathematical model of Mi's ideas as this will be discussed in the next publication.

If the reader has read the Mi book then the absence of one very important topic will be obvious, Mi's answer to the two simultaneous equations. Since these were similar to geometrical constructions they will be discussed in the third book 'GeoMitry'.

Finally, a word about the writing of the equations. The keyboard hyphen and minus sign, '-', are indistinguishable from one another when printing, so I have <u>elevated</u> the minus sign in a text line by one point, the difference being '-' & '‑': this is used for 'in-line equations'. Separate numbered 'display' equations have been written using the MathType 5 program where the minus sign is similar to the MS Word Endash '–'. In this book I have chosen not to use the MathType 5 program for 'in-line equations'.

If you would like to contact me the e-mail address is mimath224@hotmail.com, which is for 'Mi matters' / strange encounters only.

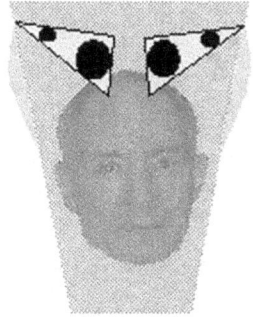

The encounter with Mi now surrounds my life

Mi Mathematics

Book 1 Page 1-15
Summary of the Mi Entity Experience

Book 2 Page 16-243
Numerical Synchronicities

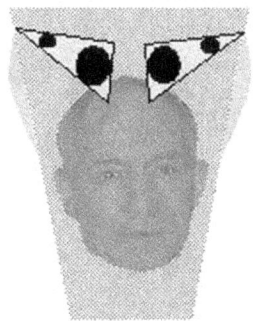

Summary of the Mi Entity experience

One evening during the first half of August 1978, the children in bed, I was sitting in my usual place close to the lounge door. My wife would have been sitting on the opposite side facing the TV set. We were watching the program that came before the late evening News when, without saying anything, I got up and went upstairs. On returning just a few moments later I again said nothing and returned to the chair. After a few seconds I did a repeat performance, only this time on returning to the lounge, I made a body gesture indicating some confusion. I told my wife that I could hear one of the children crying, but that on reaching the top of the stairs the crying had stopped, so I returned to the lounge. My wife remarked that she did not hear anything.

On hearing the crying again I walked slowly up the stairs, where I found that the crying was at a maximum about halfway. As I moved upward the sound decreased. The crying sound was not a full cry but more of a lengthy sobbing, and I heard this again a few times in the coming weeks until the latter half of September.

My wife was a Nursing Assistant at a Terminal ward and after returning home from an evening shift at about 11.30-midnight, she found that the children and I were in bed. However, during the early hours I felt that I had to go downstairs. I slowly opened the living room door and turned on one of the lights. In front of the TV set to the left and diagonally opposite, was a full size, transparent image of my father. His eyes were bulging as when angry but there was no movement or sound. I could see the TV and the wall behind quite clearly through the image but as I made a step towards the image it immediately disappeared. Before going to work, I checked the living room, and on the TV set was a potted plant, which had not been there the night before. Nor had I seen it when I saw the transparent image of my father. My wife told me that one of the patients she had been nursing died during her shift and the potted plant had belonged to the patient. The date, 12th of August.

I had previously become a member of the British UFO Research Association and it was during this time that I worked closely with Norman Oliver. Although I left BUFORA Norman

Summary of the Mi Entity experience

and I kept in touch and it was during the latter part of 1993 that the first of the 'coincidences' occurred. On returning home from Tae Kwon Do training I was in the house alone. After a meditation session and feeling very uneasy, I said 'Mum, tell me what to do'. A few days later I received a letter from Norman suggesting that if I was interested, I could be introduced to his Thai sister-in-law. I contacted Norman almost immediately and accepted the idea of an introduction by letter. Norman invited me to go and stay with him for a couple of days at the time of the New Year, and it was here that a second 'coincidence' happened. Amongst other details Norman told me that the birthday of the lady in question was the 23rd of January, the same birth date as my mother.

Norman went to Thailand, but because I had a male cat I was unable to care for Norman's male cat. Norman was upset about leaving his cat, but a short time after this my cat died, whereby I was able to look after Norman's cat, until I left for Thailand on Saturday April 8th 1995. Norman and I first met when I joined BUFORA in the early '70's, and now by marriage, we were brothers-in-law. We shall see later how BUFORA and Thailand are placed relative to the two of us. Norman later returned to England and divorced, whereby the brother-in-law aspect was dissolved, but we kept in touch.

In my e-mail to Norman 12-2-2000, and after referring to the first 'crying', "... until a couple of weeks ago. I have now heard it recently for three times – at night when I am asleep. I cannot hear the crying outside the bedroom but when I walk back into the bedroom I can hear it again. The crying lasts for about five minutes and then stops........." I heard the 'crying' again on March 7th and March 25th. On March 25th it was about noon that I heard the crying, while I was moving around in the bedroom. I stood at the point where the crying seemed to be at a peak, but this time there was a tingling sensation all over and I suddenly saw what looked like a face, though it had characteristics that were unknown to me (see Figure En.1).

I experienced very strange feelings, and it felt like things were being put into my mind. A feeling about 'time' and a feeling

2

about 'equation' are the two remembered items, though there was a lot more going on than just these. The most striking feature of the entity was that there were two pupils in each eye. A series of 'dots' were in the mouth position, and two 'extensions' at the side. There was a lighter elongated central region.

On the March 27th, Norman wrote an e-mail with the reference 'twin pupils', where I had previously written 'double pupils'. Norman's terminology turned out to be prophetic and important later.

Figure En.1

In the original colours the darkest area was a purple colour, while the lighter central and side portions were bluish. What would be the whites of the eyes were a green colour and the pupils black. The features were 'soft' and the whole seemed rather streamlined.

Why was there contact in Thailand and not in England? Was the entity unable to make contact in England? Did the entity therefore orchestrate my life so that I would go to Thailand? It was at this point that Norman was quick to point out the coincidence about my Thai wife's birthday and the coincidence concerning our cats.

During meditation I entered some kind of entrance, and saw that before me was a screen with the entity's image on it. It became obvious that I was not going to be allowed to proceed until I had done some appropriate thing. I asked about the identity of the entity, to which came the reply 'Me', although this could be written 'Mi' or even 'Mee'. Another question was whether or not the entity was human and the answer was 'No'. To the question

Summary of the Mi Entity experience

concerning the whereabouts of the entity the answer was to say the least, teasing, 'can everywhere to 24'. It seemed to me at this point that not only was there some kind of language problem, since the answer 'can everywhere to 24' could hardly be considered good English, but it also meant something else far more important. The answers were obviously not a *mental meaning or thought transfer* since this would not require a specific language. So it meant that the entity was fallible. It is also true to say that I did not 'hear' the answers either but rather more like a kind of insertion. To avoid confusion I chose the spelling 'Mi', and this turned out to be prophetic. [I now believe that I was influenced by Mi to spell the name this way.]

Mi was convinced of the existence of another Time aspect, and according to Mi, our version of Time was no more than a historical reference system. In addition, Mi stated that 'Mi life' does not use numbers. I decided to ask questions involving numbers anyway, since any result might be interesting. The second question was – if: -

$$3a + 4b - 2c = 4$$
$$5a + 2b + 3c = 10$$
$$4a - 3b + 4c = 15$$

what are the values of *a*, *b* and *c*? Mi's solution was nothing like the first one and most definitely not as easy to understand. I spent considerable time working through this one with Mi's guidance, though this was minimal. This might have been a deliberate ploy by Mi to remove the 'cobwebs' from my mind.

Further questions were related to other ideas, for example, that of Time. In terminology that may not be completely accurate, Mi communicated ideas of 'Active' and 'Passive' Time. According to Mi, Now and the Past belong to Active Time while the Future is Passive Time. This might mean that in some way the areas of Now and the Past have become 'activated' while the Future remains 'unactivated'. Mi communicated the idea of a fourth Time area

Summary of the Mi Entity experience

which also belonged to Passive Time and I can only loosely identify this as 'Unused' Time. This non-active Time can permeate the other three mentioned and also be external to them. Each of the four has different 'signatures' which is capable of and indeed does change: it is this signature that is the 'Flowing' element of Time. Mi also stated that everything has a unique 'Component Time' signature.

In my e-mail to Norman on the 21st June 2000, I wrote:

"Communication with the 'Mi program' has been completed. I am not sure 'completed' is the right word, and the image is no longer with me"

On the 8th of August I sent another e-mail to Norman saying that a strange thing had happened. All recall regarding the program had been 'lost' and that apart from the copious notes, no memory remained. The 'memory loss' also appeared to have affected some Tae kwon Do Patterns. This was the 'end' of the Mi experience, but other, and what appeared to be unrelated strange occurrences, began (see below). However, it seemed that I was clearly now in a 'Post Mi' situation. One attitude did seem to remain with me, however. Present was a driving force, or thirst, to try to understand what had happened.

In a later e-mail Norman had this to say: -

"As maybe I've suggested before, to my mind the really puzzling thing has nothing to do with actual content: this is the question as to why MI takes a heck of a lot of trouble to contact you, then lets YOU ask the questions, which 'HE' may or may not decide to answer. It would therefore …………"

There came a series of strange sightings. I taught Tae kwon Do in a large Basketball hall in the main school in Udornthani, not far from where I live. One evening in September, while talking to one of my students, I noticed out of the corner of my right eye, a lone person sitting up on my right in the concrete spectator area. I turned my head and noticed that she was sitting quite naturally, dressed conventionally in a skirt, and appeared to be Thai, that is she had a tanned skin and long dark hair. This mysterious lady was seen again several times, though not recently.

Summary of the Mi Entity experience

After this time other strange happenings included walking 'in and out of dreams' during waking hours and the presence of a kind of a fast moving dark grayish blur. The occurrence of the blur seemed to diminish in frequency until the last occurrence on Friday 1st of March 2002.

Late in the year 2000 after storing many of my notes on to floppy disc, I placed most of my 'scribbling' outside at the back of the bungalow, a place where I frequently kept records of Tae kwon Do etc. One day, while sorting out clothes that had been brought from England, I came across some long-sleeve shirts I had not worn for a long time. I picked up one of my favorites, which had a single chest design not unlike that of the clef symbol used in music, only it was facing in the reverse direction. As I picked it up a strange chill hit me and I started to think about the notes I had just stored away.

This was the beginning of what has now materialized as this book, because I was now comparing some of my 'scribbling' to a musical clef which ultimately led me to the star Mira Ceti, (Omicron Ceti), the 15th catalogued light source in the constellation of Cetus.

The numbers 3 and 8 seemed to be occurring – my birthday on the 8th: my first marriage on the 8th. (I had *three* children. It was the third youngest child who was responsible for me getting out of my seat to check her when I heard the 'crying'). My departure from England on the 8th for Thailand, where Mi made contact. The number 23 from both my mother's and my third wife's birthday and that from the 8th of December there are 23 days to the last day of the year. Another 23 came later in connection to Norman.

The Tonic Sol-fa, notes are arranged in Octaves. It is vibrations that cause the sounds, which brings us into the study of Harmonics in Physics and Mathematical Progressions, also known as Harmonics. The patterns of Tae kwon Do are based on the philosophy of the 8 Trigrams from the Chinese I Ching, and each Trigram is made up of 3 lines, a total of 24 lines. Norman and I, with the aid of 'askjeeves.com' found only one place in the world that had the single name of 'Mi', S.E. China. However, most maps do not show this town and its apparent location coincides with a town called Chang Sha, which has ancient origins. It seems that Chang Sha has long been an important transportation point. There is no explanation given why the map shown translates the Chinese area as 'Mi', but it does so happen that one of the most important commercial activities in Chang Sha is rice. There are several Chinese words with the transliteration of 'Mi', perhaps the most common one meaning 'rice'. Other meanings range from 'honey' to implications of divine processes. The 'i' in Chinese has two pronunciations, but when it comes after 'm' the 'i' is pronounced as 'ee'.

By working with simple Harmonic Progressions using '8' and '3' the result is 27.24, a figure which is close to the Moon's sidereal period of revolution, 27.23 days. The Moon has eight named phases – Crescent, First Quarter, Gibbous, Full, Waning, Last Quarter, Old and New Moon. One morning while shaving and thinking of the 'mirror image' staring back at me, what if I used the Earth as the original, showing Mi in China as being in the S.E quadrant, what area on the Moon might this coincide with? From my Astronomical Atlas, in the S.W. quadrant of the Moon, there is a feature called 'Mee'.

With the memory of the experience 'deleted', the contents of my original scribbling and notes that had been put on to floppy disc also mysteriously disappeared. Norman mentioned several possible alternatives of what may have happened to the files including ideas that might have involved Mi, but It seems now that we will never know the truth. However, all new notes and researches remained.

Using the idea of letter counts for names, 'Lawrence Dale' equals 103, which coincidentally is the atomic number of the chemical element Lawrencium, which in turn has a letter count of 119. This added to 'Mira Ceti' equals 197, plus 103 totals 300. This gave rise to whole group of synchronicities including the elements from which Lawrencium was produced, Californium and Boron. This led to the construction of a diagram, the 'reaction chamber' which shows the relationships between the name counts in both English and Thai languages.

While exploring various avenues I noted that adding 'Mira', 41 and 'Mi', 22 equals 63 (BUFORA) and then adding 24 to 'Ceti' and 'Mira', gave 61 and 65 respectively, I wondered whether there was another word I hadn't considered and that would give yet another triad, 37, (?) and 41. I began looking for a word that would have a count of 39. After various considerations I decided to e-mail Norman and asked if he could find a word with a count of 39, though I did not tell him why I wanted it. After a day or two, Norman replied with Enki, which has counts of 39 and 21. Not only would the numerical count for 'Enki' turn out to be important but also the accounts concerning this Sumerian deity had a connection with the constellation of Cetus. The study of the Sumerian culture would also uncover various numerical synchronicities. During this phase of research the fractions $^{22}/_{6}$ and $^{6}/_{22}$ were considered and were given symbols and names, $\overline{\overline{\partial}}$, Tridel 1, and $\overline{\overline{2\partial}}$, Tridel 2 respectively. Various synchronicities were found using these fractions.

A lot of time and effort was spent in studying Mi's answer to the simultaneous equations and this eventually leads to a study of 'mirror image' numbers and a 'mirror image' process which might be another method to solving simultaneous equations. Mi's explanation of how Mi life calculates positions was just as difficult to understand, and my various analogies helped – but only up to a point.

We consider ourselves as Carbon based life forms, and though there are other 'trace elements' involved, the main constituents are Hydrogen, Nitrogen and Oxygen, and it is Carbon that is the main carrier, or hub, for the others. The Molecular Weight for CO_2 is 44. The Atomic Weight of Carbon is 12, and it is from here that the word counts for 'Mi', 'twin' and 'Mira Ceti', as well as $\overline{\overline{\partial}}$ can be derived. There is yet a more important synchronicity concerning the *Peptide* bond: -

Summary of the Mi Entity experience

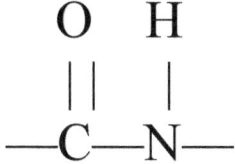

This shows several numerical synchronicities.

An examination of Kepler's third law also leads the way to several important synchronicities, though a simple look at a star map illustrates a visual synchronicity. Looking at the star map of Cetus, Southern Hemisphere, χ Ceti can be seen and just below is ζ Ceti. χ, Chi is the 22nd letter of the Greek alphabet while ζ, Zeta, is the 6th letter of the Greek alphabet, which gives an idea of the inverse of $^{\equiv}\partial$.

During my mathematical studies I became aware that I was soon to hit a 'brick wall', so to speak, because I could not really justify expressions concerning Mi's four Time categories. I did have some ideas worked out based on a tetrad system, numbers from the name counts that differed by a count of 2, but I felt that they were not adequate in providing little more than a overall intuitive grasp of the problems. Now two years after the experience, in the early part of 2002, I was beginning to think that I had gone as far as I could. Then something quite incredible happened to Norman at his home, which provided me with a new impetus and direction without which most of Mi Mathematics could not have been written. Below are copies of e-mails from Norman to me, giving the full account of his experience.

The incidents concern chimes from my doorbell – or, to be more precise, apparently emanating from a source close to and from the 'remote' speaker in our lounge. The first of these occurred on Sunday 3rd March 2002, after which I sent the following e-mail to Larry: -

"....At 12.42GMT I was coming into the lounge from the kitchen when the doorbell chimed – only it wasn't the doorbell! About two months ago we fitted a new doorbell with a 'remote'

speaker that you can take from room to room – but we usually leave it on the music centre in the lounge by the door to the passage, where it was today and most days. This doorbell has a two-tone chime – ding-dong – (two notes). However, what we heard today was TWO sets of FOUR chimes, much deeper and louder than is normal (Think of Big Ben striking the half-hour and you won't be far out!). My wife got up and went to the door – which is some 20-25 yards up the drive from the gate. I followed her. No-one was at or anywhere near the door in any case and the gates were shut."

"....No neighbors were around. We thought of an ice-cream van, but none was in the vicinity and no engine noise had been heard at the time anyway. Also, I fancy an ice-cream van's chimes would have gone on longer. Electrical equipment in that part of the lounge consists of the doorbell 'speaker': a music center (both already referred to) and a TV and Video Recorder. The recorder was switched off, though 'on' at the power point. I'd switched on the TV at 12.30 to watch the Australian Grand Prix – replayed by ITV from the night before: (earlier in the day, actually, because it had been shown 'live' around 2 a.m.), but I'd gone out to the kitchen to get something before the race actually began. The music center was switched off at the power point."

"....To my mind, the source of the chimes seemed not actually to be the 'speaker', but to be two or three feet above and away from the music center, this being next to the speaker."

"...O.K. That was odd enough, but at 1.12 p.m. (13.12), precisely half-an-hour later, the same thing happened. I was sitting in an armchair by the window: my wife was in an armchair by the far wall. It's a very large lounge, and she would have been eighteen to twenty feet from the sound, and I'd have been eight to ten feet (always assuming that my estimate of source – which seemed to be precisely as before – is correct)."

"...I then thought that since it seemed the second chimes had occurred precisely half-an-hour after the first, that they could well recur again, and at 1.40 p.m. (13.40), took up a position underneath where I thought the sound had come from, this being

Summary of the Mi Entity experience

about an arm's length from the doorbell speaker, which I proposed to grab hold of and move if the chimes recurred, to see what the result, if any, would be. It seemed to me that the only possible piece of equipment had to be the speaker – which, being a mobile operated by a battery-powered beam from the doorbell, I thought just possibly might have picked up emanations from a neighbor's doorbell or some other electrical equipment – though it would have had to be a pretty strong source, for the chimes were very loud, louder than the doorbell itself, which, even with four batteries, won't activate the speaker from a distance greater than 60ft."

"...However, no further chimes. I'm wondering, though, if they might recur at the same time early tomorrow morning, or perhaps precisely 24 hours later...."

Saturday 4th of May 2002

Well, they didn't recur 24 hours later. I made all the obvious checks – including asking the makers whether the speaker should actually be *able* to emit the eight notes – was it within its 'remit' to do this? According to them, it was, so far as they were aware, not possible. The incident had slipped to the back of my mind when, at two minutes past six (18.02) on May 4th they occurred again. The conditions were precisely as before, but this time there was no 'follow-up' half-an-hour later. Interestingly, about three hours previously there had been an 'ordinary' ring at the door without anyone apparently present. ('Ordinary' being two notes, the chimes at 6.02 p.m. again having eight notes – six of which the speaker shouldn't know about). This time, my wife and I were sitting in armchairs about fifteen feet apart. At precisely two minutes past ten (22.02) we were again treated to a repeat performance, hearing them from precisely the same positions. As I put in a further e-mail to Larry a day later, 'The 'ordinary' chime of the bell is 'ding-dong' – high note/lower note. The 'alien' chimes consisted of eight notes in two sets of four in a different cadence to the 'ordinary', the two sets being different to each other. Nothing further till........

Sunday 8th December 2002

Summary of the Mi Entity experience

One set of four chimes was heard at 10.45 a.m. GMT when we were both in different rooms to the speaker and to each other. My wife was in the kitchen, outside which is the bellpush. I was in a bedroom. There was no one at or anywhere near the door.

<u>Sunday, 2nd of February 2003</u>

This occurred at 8.30 p.m. (20.30GMT). This time they again reverted to eight notes (as far as one could tell, the same eight notes). Again no one around anywhere at all. On this occasion there was deep snow all around and there were no footprints at all, other than my own, the whole 50-60 feet to the gate! The weather also excluded the 'ice-cream van' hypothesis.

Finally – to the time of writing, (December 2003), they occurred again on Saturday 3rd of May, 2003, when I sent the following e-mail to Larry: -

"...Thought you might like to know that the chimes recurred today about half-an-hour ago (Saturday, May 3rd 2003 – 03.05.03 at 3.54 p.m. BST -15.54). Eight notes – two sets of four, separated by a second's pause, as on the half-hour. Seating arrangements precisely as before – my wife reading a newspaper and me doing a crossword. Position of speaker as previously.

My wife went to the door but no-one was there. Actually, it is now impossible for anyone to ring the bell in any case, since about ten days before we went to the USA I found there was no bellpush! This had been affixed to a square of wood by superglue. In turn this square was screwed in with rawlplugs to the brickwork. The square of wood remains, but the bellpush is, as I say, no longer there. Nor, when I noticed the absence of the bellpush about a month ago, was it to be found on the path below. Am tempted to carry the speaker around with me or in the car. Could raise some interest if it recurred whilst shopping or having my hair cut!

Best   Norman PS.

"As I type this, it's just done it again at 3.18 p.m. (15.18BST) and at 3.21 p.m. (15.21BST). Me at the computer both times. My wife in the garden at 15.18 and in the kitchen at 15.21. On the last occasion got to the speaker in time to hear the last chimes –

definitely they come from the speaker itself, not anywhere else –
N.."

Precisely the same thing occurred again at 8.45 p.m. (20.45) and 8.52 p.m. (20.52) the same night. Following these two occurrences, Larry suggested I have a bell handy and ring it after they occur. Well, we do have a cowbell hanging in the hall but, to date, there has been no repeat of the chimes, so no occasion to use it.

There, for the moment the matter rests. The problem, of course, is that it's impossible to predict when they're going to recur, and they're over so quickly that, by the time one has reached the apparent point of origin, they've finished. By the same token it's also impossible to record them! I'm hesitant, even now, definitely to ascribe them to a 'non-material' source such as MI, even though, from Larry's deductions, it would so appear. The one common fact is, perhaps, that they were all heard at the weekend – on a Saturday or Sunday, which MIGHT just have a significance should someone around, normally at work during the week be indulging in some form of electronic experimentation. However, I could find no neighbor who would admit to such, and, as the bungalows around are quite widely spaced, this would mean that only three of them could be the source anyway.

One last point – followed by a table. I originally thought that we heard four sets of chimes on the first occasion, but for some reason, by the time I e-mailed Larry, began to doubt this – why, I don't know, and was then more inclined to there having been only two sets – the 'half-hour' rather than the 'hour'. However, in response to the e-mail from Larry where he refers to following the 'table' – asking if I could identify the notes, I included my interpretation of all four sets, taking them as having had precisely the same cadence as the 'Big Ben' chimes since this is how they came over to me. It is odd that I have this dichotomy of memory for that first occasion – my wife could not be sure either. Memory can be a tricky thing! For this reason I would not personally be absolutely sure that numerological possibilities and sequences derived from their notes must of necessity be completely accurate, though I have to agree that all forms of 'normal' explanation for the chimes themselves seem to have been exhausted. 'MI' would certainly appear to be the most likely possibility, therefore.

Table of dates for Chimes

Sunday 3rd of March 2002 12.42.GMT two/four(?) sets of four chimes
13.12.GMT   Ditto

Saturday 4th of May 2002 18.02.BST, two sets of four chimes
22.02.BST   Ditto

Sunday 8th of December 2002 10.45.GMT, one set of four chimes
Sunday 2nd of February 2003 20.30.GMT, two sets of four chimes
Saturday 3rd of May 2003 15.54.BST, two sets of four chimes
20.45.BST   Ditto

Aside from 'weekends' being prominent, one thing perhaps of note from the table is that all dates were quite early in the month and, indeed, two of them were within one day of each other, but in different years (May 4th 2002 and May 3rd 2003 respectively.)

In September I wrote for details on the notes played by the chimes, and on receiving this information from Norman I replied with the following.

21-9-2002

"Dear Norman, thank you for the e-mail concerning your chimes. What I am doing is that I am only taking notice of your first alternatives. That is CGAD DEFD CGAD DEFD (or CBAD), and BFGC CDEC BFGC CDEC (or BAGC). I will not try to evaluate the other alternatives, because I will probably find at least one that fits what I am looking for. What I am saying is that I will consider your first impressions as being closer to the truth, as it were. Just to consider these is going to take some considerable time. At this time, based upon the first four I have a small indication that Mi may be referred to, as well as Lawrence and Oliver. I will let you know more once I have had the chance to study them in more detail. All the best. Larry"

Summary of the Mi Entity experience

Eventually the Chimes Expression, 2a-2b-4c+4d, was formulated, and I gave reasons why I thought that Mi was involved in Norman's Chimes Experience. However, more than two years after our experiences Norman came up with something else that I was totally unprepared for.

Norman had been studying the situation concerning the laboratory at Montauk (Long Island, USA) and the Philadelphia Experiment and during August of 2002 Norman, in an e-mail to me, asked about my ideas on the dates 12-8-1943 and 12-8-1983. After giving my reply we again exchanged various e-mails and it soon became an idea that with many synchronicities between them, my Mi experience and Norman's studies might be connected. This is not the end of the story because Norman is engaged in another case study of a different kind, yet the synchronicities persist. For example, Norman gave me the names of three places important in his study, and they all have exactly the same word count which just happens to be the same count as 'Mira'.

During the numerical study, one must ask the question of why the name counts should produce any synchronicities at all. One possible theory is that our language has been influenced by agencies other than natural evolution. If this is so, did Mi know? If Mi *didn't* know, then that raises an even bigger question.

Notes

On page 6 reference is made to the star Mira Ceti, but the complete account, given in the Mi book, states that Mira Ceti is the only star in the Constellation of Cetus that has a name. What I meant to say was that Mira was the only star in Cetus with a *Latin* name that I knew of. Alpha Ceti & Beta Ceti are also known as Menkhar and Kaitos respectively, but these names are Arabic.

Mi Mathematics Part 1
Details omitted from the Mi book

Section 1

From the early stages in the analysis sequences of 8's and 3's became apparent and continued throughout the book. These were used in a simple harmonic equation: -

1.1

$$\frac{8}{8}+\frac{8}{7}+\frac{8}{6}+\frac{8}{5}+\frac{8}{4}+\frac{8}{3}+\frac{8}{2}+\frac{8}{1} = 21.742857143$$

$$\frac{3}{3}+\frac{3}{2}+\frac{3}{1} = 5.5$$

$$5.5 + 21.7428571428 = 27.2429$$

The result, to four significant places, is close to the *nodal* period of the Moon and is just under 0.3% of the sidereal period, 27.3217. This might be an indication that time was involved and as the Moon is the Earth's companion perhaps a closer look was required.

1.2

$$\frac{\sqrt{21.742857143}}{\overline{\overline{\partial}}} = 1.271706455\left(\sqrt{1.617237308}\right)$$

$$\sqrt{\frac{57}{1.271706455^6}} = 3.670935895$$

$$((52+57)\overline{\overline{\partial}}) - 374 - 22 = \overline{\overline{\partial}}, \frac{2(54\times52)}{+365.25\overline{\overline{\partial}}} = 3.665841809$$

$$((52+57)\overline{\overline{\partial}}) - 182 - 66 - 39 - (52+57) = \overline{\overline{\partial}}$$

$$\sqrt[36]{((52+57)54)} = 1.27267417\left(\sqrt{1.61969954}\right)$$

$$\sqrt[36]{((52+54)57)} = 1.273599259\left(\sqrt{1.62206}\right)$$

$$\frac{1.61969954 + 1.617237308}{2} = 1.618468424$$

Mi Mathematics Part 1
Details omitted from the Mi book

(1.2 continued)

$$\frac{\mp365.256}{8(54+46)} = \sqrt{1.618680495} \cong \stackrel{\equiv}{_2}\partial, \sqrt{\mp365.25}\stackrel{\equiv}{=}\partial = 39.14053,$$

$$\sqrt{\frac{\mp(54+52)}{8}} = 9.400797838, \sqrt{\left(\frac{8\times3}{8+0.8}\right)^{-1}} + 8\times3\stackrel{\equiv}{=}\partial = 9.400354603,$$

$$\left((\mp54+\mp46)-\mp(54+46)\right)\stackrel{\equiv}{=}\partial - 374 = 22,$$

$$\frac{\mp\left(\mp182-\left((\mp54+\mp46)-\mp(54+46)\right)\stackrel{\equiv}{=}\partial\right)}{39} = \stackrel{\equiv}{=}\partial$$

It is clearly shown in eq.1.2 that there are a considerable number of synchronicities with regard to figures involving the name counts of 'Earth', 'Moon' and 'Sun', such that these simple computations illustrate the idea of an '8 and 3 syndrome'. Possible connections to either Tridel 1, $^{11}/_3(\stackrel{\equiv}{=}\partial)$, or Tridel 2, $1 + {}^3/_{11}$ ($\stackrel{=}{_2}\partial$), are also seen. It is possible that some objection could be leveled at eq.1.2 because three quarters of the computations involve mirror image numbers (symbol $\mp$; 'I' mid-bar, for which there is yet to be shown any analysis: $46 = $ 'Sol') but eq.1.3 cannot be ignored because it involves physical events. The figures of (9.400…) are important in Part 3 to Part 5.

1.3

$$\sqrt{\frac{365.256}{27.2429}} = 3.6616, \sqrt{\frac{365.256}{27.3217}} = 3.6563$$

$$\frac{\left(\dfrac{4}{\pi}365.256\right)-365.256}{27.2429} = 3.66343$$

$$\frac{\left(\dfrac{4}{\pi}365.25\right)-365.25}{27.3217} = 3.6528$$

17

Mi Mathematics Part 1
Details omitted from the Mi book

If $\overset{\equiv}{\partial}^2$ is set as a 'standard Time element' then the Moon's 'standard' sidereal motion will be about 27.1674 to 27.1678, depending on what yearly figure is used. Also $(27.1674+27.3217) \div 2 = 27.245$. The equations of 1.2 now become more interesting because eq.1.3 add support with synchronicities involving time. In addition, note the similarity between 27.24 with the inverse of $\overset{\equiv}{\partial}$. So, at a very basic level, the trio 'Earth', 'Moon' and 'Sun' sustain a relationship that is close to $\overset{\equiv}{\partial}$ and $\overset{\equiv}{\partial}^2$. This relationship, at least in part, justifies the introduction and use of $\overset{\equiv}{\partial}$. However, in the Mi book the author maintained that Norman was 'chimed' by Mi, so there is a need to find the relationship between Norman, the author and $\overset{\equiv}{\partial}$, if indeed there is such a connection.

1.4(Parent name counts)

$$\frac{246}{39}+\frac{157}{22}=13.44405594,\quad \frac{234}{22\times 39}=\frac{1}{\overset{\equiv}{\partial}}$$

$$182+(110+40)=332,\frac{\pm(110+234)-40}{332}=2.25$$

$$^{2.25}\!\sqrt{(110+234)}=13.4078551,\quad \left(\frac{1}{2}\overset{\equiv}{\partial}\right)^4\times 2.25=25.418$$

$$\frac{\pm(110+234)-40}{25.418}=29.38815655\cong 8\overset{\equiv}{\partial}$$

The equation set 1.4 basically means that to three decimal places the first multiplied by the second is equal to $\overset{\equiv}{\partial}$, while the other computations show further synchronicities.

Having begun this section with a sequence we will take a brief look at a Fibonacci recursion sequences.

1.5

$$F_n = F_{n-1}+F_{n-2}, n\geq 2 : F_0 = 0, F_1 = F_2 = 1, F_0 = 0, F_1 = F_2 = 11$$

$$0,1,1,2,3,5,8,13,21,34,55,89,144,233,377$$

$$0,11,11,22,33,55,88,143,231,374,605,979,1584,2563,4147$$

18

(1.5 continued)

$$\frac{F_{n+1}}{F_n} = \frac{F_{n-1}}{F_{n-1}} + \frac{F_{n-2}}{F_{n-1}}, \frac{F_2}{F_1} \cdots \frac{F_{15}}{F_{14}} =$$

$$1 + 2 + 1.5 + (^{\equiv}\partial - 2) + 1.6 + 1.625 + 1.615385 + 1.619048$$
$$+ 1.617647 + 1.618182 + 1.617978 + 1.618056 + 1.618026$$

$$1 + 2 + 1.5 + (^{\equiv}\partial - 2) + 1.6 + 1.625 + 1.615385 + 1.619048$$
$$+ 1.617647 + 1.618182 + 1.617978 + 1.618056 + 1.618026$$

$$\bar{X} = 1.593537432, \sum_{i=1}^{13} X_i = 20.71598661$$

Immediately we notice that 22,143,144 ('Mi', 'Enki' $\times$ $^{\equiv}\partial$, 222-78) and 374 (Norman's full name count) are present in the sequences. Although the author's name count is not present it can be calculated by 374 + (143 $\div^{\equiv}\partial$) - 231.

However, perhaps more importantly: -

1.6

$$\frac{\sqrt[4]{556}}{3} = 1.61863 \cong \frac{1.619048 + 1.618182}{2}$$

$$\sqrt{1.61863} = 1.272537, \sqrt[8]{47} = 1.618125613$$

One wonders if $^{\equiv}_2\partial$ is a precursor to some formulation or a term in a solution to some important equation. The appearance of a number close to the Golden Ratio, τ (sometimes written as ϕ), suggests that that an interval like $[^{\equiv}_2\partial, {}^{\equiv}_2\partial^2, \tau]$ is important, an idea supported by: -

1.7

$$\sqrt{\frac{\tau + \left(\dfrac{4}{\pi}\right)^2}{2}} = 1.272629743 \approx {}^{\equiv}_2\partial$$

Further Fibonacci recursion sequences are considered later.

Mi Mathematics Part 1

Both Norman and the author usually use just two names for general purposes, so: -
1.8

$$\frac{156^{\equiv\partial}}{\pi} = 182.07, \quad 103^{\equiv\partial} - {}^{\equiv\partial} = 374$$

Equation 1.8 gives an almost perfect reciprocal arrangement with regard to the usual and full name counts – which must rank as being high on a scale 1-10 in terms of synchronicity. What about our other names?
1.9

$$\frac{142 + 76 + 79}{\equiv\partial} = 81 \quad \left(\frac{81}{22} = 3.6818182\right)$$

The remaining middle names divided by ${}^{\equiv\partial}$ result in the count for 'Lawrence' or 'Oliver', with the fraction that both the counts of 81 and 22 give a figure only 0.4% above ${}^{\equiv\partial}$ (but figures of 3.68... become important later).
1.10

$$\frac{182}{39} = 4.666\dot{6} = {}^{\equiv\partial}+1, \quad \frac{182}{22} = 8 + \frac{1}{\equiv\partial}$$

Even if eq.1.10 is a bit fortuitous, ${}^{\equiv\partial}$ has shown that it can connect Norman's and the author's name count. However, to dispel any lingering doubts we can consider a further example: -
1.11

$$182 \times 22 = 4004, \quad 374 \times 39 = 14586$$

The interesting point in eq.1.11 is that while the product, 4004, is not exactly divisible by 39, dividing first by ${}^{\equiv\partial}$ the result, 1092, is, and that the quotient of 14586 divided by ${}^{\equiv\partial}$ remains divisible by 39. $14586 \div 4004 = 3.642857$. So, the combined word counts of Norman, Enki, Mi and the author are related by means of ${}^{\equiv\partial}$.

Mi Mathematics Part 1
Details omitted from the Mi book

Furthermore $182 \times 374 = 68068$, 1001 times the word count for Cetus. However, these figures show a connection to $\overset{=}{\partial}$ with: -

1.12

$$\frac{4004 + 14586}{68068} = 0.27311 \cong \frac{1}{\overset{=}{\partial}}$$

Did Mi use this, or some similar type of procedure, to select both Norman and the author? Mira Ceti, Norman reminds us in an e-mail, is a Binary star system. So here, Norman's input of 'twin' can be used again as Binary Star = Twin Stars. The word count for Twin Stars is 143, which is equal to 'Enki'× $\overset{=}{\partial}$, and the word 'stars' gives yet another twin total of 77. Another curious point is $\overset{=}{\partial}$ to the power of $\overset{=}{\partial}$ = 117.218 – very close to $39 \times 3 = 117$.

Section 2

Section 1 was basically about connections simply by the use of actual numbers, but in this section we form a generating function, with the number 3 as a root. After differentiating we convert back into a number using the original root.

Firstly, Lawrencium, using the highest possible power on $119 = y$ where y is a Polynomial expression in x.

1.13

$$y = x^4 + x^3 + x^2 + 2, \frac{dy}{dx} = 4x^3 + 3x^2 + 2x = 141$$

There are two ways to look at this result. It could represent the sum of 'Lawrencium' and 'Dale', $119 + 22$, but 22 might also represent 'Mi'. A third way of interpreting the result might be $78 + 63$, 'Mira Ceti' + 'BUFORA', though this would then require a 'Lawrencium', 'Mira Ceti' and 'BUFORA' connection. Apart from the result of 141 we are not yet able to make this connection, so for the time being we will discount this third alternative. (The figure of 141 becomes important later) We are left with the idea that the derivative of 'Lawrencium' includes 'Lawrencium', and since the theory is that Lawrencium and Mira Ceti were central 'characters', we should perform the same procedure on '78' to really confirm or contradict that theory. What we need is 78 + 22 = 100.

1.14

$$y = 2x^3 + 2x^2 + 2x = 78, \frac{dy}{dx} = 6x^2 + 4x + 2 = 68$$

This is only a partial confirmation because 68 is the count for Cetus, which has the obvious connection, but we cannot claim that 78 is included in 68. However, 78 + 68 = 146 = 124 + 22 which has a similar structure to that of eq.1.13. So for 'Omicron Ceti': -

1.15

$$y = x^4 + x^3 + x^2 + 2x + 1, \frac{dy}{dx} = 4x^3 + 3x^2 + 2x + 2 = 143$$

The result of eq.1.15 seems more likely to involve 'Enki' than 'Mira', but in this lies the proof that the above procedure is synchronistic. 'Mira Ceti' = 2 ×'Enki' → ½$\overset{=}{\partial}$ 'Mira Ceti' = 143 – quod erat demonstrandum. (For older readers – sorry, can't use Q.E.D. as this is now an abbreviation for Quantum Electro Dynamics). With x = 8 eq.1.15 is 4689 and 2258 respectively and $(4689 - 2258)^{\frac{1}{6}}$ =3.6668867, very close to $\overset{=}{\partial}$.

Now, Lawrencium can be identified just by its position in the Periodic Table, 103, and has no other references but the same cannot be said for Mira which might refer to the Latin language or the star. Hence, the minimum number for these would be 103 + 78 = 181 (181 is close to $\overset{=}{\partial}{}^4$). Using powers of x we obtain: -

1.16

$$2x^4 + 2x^2 + 1 = 181 \therefore 2x^4 + 2x^2 = 180$$

The author's name count, 182, would give the same result: -

1.16b

$$2x^4 + 2x^2 + 2 = 182 \therefore 2x^4 + 2x^2 = 180(180° = \pi \ radians)$$

Mi Mathematics Part 1
Details omitted from the Mi book

The RHS of eq.1.16 is not of much use as it is, so we construct a graph of the equation (which is of course parabolic) and then calculating the area of this quadrant using elementary calculus the resulting area is 424.8 square units. For two quadrants we have: -
1.17

$$\left| \int_b^a y\,dx \right| + \left| \int_{-b}^a y\,dx \right| =$$

$$\left\| \int_{-3}^3 \left(2x^4 + 2x^2 - 180\right)dx \right\| = \frac{2x^5}{5} + \frac{2x^3}{3} - 180x \Big|_0^3$$

$$+ \frac{2x^5}{5} + \frac{2x^3}{3} - 180x \Big|_{-3}^0 = \left| -424.8 - 424.8 \right| = 849.6$$

Completing the ellipsoid we have an area of 1699.2 square units. The true ellipse for 180 is $\pi ab = 1696.46$. For $222 + 78 = 300$: -
1.18

$$\int_0^3 \left(x^5 + 2x^3 + x - 300\right)dx =$$

$$\frac{x^6}{6} + \frac{2x^4}{4} + \frac{x^2}{2} - 300x \Big|_0^3 = -733.5$$

Completing the ellipsoid we have an area of 2934 square units. The true ellipse has the area of 2827.43 square units. The areas of the rectangles 360×6 and 600×6 are 2160 and 3600 square units respectively so that the proportions are: -
1.19

$$\frac{2160}{1696.46} = 1.27324, \quad \frac{2160}{1699.2} = 1.27119,$$

$$\frac{3600}{2827.43} = 1.27324, \quad \frac{3600}{2934} = 1.22699$$

To examine the importance of these results we need to digress a little. $^4\!/\pi$ is well known in mathematics, but if $^{\equiv}\partial$ is important, then we should be able to express $^4\!/\pi$ in terms of $^{\equiv}\partial$. We could state the obvious easy way, that to three significant decimal places –

1.20

$$\frac{4}{\pi} = \left(1 + \frac{1}{\overset{\equiv}{\partial}}\right) = 1.273$$

– but this would not really meet our critique, so we continue on with eq.1.21.

1.21

$$\frac{4}{\pi} - \left(1 + \frac{1}{\overset{\equiv}{\partial}}\right) = 1.273239545 - 1.272727273 = 0.000512272$$

$$\sqrt[32]{\frac{1}{0.000512272}} = 1.267150226^{\dagger}$$

$$\frac{4}{\pi} = \left(1 + \frac{1}{\overset{\equiv}{\partial}} + 1.267150226^{-32}\right)$$

1.267150226 is about 99.6% of 1.272727273 and therefore is a good approximation. However, because 4 & 32 have a numerical connection to 8, then $(^4/_\pi)^{32}$: -

1.22

$$\left(\frac{4}{\pi}\right)^{32} \times 1.267150226 = 2275.746 \times 1.267150226 = \underline{2883.712}$$

$$\overline{X}(2934 + 2827.43) = \underline{2880.715}$$

The synchronicity here is that the average of the two ellipsoid areas on the previous page is very close to $(^4/_\pi)^{32}$ multiplied by '†' of eq.1.21. We can therefore conclude that the connection between $^4/_\pi$ and $^{\equiv}\partial$ is established.

  This is a convenient place to state: -

  1. The Circumference of a circle enclosed exactly by a square (inscribed) is equal to the perimeter of the square multiplied by $^\pi/_4$ (three decimal places 1.273^{-1}).

Mi Mathematics Part 1
Details omitted from the Mi book

2. From '1' a consequence is that the area of the enclosed ellipsoid is equal to the area of the enclosing rectangle multiplied by $\pi/4$.

1.23

$$P_e = \pi(a+b), P_\square = 2x + 2y: a+b = \frac{1}{2}x + \frac{1}{2}y$$

$$P_e = \pi\left(\frac{1}{2}x + \frac{1}{2}y\right) = \frac{1}{2}\pi(x+y)$$

$$2P_e = \pi(x+y) \therefore \frac{2}{\pi}P_e = x+y \therefore \frac{4}{\pi}P_e = 2x + 2y$$

$$\therefore P_e = \frac{\pi}{4}(2x+2y) \quad \blacksquare$$

$$A_e = \pi ab, A_\square = xy: ab = \frac{1}{2}x\frac{1}{2}y : \pi ab = \pi\frac{1}{2}x\frac{1}{2}y$$

$$\therefore \frac{1}{4}\pi xy = \frac{\pi}{4}xy : A_e = \frac{\pi}{4}xy \therefore A_e\frac{\pi}{4} = A_\square \quad \blacksquare$$

The proofs of equations 1.23 are very simple (but personally the author has never seen them in any mathematical texts – perhaps you have. They might be in some mathematical encyclopedia.) However, the topic of Work and Energy can be calculated in a similar way to eq.1.17, $\int_a^b Fdx$. So ends this short digression.

1.24

$$\frac{22^{\equiv\partial}}{\equiv\partial^3} = 1695.9,\ 1696.46 - 1695.9 = 0.56$$

$$\frac{1536}{\left(\frac{4}{\pi}2160 - 2^{\equiv\partial}\right)} = 0.56$$

The figure of 1536 will be derived later as one result of Norman's Chimes experience. Further synchronicities concerning SETI signal (mentioned in the Mi book) occur in the equations of 1.25, which in part also connect with previous equations.

Mi Mathematics Part 1
Details omitted from the Mi book

1.25

$$1679, 1 + 6 + 7 + 9 = 23$$

$$\frac{2160 - 23}{{}_2^{\equiv}\partial} = 1679.07$$

$$\frac{1679 - 1536}{{}^{\equiv}\partial} = 39, \quad \left(111 + \frac{{}_2^{\equiv}\partial}{{}^{\equiv}\partial}\right) = \partial^2 + 182 = 1679$$

When ignoring the second decimal place in the second line of eq.1.25, we have the identities: -

1.26

$$\frac{2160 - 23}{{}_2^{\equiv}\partial} = (1536 + {}^{\equiv}\partial 39) = \left(111 + \frac{{}_2^{\equiv}\partial}{{}^{\equiv}\partial}\right){}^{\equiv}\partial^2 + 182$$

The first identity involves ${}_2^{\equiv}\partial$, the second ${}^{\equiv}\partial$ and the third involves both. The figure of 111 was also discussed in the Mi book. Another synchronicity involving the number 1679 using the count common to both Norman's and the author's name and the combined full name counts is: -

1.27

$$\sqrt{\log_n\left((556 - (2 \times 81)) \times 1679\right)} = 3.66091581 = 0.998432{}^{\equiv}\partial$$

Section 3

Here we discuss the details that involved a brief look, in the Mi book, at the topics of Chemistry, Astronomy, and Physics.

1. Adding the Atomic Number of the four elements Carbon, Hydrogen, Nitrogen and Oxygen, $6 + 1 + 7 + 8 = 22$.
2. The ratio of the Atomic number list to Carbon is $^{22}/_6 = {}^{\equiv}\partial$.
3. With the molecular weight of H_2O, $18 \times {}^{\equiv}\partial = 66$.
4. The ratio of CO_2 to Carbon is $^{44}/_{12} = {}^{\equiv}\partial$.
5. And the addition $(44 \div {}^{\equiv}\partial) + (18 \times {}^{\equiv}\partial) = 78$.

Mi Mathematics Part 1
Details omitted from the Mi book

6. Below is the basic structure of Amino Acids and each A.A. differs only in the 'X' position. The Atomic number count for the basic unit is 39 (Enki?). The basic building blocks of human beings is then represented by the numbers 22 and 39. The '3' and '8' syndrome is also represented along with $\overset{\equiv}{\partial}$.

$$\text{H}_2\text{N} - \overset{\overset{\displaystyle X}{|}}{\underset{\underset{\displaystyle H}{|}}{C}} - \overset{\overset{\displaystyle O}{\|}}{\underset{\underset{\displaystyle OH}{|}}{C}} \qquad \frac{\sqrt{22 \times 39}}{8} = 3.661454629, \quad \frac{22 \times 39}{3 \times 78} = \overset{\equiv}{\partial}$$

$$\therefore \left(\frac{\sqrt{22 \times 39}}{8} + \frac{22 \times 39}{3 \times 78} \right) \Big/ 2 = 3.664060648$$

7. The first result is close to $\overset{\equiv}{\partial}$. The second and third results are synchronistic with important derivations in Part 3.

$$2 \left(\sqrt[8]{(22 \times 39) - (2 \times 365.25)} \right) = 3.666178947$$

$$\frac{(22 \times 39)}{4 \times r_\odot} = 3.689859166, r_\odot = 58.1323$$

$$\sqrt{(22 \times 39) - (31 \times 27.24)} = 3.682390528$$

58.1323 is the Sun-Earth distance in days: 31 – the number of days in August. Cross-dividing atomic numbers with atomic weights: - 1.28

$$2 \left(\sqrt[8]{\frac{103 \times 22}{18}} \right) = 3.6604$$

While $\overset{\equiv}{\partial}$ might relate to mankind, the results 3.68…will be seen later as an integral part of the analysis.

Moving on to the astronomical connection, we compare a star map (drawn by the author) with the author's rectangular

Mi Mathematics Part 1
Details omitted from the Mi book

diagrammatic representation (omitted in the Mi book) shown on pages 29 & 30. On the star map are 22 and 6, 'χ Ceti' and 'ζ Ceti', along with '66', 'Mira', 'M77' (on the Celestial equator), which will help locate these positions on a star map. One should be mindful that we are looking below the celestial equator, so that χ Ceti is slightly more southerly than ζ Ceti, or to put it another way 6 over 22. Mira Ceti is closer to the celestial equator and just to the left is a star designated as 66 Ceti. NGC 1068 (M77) is further to the right of Mira Ceti and touches the celestial equator.

Now, looking at the diagram, there is a triangle that would, to the nearest degree in Declination, enclose the objects under consideration. The hours of Right Ascension have been converted to degrees, 1 hour = 15°, and used for 0° to -11° Declination and a full hour of Right Ascension, 1hr.49 min. to 2hr.49 min., or 15°. The 1hr.49 min just about encloses the two stars χ Ceti and ζ Ceti and the figure of -11° Declination does also in a similar manner. The position of Mira is chosen as -3° Declination. Choosing this point of view is not because it conveniently fits, but because different sources give different values. One star map that the author has puts Mira at -3° 12 min., and another source from the Internet quotes -3° 5 min and yet another source puts Mira closer to -3°. However, what they all agree on is -3°. Any amateur, such as myself, would almost certainly set their equipment on -3° to view Mira.

Two points can be seen immediately. -11° Declination divided by Mira -3° Declination, $^{-11}/_{-3}$, is equal to $^{\equiv}\partial$. The proportion of the 0 to -11° line from 0 to -3° to -11° equals 0.2727 to 0.7272, which are mirror images.

Other features not immediately obvious are that: -
- The area of the larger rectangle is, 15 × 11 = 165, so that the area of the triangle from this equals 82.5. This, when divided by the area of the lower left rectangle, as determined by Mira, is 3 × 7.5 = 22.5, $^{82.5}/_{22.5} = {}^{\equiv}\partial$, or $^{165}/_{22.5} = 2{}^{\equiv}\partial$.
- The area of the triangle Mira, M77, and 22 Ceti equals 10.725. This plus the area of triangle -11°, 15° and M77 equals, 10.725 +

Mi Mathematics Part 1
Details omitted from the Mi book

$10.275 = 21$, $21 \times {}^{\equiv}\!\partial = 77$.

- The area corresponding to the word count of 'Enki', 39, is made up by triangles M77, Mira, 7.5° and Mira, 22 Ceti, -3°.

So it would seem that there are several interesting synchronicities here, particularly those involving ${}^{\equiv}\!\partial$, and there is almost a feeling that some kind of 'cycle' is present. The numbers 21 and 24 when multiplied by ${}^{\equiv}\!\partial$ give 77 and 88 respectively and this is suggestive of a 24 hour clock, so would a 'clock' design reveal other details? On page 31 we examine the 'star map' using the idea of a clock.

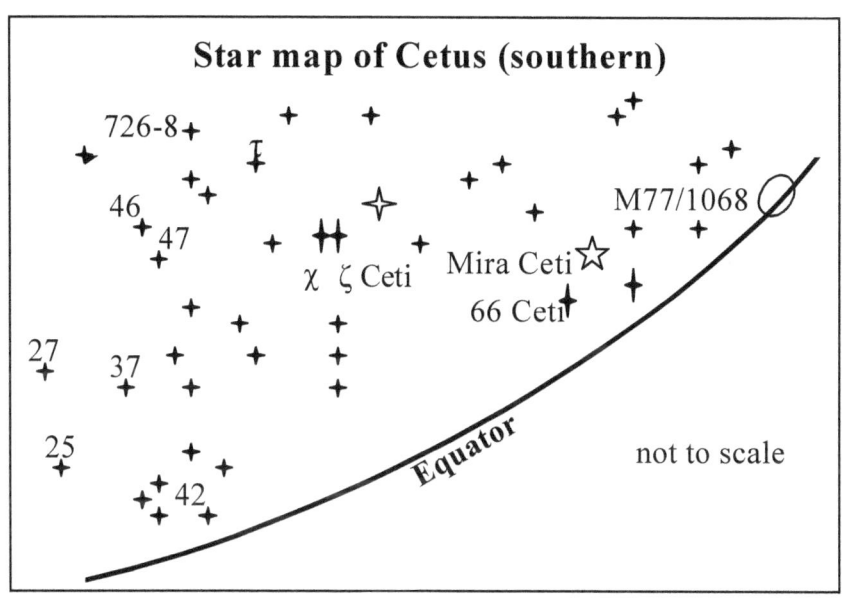

Star map of Cetus (southern)

Mi Mathematics Part 1
Diagrammatic representation of star map

$$\frac{3^0}{11^0} = 0.272727^0, .\frac{8^0}{11^0} = 0.727272^0, \frac{11^0}{3^0} = 3.666667^0$$

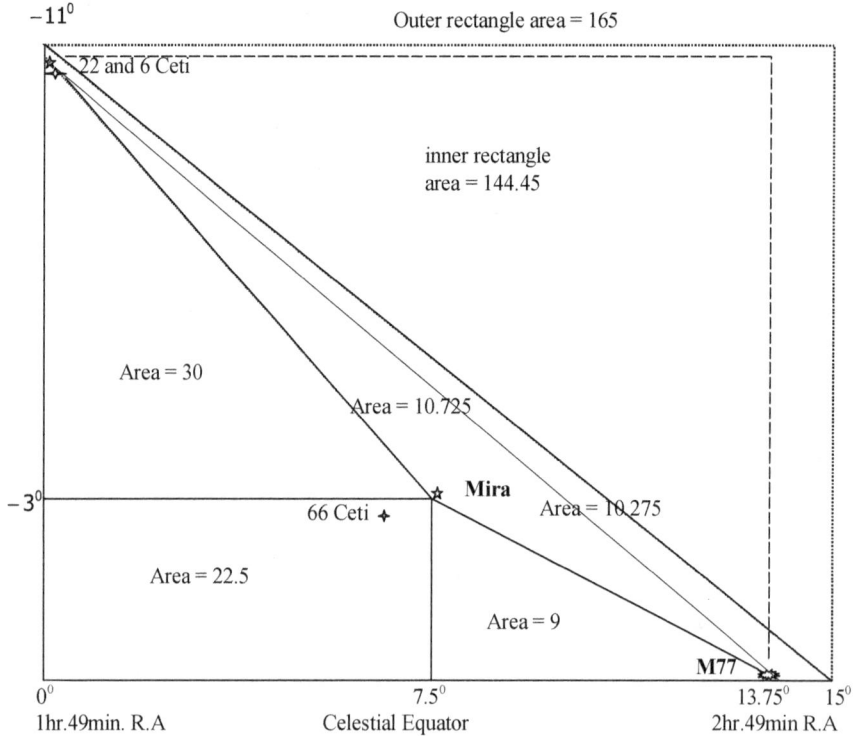

Mi Mathematics Part 1
Clock diagrams

Clock 1

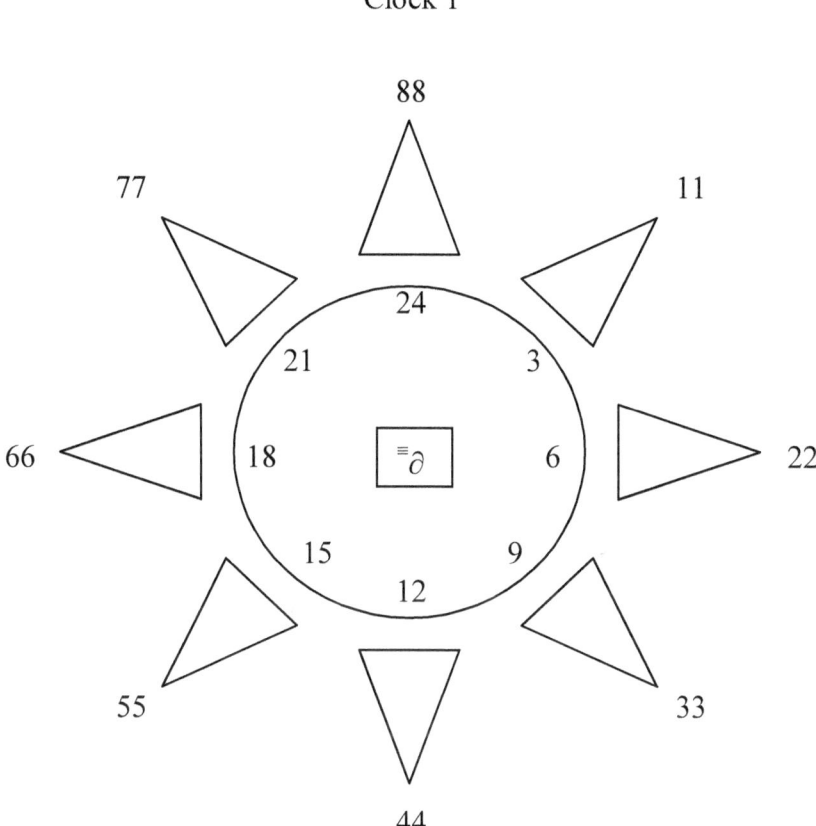

Clock 2

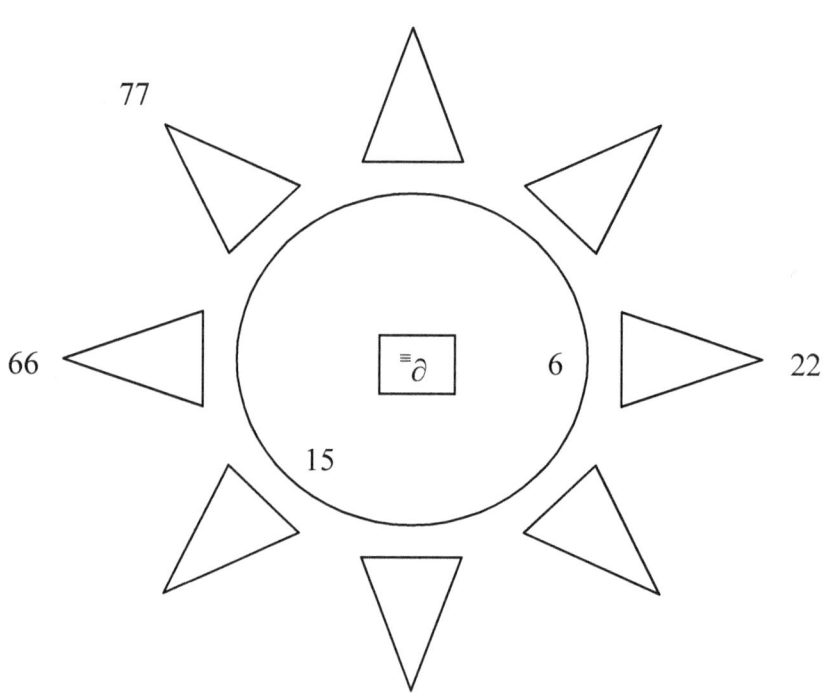

Clock 3

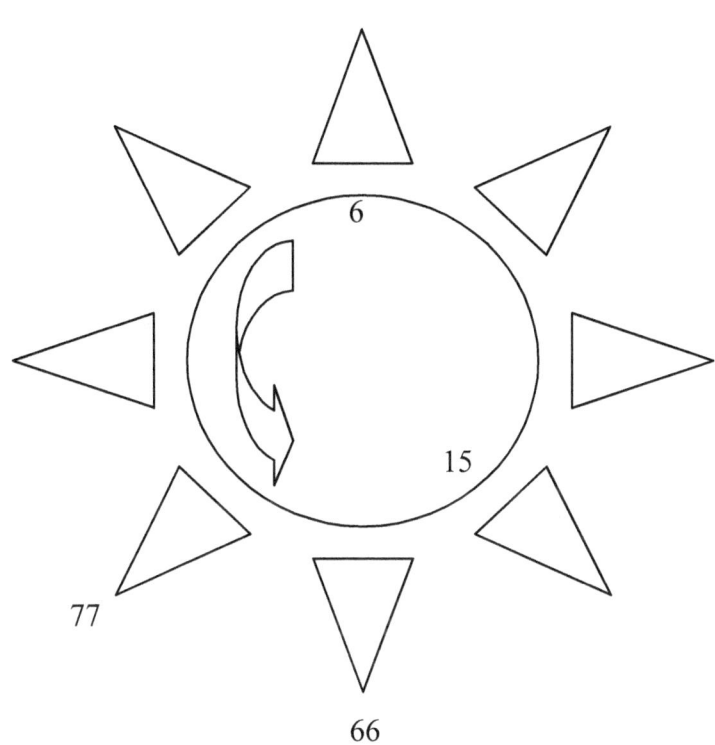

Clock 4

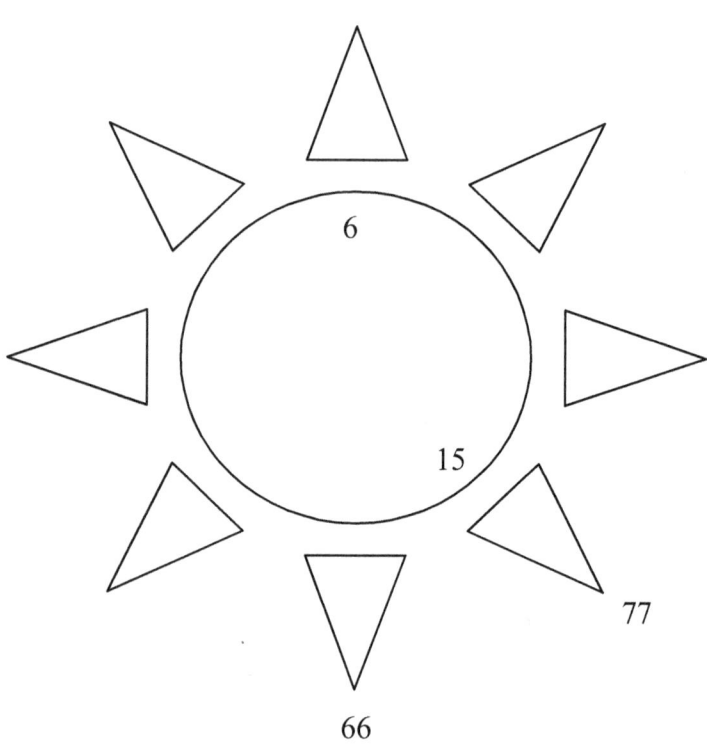

6

15

77

66

Mi Mathematics Part 1
Details omitted from the Mi book

On pages 31-34 we have a 24-hour clock face with intervals of three hours. Clock 1 shows the intervals of three on the inner numbers while the outer numbers are all twins. Each interval of 3 when multiplied by $\overline{\overline{\partial}}$ gives the appropriate 'twin'. $3 \times \overline{\overline{\partial}} = 11$, $6 \times \overline{\overline{\partial}} = 22$, and so on until $24 \times \overline{\overline{\partial}} = 88$. Hence, we find another important aspect of Norman's idea of 'Twin'. The '24' is intended to represent Mi's ' …to 24'.

On Clock 2 are only the numbers which seem to be important on the star map, such as 6 and 22 together. 15 is Mira Ceti's Greek alphabet number, Omicron, while 77 represents M77. The twin 66 is kept to remind us that Norman's 'twin' is close, on the map, to Mira.

For convenience Clock 2 is rotated to make Clock 3, and here we can see that the stars are all in a similar position, relative to one another, as on the star map. However, 77 is not. The number 77 is on the left whereas if relative to others it should be on the right. Clearly, this attempt to construct a Clock to represent the star map and diagram contains a flaw so we need to compare the basic Clock idea with the diagram.

Firstly $77 + 88 = 165$, which happens to be the area of the larger rectangle on the star map diagram. This might indicate that M77 lay within 24 since 77 precedes 88.

Next, if the 77 form M77 indicates being inside of the 24 (88) zone, then 1068, from the calculation ['Mira' × 'Lawrecium'] minus ['Ceti' × Proton number] = $(41 \times 119)-(37 \times 103)$ and the NGC number, should also show some sign of this. If it does not then the theory of the clock is not complete. So add 24 to $1068 = 1092$, and $1092 = 28 \times 39$: to look at it another way, $(15 \times 78)-1092 = 78$, the word count for Mira Ceti. 15 represents the number of degrees in 1 hour R.A. Two other points become apparent when using the word count for twenty four‡, 167: -
1.29

$$167 - 24 = 143, \quad \frac{143}{\overline{\overline{\partial}}} = 39, \quad \frac{(167 \times 24) - 2160}{24} = 77$$

Mi Mathematics Part 1
Details omitted from the Mi book

So, if the clock idea is correct, something about 77 must indicate that M77 should be treated differently. Although M77, or NGC 1068, is in the Constellation of Cetus, it does not have a Ceti designation. 77 and 1068 are catalogue numbers that do not refer to Cetus and in any case M77 is a different galaxy altogether. This might suggest that some separate process must be performed on M77 to place it in a position relative to the other objects.

As can be seen in Clock 3, if 77 were flipped over to the other side of 66 the positions on the clock would be relative to the positions of the objects concerned. The idea of a 'mirror image' has shown synchronicities in some numbers, and it was responsible for locating the area 'Mee' on the Moon as mentioned in the Mi book. Indeed, one might wonder if the letters 'Mi' might be an abbreviation for 'mirror image'(or 'symMitry'). So it would seem reasonable to just perform the mirror image on the number 77.

We should, however, not be satisfied with doing that unless we have something else in support. The support is found by using $\overset{=}{\partial}$ on the number 1092 mentioned on the previous page, that is $1092 \times \overset{=}{\partial} = 4004$, which can be split into a mirror image. 'Enki', 39, also provides us with the closest number we can get to 103 on the clock scale of $\overset{=}{\partial}$. Position 28 on the clock would be $28 \times \overset{=}{\partial} = 102.6666667$, and therefore it is not surprising that $39 \times 28 = 1092$. As additional possibilities, $^{1092}/\overset{=}{\partial} = 297.818181\ldots$ strange that the decimal parts are reminiscent of $^{297}/_{81}$.

So splitting 4004 and 22 into their images we have:
1.30

$$\frac{40}{2} = 20 \text{ and } \frac{4}{2} = 2, \ 20 + 2 = 22, \frac{4004}{22} = 182$$

182 is the word count for the author's full name. One wonders if Mi Life exists within a 'Mirror Image Universe' at the point of *our* Universe known as M77 or NGC 1068, almost sixty million light years away.

Therefore, it would seem that the rotation of 77 in the clock diagram is, in the present context, justified.

Mi Mathematics Part 1
Details omitted from the Mi book

Turning now, briefly, to the topic of Physics, an attempt is made to see if $\overline{\overline{\partial}}$ can be used in equations involving Gravity, though at this stage no complex equations are examined. Here we are calculating the height of an artificial satellite for which the general expression is: -

1.31

$$R = \sqrt[3]{\frac{T^2 gr^2}{4\pi^2}}$$

The obvious unit to start with is that which involves π, and very quickly we find that this unit is almost exactly equivalent to a number referred to in the Mi book, 'BUFORA' or 'Mira' plus 'Mi', that is, the number 63.

1.32

$$R = \sqrt[3]{\frac{T^2 gr^2}{\left(\overline{\overline{2}}\partial\pi^3 + \frac{1}{63}\right)}}, \quad \left[4\pi^2 - \left(\overline{\overline{2}}\partial\pi^3 + \frac{1}{63}\right) = 0.000010623\right]$$

The difference is 1.000000269%, which for the purpose here we might regard as sufficient evidence for replacement. Having said that it is a straightforward rearrangement of eq.1.31 that produces another definition of $\overline{\overline{\partial}}$. First, however, we need to digress a little to give a very trivial example followed by an equally trivial proof, to illustrate where any substitution might come from.

Constructing a rectangle (see below) with the same units of eq.1.17, the resulting area is 2160 square units. Later it will be shown that the choice of this rectangle is not arbitrary. Using a similar procedure as that for the area of an ellipse by using the 'half lengths' of the sides, that is 3 and 180, and $\overline{\overline{\partial}}$, we arrive at the same answer. (This was intended for original Mi book manuscript but was omitted in the final version for reasons stated elsewhere.)

1.33

$$A = xy = 4ab = {}^{\equiv}\partial ab + \left(\frac{ab}{3}\right)$$

$$x = 2a, y = 2b$$

For completeness an example: -

1.34

$$x = 46, y = 6 \therefore xy = 276$$

$$\left({}^{\equiv}\partial \times 3 \times 23\right) + \left(\frac{3}{3} \times 23\right) = \left({}^{\equiv}\partial \times 3 \times 23\right) + 23 =$$

$$\frac{22}{6} \times 69 + 23 = 253 + 23 = 276$$

An infinite number of identities could be chosen to equal four, but choosing ${}^{\equiv}\partial$ is consistent with the idea of threes and, as mentioned in the Mi book, it has a similar structure to that of π. The proof is just a rearrangement of eq.1.33. Equation 1.31 can now be restated to include ${}^{\equiv}\partial$.

1.35

$$R = \sqrt[3]{\frac{T^2 gr^2}{\left({}^{\equiv}\partial + \frac{1}{3}\right)\pi^2}} \quad \therefore \quad \left({}^{\equiv}\partial + \frac{1}{3}\right)R^3 = \left(\frac{T^2 gr^2}{\pi^2}\right),$$

$$^{\equiv}\partial R^3 = \left(\frac{T^2 gr^2}{\pi^2}\right) - \frac{1}{3}R^3, \left(\frac{T^2 gr^2}{R^3 \pi^2}\right) - \frac{1}{3} = {}^{\equiv}\partial$$

Equation 1.35 is neat and exact and demands no more understanding than eq.1.31. Equation 1.32 on the other hand, is arguably less 'attractive' due to a minute remainder and adds another 'probability factor' to any result. However, perhaps the most important feature is that ${}^{\equiv}\partial$ provides another way of explaining the way π 'affects' us. For example, our one-day is twenty-four hours long, this equating with the circumference of the Earth, and the radius is then $(2\pi)^{-1}$ days. To illustrate that the *author's* name count is perhaps a synchronicity with $\overset{\equiv}{\partial}$, 365.256 days and eq.1.31: -

1.36

$$\frac{365.256 \times \overset{\equiv}{\partial}}{2 \times 182} = \frac{\left(\left(\frac{T^2 g r^2}{R^3 \pi^2}\right) - \frac{1}{3}\right) \times 2\pi 58.1323}{2 \times 182} = 3.679318681$$

The second part of eq.1.36 is just an expansion of the first part in terms of eq.1.35 and the result is close enough to $\overset{\equiv}{\partial}$ to be significant (if not downright uncanny). Gravity is also included, which adds to the possible significance of $\overset{\equiv}{\partial}$.

The number 182 is not that far from $\overset{\equiv}{\partial}^4$, $+1.246913579$ in fact, and $(1.246913579)^{32}$ is approximately 1166.2 – another number that will appear later.

‡ From page 35

That Mi life does not use numbers Mi's reply '…up to twenty four…' must have had some significance to Mi: perhaps to signal some direction or connections. It turns out that eq.1.29 is just 'the tip of the ice berg' and the synchronicities connect to almost every part of this study. In addition to eq.1.29 we have such items as: -

$$\frac{167}{\overset{\equiv}{2}\partial^2} = 103.1, \frac{167}{\overset{\equiv}{2}\partial^3} = 81.005, \frac{222 - 167}{15} = \overset{\equiv}{\partial}$$

The first two items in the above relate to Lawrencium and the count of names coincidental to both Norman and the author. The third is perhaps more significant because if the count for Lawrencium is considered as degrees R.A., then we have $\overset{\equiv}{\partial}$ hours R.A. Further study of 167 will appear in the next book, GeoMitry.

Mi Mathematics Part 1
The Sumerian number system

Although China can be said to be the cradle of the species Homo Erectus, and apparently from 10,000 BC Neolithic villages were springing up, it seems that China did not have a well-developed society until very much later – perhaps due to its vastness. Some think that China's eventual superior agricultural system was due to a much earlier influence. Apparently it was at Sumer that the first civilization grew into a sophisticated society.

Sumer was founded between the rivers Tigris and Euphrates that flow toward the Persian Gulf, an area known as the Fertile Crescent. Sumer was later absorbed by the Babylonian civilization.

The history of Sumer was unknown to modern society until about the mid-nineteenth century, and then only from fragmentary writings on clay tablets, with other evidence discovered by modern archaeologists. The name 'Sumer' seems to date from about the beginning of the 3rd millennium BC. Somewhere about 3250 BC people from the north mixed with the local people and it was the newcomers that were called Sumerians, and they spoke a language unrelated to any other known language.

The Sumerians developed an advanced society (for that period), including schools, lawyers, Art and architecture, crafts, religion and so on, and had the first domesticated animals and plants. The Sumerian language became the main language, and the cuneiform script was developed. This script became the prominent means of written communication throughout the Middle East for about 2000 years.

However, they do not appear to have been a powerful people and around 2300 BC they were no longer able to defend themselves against aggressive invaders. The people of northern Sumer and the invaders intermixed, and became known ethnically and linguistically as Akkadians whereby the land of Sumer was given the name of both Sumer and Akkad. Somewhere between 1820 and 1760 B.C. is the date that sees the end of the Sumerian State, but its civilization was completely adopted by the Babylonians.

Mi Mathematics Part 1
The Sumerian number system

Comparing the ancient Chinese language and Sumerian, one immediately recognizes just how very different they were, even though they had basically risen from a similar idea. Both used the idea of a type of imitative symbol and both exhibited more curved lines in the early writings converting to straight lines in later writing evolution. However, the Chinese language developed by adding more symbols while Sumerian developed by use of vowels and consonants, which in total numbered 144 symbols. By contrast the Chinese symbols grew in number so that by about 210-215 BC there were more than 3,000 symbols. By the 18th century the number of symbols had increased so much that a dictionary revealed that the Chinese language had some 40,000 characters. At this point, close examination revealed 34,000 were doubles and were really unnecessary. At present the Chinese language has about 4,000 characters and many are being written in a 'short' form for ease of writing and memory.

The Sumerian mathematical system was discovered by detailed study of Babylonian texts, and it seems to have been a dual system. For everyday, or lay purposes a mixture of the decimal and sexagesimal systems was used, whereas for the learned fraternity only the sexagesimal system was used. As an example, one tablet of clay found at the Mari location [Mari =Mira = 41], dated early second millenium BC, shows terms of an geometrical progression with a common ratio of 9 and reads, left – sexagesimal, right – decimal: -

Sumer 1

1 39	99
14 51	891
2 13 39	8019
20 02 51	72171
3 00 25 39	649,539

In Sumer 1 we have on the right 99, 99×9, 99×9^2, 99×9^3 and 99×9^4, while on the left we have $(1 \times 60) + 39 = 99$

Mi Mathematics Part 1
The Sumerian number system

$(14\times60)+51 = (39\times9)+ (1\times60\times9)$
$(2\times60^2)+(13\times60)+39 = (1\times60\times9^2)+(39\times9^2).$
$(20\times60^2)+(2\times60)+51 = (1\times60\times9^3)+(39\times9^3)$
$(3\times60^3)+(0\times60^2)+(25\times60)+39 = (1\times60\times9^4)+(39\times9^4)$

Oddly enough there are synchronicities here. Firstly, all numbers on the decimal side are one-time devisable by $^{\equiv}\partial$ – and: -

Sumer 2

1    $\sqrt[4]{\dfrac{649539}{60^2}} = 3.6650144, e^{3.6650144} = 39.0557,$

2    $\dfrac{649539}{(39)^2 \,^{\equiv}\partial} = 116.4675, \sin^{-1}(\sin 649539) = 81$

3    $99 + 891 + 8019 + 72171 + 649539 = 730719$

$\sqrt{\log_n 730719} = 3.674477,$

4    $\dfrac{\sqrt[4]{\dfrac{730719}{374\times78}}+1}{2} = 1.618577432$

5    $\dfrac{730719}{182^2} = 22.06$

    In Sumer 2(1) we see that by using the sexagesimal system to divide the decimal, the answer is about $0.99955^{\equiv}\partial$, and the anti-$\log_n$ of this is very close to the count of 'Enki' (the exact figure is $e^{3.663561646} = 39$). Sumer 2(2) shows that by dividing the decimal figure by 'Enki'$\times^{\equiv}\partial$ gives a result that is very close the diameter of the Earth's orbit around the Sun, in days, whereas in the second part the result is 81, Norman's last name count, and the author's first name count. In Sumer 2(3) the natural logarithm of the decimal total is also close to $^{\equiv}\partial$. The Golden Ratio, represented here as τ, can be derived from $((\sqrt5)+1)\div2$, and in Sumer 2(4) using Norman's full name count with that of Mira Ceti in a similar construction the answer is also very close to τ. Lastly, and very direct, in Sumer 2(5) is the author's full name count squared

Mi Mathematics Part 1
The Sumerian number system

dividing the decimal total, giving almost exactly the count for 'Mi'. The reason why this particular example was chosen in the first place is because there are 9×60^2 seconds in 9hrs. and the 8th root of that figure is 3.6628415. (9hrs. will be discussed in more detail in Part 3.) What happens when we reverse the procedure?

Sumer 3

$$1 \quad 374 = (3 \times 60^2) + (7 \times 60) + 4 = 11224$$

$$1a \quad \frac{11224}{2^{\equiv}\partial} = (39.12218622)^2$$

$$1b \quad \frac{11224}{\equiv\partial^3} \times \frac{360}{365.256} = 224.41$$

$$1c \quad \sqrt[8]{11224} = 3.2083$$

$$2 \quad 182 = (1 \times 60^2) + (8 \times 60) + 2 = 4082$$

$$2a \quad \frac{4082}{60} = 68.03\dot{3}$$

$$2b \quad \frac{4082}{556} = 7.341726619 \approx 2^{\equiv}\partial + \frac{1}{119}$$

$$2c \quad \frac{4082}{39} = 103 + \left(\equiv\partial - 2\right)$$

In Sumer 3(1 & 2) Norman's and the author's full name counts have been converted to the sexagesimal system. 1a shows that by using $\equiv\partial$ a figure close to the count of 'Enki' squared can be derived: 1b converts to a figure that is similar to day 224, the 12th of August, although the dimension is degrees and not days. 1c using the octave idea, results in 'a' of the simultaneous equations. Using a sexagesimal denominator in 2a the integer is the count for 'Cetus', while in 2b using the addition of Norman's and the author's full name counts, the answer is almost exactly twice $\equiv\partial$ plus the inverse of the count for 'Lawrencium'. In 2c using the count for 'Enki' in the denominator Lawrencium's periodic number plus a contraction of $\equiv\partial$ is derived.

Mi Mathematics Part 1
The Sumerian number system

One begins to wonder just how far these synchronicities go, although the meaning might be as that mentioned in the Mi book – that Norman was meant to offer the name of 'Enki'. In trying another name with a count of 152, belonging to the author of the books on the Montauk affair (presented in the Mi book) the above synchronicities do not occur. Yet as soon as we use the name of Norman's contactee case we are given $^{(11224 \times \equiv \partial)}/_{110} = 374.1333\ldots$ These synchronicities involving Norman's name count cannot simply be ignored or explained away, instead they imply a connection between the counts of Norman's name, 'Mi' and 'Enki', which becomes immediately clear with: -

$$\frac{374 \times 39}{22} = 3.66693073^5$$

With a result of almost exactly $^{\equiv}\partial^5$ this basic formulation connects to just about everything written in this and the Mi book, but that raises perhaps the biggest question of all – was Mi involved with evolution of Sumer? Admittedly Mi may have learnt about Sumer in the same way that we can, but then this would not explain the synchronicities and how they came to be. (If Mi was involved with Sumer perhaps Mi influenced other ancient civilizations as well, The Maya for example. The count for 'Enki' is 39 and the count for the supreme Mayan deity, 'Hunab K'u' is 78, equal to 2 × 'Enki' or equal to the count of 'Mira Ceti'. The ancient Maya calendars also produce synchronicities but their measure will have to wait for next book.)

There are other instances that imply a circular nature both in the answer to this question and the above synchronicities, but such a discussion will be have to be deferred without a promise of complete satisfaction.

Mi Mathematics Part 2

Section 1

Below is the second set of simultaneous equations, S_i, presented to Mi along with the two original methods of solution. Other methods of solution are also shown in the hope that some pattern might emerge.

2.1

Method of Elimination

$$S1.\ 3a + 4b - 2c = 4$$

$$S2.\ 5a + 2b + 3c = 10$$

$$S3.\ 4a - 3b + 4c = 15$$

Eliminating c from S1 and S2: -

$$(3a + 4b - 2c = 4) \times 3 = 9a + 12b - 6c = 12$$

$$(5a + 2b + 3c = 10) \times 2 = 10a + 4b + 6c = 20$$

$$S1 + S2 = 19a + 16b = 32$$

A similar procedure including S3: -

$$(5a + 2b + 3c = 10) \times 4 = 20a + 8b + 12c = 40$$

$$(4a - 3b + 4c = 15) \times 3 = 12a - 9b + 12c = 45$$

$$S2 - S3 = 8a + 17b = -5$$

$$S4 = 19a + 16b = 32,\ S5 = 8a + 17b = -5$$

$$(19a + 16b = 32) \times 8 = 152a + 128b = 256$$

$$(8a + 17b = -5) \times 19 = 152a + 323b = -95$$

$$S5 - S4 = S6 = 195b = -351$$

$$\therefore\ b = \frac{-351}{195} = \frac{-9 \times 39}{5 \times 39} = -1.8$$

Substituting into S5: -

$$8a + (17 \times -1.8) = -5$$

$$8a - 30.6 = -5, \; a = \frac{25.6}{8} = 3.2$$

$$3a + 4b - 3c = 4$$

$$(3 \times 3.2) + (4 \times -1.8) - 2c = 4$$

$$c = \frac{-1.6}{2} = -0.8$$

2.2 Matrix Method

$$SE2 = \begin{bmatrix} 3 & 4 & -2 \\ 5 & 2 & 3 \\ 4 & -3 & 4 \end{bmatrix} \begin{bmatrix} a \\ b \\ c \end{bmatrix} = \begin{bmatrix} 4 \\ 10 \\ 15 \end{bmatrix}$$

Det.SE2

$$\begin{vmatrix} 3 & 4 & -2 \\ 5 & 2 & 3 \\ 4 & -3 & 4 \end{vmatrix} = 3 \times \begin{vmatrix} 2 & 3 \\ -3 & 4 \end{vmatrix} - 5 \times \begin{vmatrix} 4 & -2 \\ -3 & 4 \end{vmatrix} + 4 \times \begin{vmatrix} 4 & -2 \\ 2 & 3 \end{vmatrix} = 65$$

$$SE2^c = \begin{bmatrix} 17 & -8 & -23 \\ -10 & 20 & 25 \\ 16 & -19 & -14 \end{bmatrix}^T = \begin{bmatrix} 17 & -10 & 16 \\ -8 & 20 & -19 \\ -23 & 25 & -14 \end{bmatrix},$$

$$SE2^{-1} = \frac{\begin{bmatrix} 17 & -10 & 16 \\ -8 & 20 & -19 \\ -23 & 25 & -14 \end{bmatrix}}{65}$$

Solving: -

$$\begin{bmatrix} 4 \\ 10 \\ 15 \end{bmatrix} \times \left(\begin{bmatrix} 17 & -10 & 16 \\ -8 & 20 & -19 \\ -23 & 25 & -14 \end{bmatrix} \middle/ 65 \right) = \begin{bmatrix} \dfrac{208}{65} \\ \dfrac{-117}{65} \\ \dfrac{-52}{65} \end{bmatrix} = \begin{bmatrix} 3.2 \\ -1.8 \\ -0.8 \end{bmatrix}$$

The method of reduction by elementary row operations followed by the Gause-Jordan elimination is used to check the above, by coincidence, in eight steps.

2.3

$$\begin{bmatrix} 3 & 4 & -2 & | & 4 \\ 5 & 2 & 3 & | & 10 \\ 4 & -3 & 4 & | & 15 \end{bmatrix} r1 \times 2 \rightarrow \begin{bmatrix} 6 & 8 & -4 & | & 8 \\ 5 & 2 & 3 & | & 10 \\ 4 & -3 & 4 & | & 15 \end{bmatrix} r1 - r2 \rightarrow$$

$$\begin{bmatrix} 1 & 6 & -7 & | & -2 \\ 5 & 2 & 3 & | & 10 \\ 4 & -3 & 4 & | & 15 \end{bmatrix} r2 - r3 \rightarrow \begin{bmatrix} 1 & 6 & -7 & | & -2 \\ 1 & 5 & -1 & | & -5 \\ 4 & -3 & 4 & | & 15 \end{bmatrix} r2 \leftrightarrow r1 \rightarrow$$

$$\begin{bmatrix} 1 & 5 & -1 & | & -5 \\ 1 & 6 & -7 & | & -2 \\ 4 & -3 & 4 & | & 15 \end{bmatrix} r2 - r1 \rightarrow \begin{bmatrix} 1 & 5 & -1 & | & -5 \\ 0 & 1 & -6 & | & 3 \\ 4 & -3 & 4 & | & 15 \end{bmatrix} r3 - 4 \times r1 \rightarrow$$

$$\begin{bmatrix} 1 & 5 & -1 & | & -5 \\ 0 & 1 & -6 & | & 3 \\ 0 & -23 & 8 & | & 35 \end{bmatrix} r3 + 23 \times r2 \rightarrow \begin{bmatrix} 1 & 5 & -1 & | & -5 \\ 0 & 1 & -6 & | & 3 \\ 0 & 0 & -130 & | & 104 \end{bmatrix}$$

$$r3 \times \dfrac{1}{-130} \rightarrow \begin{bmatrix} 1 & 5 & -1 & | & -5 \\ 0 & 1 & -6 & | & 3 \\ 0 & 0 & 1 & | & -0.8 \end{bmatrix}$$

The results follow by substitution.

2.4 Gause-Jordan elimination

$$\begin{bmatrix} 1 & 5 & -1 & \vdots & -5 \\ 0 & 1 & -6 & \vdots & 3 \\ 0 & 0 & 1 & \vdots & -0.8 \end{bmatrix} r2+r3\times6 \rightarrow \begin{bmatrix} 1 & 5 & -1 & \vdots & -5 \\ 0 & 1 & 0 & \vdots & -1.8 \\ 0 & 0 & 1 & \vdots & -0.8 \end{bmatrix}$$

$$r1-r3 \rightarrow \begin{bmatrix} 1 & 5 & 0 & \vdots & -5.8 \\ 0 & 1 & 0 & \vdots & -1.8 \\ 0 & 0 & 1 & \vdots & -0.8 \end{bmatrix} r1-r2\times5 \rightarrow \begin{bmatrix} 1 & 0 & 0 & \vdots & 3.2 \\ 0 & 1 & 0 & \vdots & -1.8 \\ 0 & 0 & 1 & \vdots & -0.8 \end{bmatrix}$$

or 2.5

$$\begin{bmatrix} a & b & c \\ 0 & d & e \\ 0 & 0 & f \end{bmatrix}\begin{bmatrix} 1 & 5 & -1 \\ 0 & 1 & -6 \\ 0 & 0 & 1 \end{bmatrix} = \begin{bmatrix} 1 & 0 & 0 \\ 0 & 1 & 0 \\ 0 & 0 & 1 \end{bmatrix}$$

$$\begin{bmatrix} a & b & c \end{bmatrix}\begin{bmatrix} 1 \\ 0 \\ 0 \end{bmatrix} = 1 \therefore a = 1, \begin{bmatrix} 1 & b & c \end{bmatrix}\begin{bmatrix} 5 \\ 1 \\ 0 \end{bmatrix} = 0 \therefore b = -5,$$

$$\begin{bmatrix} 1 & -5 & c \end{bmatrix}\begin{bmatrix} -1 \\ -6 \\ 1 \end{bmatrix} = 0 \therefore c = -29, \begin{bmatrix} 0 & d & e \end{bmatrix}\begin{bmatrix} 5 \\ 1 \\ 0 \end{bmatrix} = 1 \therefore d = 1,$$

$$\begin{bmatrix} 0 & 1 & e \end{bmatrix}\begin{bmatrix} -1 \\ -6 \\ 1 \end{bmatrix} = 0 \therefore e = 6, \begin{bmatrix} 0 & 0 & f \end{bmatrix}\begin{bmatrix} -1 \\ -6 \\ 1 \end{bmatrix} = 1 \therefore f = 1$$

$$\begin{bmatrix} 1 & 5 & -1 \\ 0 & 1 & -6 \\ 0 & 0 & 1 \end{bmatrix}^{-1} = \begin{bmatrix} 1 & -5 & -29 \\ 0 & 1 & 6 \\ 0 & 0 & 1 \end{bmatrix}, \begin{bmatrix} -5 \\ 3 \\ -0.8 \end{bmatrix} \times \begin{bmatrix} 1 & -5 & -29 \\ 0 & 1 & 6 \\ 0 & 0 & 1 \end{bmatrix} = \begin{bmatrix} 3.2 \\ -1.8 \\ -0.8 \end{bmatrix}$$

2.6 Chio's method

$$\begin{vmatrix} 3 & 4 & -2 & 4 \\ 5 & 2 & 3 & 10 \\ 4 & -3 & 4 & 15 \end{vmatrix} = \begin{vmatrix} -14 & 19 & 10 \\ -23 & 8 & 35 \end{vmatrix} = |325 \quad -260| =$$

$$325x_3 = -260 \therefore x_3 = \frac{-260}{325} = -0.8$$

$$-23x_2 + 8x_3 = 35 \therefore -23x_2 = 35 + 6.4 = x_2 = \frac{41.4}{-23} = -1.8$$

$$4x_1 - 3x_2 + 4x_3 = 15 \therefore x_1 = 3.2$$

2.7 Factors of the Matrix Method

$$\begin{bmatrix} 3 & 4 & -2 & | & 1 & 0 & 0 \\ 5 & 2 & 3 & | & 0 & 1 & 0 \\ 4 & -3 & 4 & | & 0 & 0 & 1 \end{bmatrix} r1 \times 2 \rightarrow \begin{bmatrix} 6 & 8 & -4 & | & 2 & 0 & 0 \\ 5 & 2 & 3 & | & 0 & 1 & 0 \\ 4 & -3 & 4 & | & 0 & 0 & 1 \end{bmatrix}$$

$$r1 - r2 \rightarrow \begin{bmatrix} 1 & 6 & -7 & | & 1 & -1 & 0 \\ 5 & 2 & 3 & | & 0 & 1 & 0 \\ 4 & -3 & 4 & | & 0 & 0 & 1 \end{bmatrix} r2 - r3 \rightarrow$$

$$\begin{bmatrix} 1 & 6 & -7 & | & 1 & 0 & 0 \\ 1 & 5 & -1 & | & 0 & 1 & -1 \\ 4 & -3 & 4 & | & 0 & 0 & 1 \end{bmatrix} r2 \leftrightarrow r1 \rightarrow \begin{bmatrix} 1 & 5 & -1 & | & 0 & 1 & 0 \\ 1 & 6 & -7 & | & 1 & 0 & 0 \\ 4 & -3 & 4 & | & 0 & 0 & 1 \end{bmatrix}$$

$$r2 - r1 \rightarrow \begin{bmatrix} 1 & 5 & -1 & | & 1 & 0 & 0 \\ 0 & 1 & -6 & | & -1 & 1 & 0 \\ 4 & -3 & 4 & | & 0 & 0 & 1 \end{bmatrix} r3 - 4 \times r1 \rightarrow$$

$$\begin{bmatrix} 1 & 5 & -1 & | & 1 & 0 & 0 \\ 0 & 1 & -6 & | & 0 & 1 & 0 \\ 0 & -23 & 8 & | & -4 & 0 & 1 \end{bmatrix}$$

(2.7 continued)

$$r3 + 23 \times r2 \rightarrow \left[\begin{array}{ccc|ccc} 1 & 5 & -1 & 1 & 0 & 0 \\ 0 & 1 & -6 & 0 & 1 & 0 \\ 0 & 0 & -130 & 0 & 23 & 1 \end{array}\right]$$

$$r3 \times -\frac{1}{130} \rightarrow \left[\begin{array}{ccc|ccc} 1 & 5 & -1 & 1 & 0 & 0 \\ 0 & 1 & -6 & 0 & 1 & 0 \\ 0 & 0 & 1 & 0 & 0 & -\frac{1}{130} \end{array}\right]$$

2.7b The 8 factors are: -

$$\begin{bmatrix} 1 & 0 & 0 \\ 0 & 1 & 0 \\ 0 & 0 & -\frac{1}{130} \end{bmatrix}\begin{bmatrix} 1 & 0 & 0 \\ 0 & 1 & 0 \\ 0 & 23 & 1 \end{bmatrix}\begin{bmatrix} 1 & 0 & 0 \\ 0 & 1 & 0 \\ -4 & 0 & 1 \end{bmatrix}\begin{bmatrix} 1 & 0 & 0 \\ -1 & 1 & 0 \\ 0 & 0 & 1 \end{bmatrix}$$

$$\begin{bmatrix} 0 & 1 & 0 \\ 1 & 0 & 0 \\ 0 & 0 & 1 \end{bmatrix}\begin{bmatrix} 1 & 0 & 0 \\ 0 & 1 & -1 \\ 0 & 0 & 1 \end{bmatrix}\begin{bmatrix} 1 & -1 & 0 \\ 0 & 1 & 0 \\ 0 & 0 & 1 \end{bmatrix}\begin{bmatrix} 2 & 0 & 0 \\ 0 & 1 & 0 \\ 0 & 0 & 1 \end{bmatrix}$$

No obvious pattern related to already given synchronicities has emerged, apart from the *eight* factors, although there are two possibilities that might be relevant. The numerical difference between the constants is 0.6 and this is shown in the final part of eq.2.2 as: -

$$\text{a. } \frac{208 - 117 - 52}{65} = \frac{39}{65} = 0.6, \text{ b. } 2\left(\sqrt[8]{130}\right) = 3.675131767$$

The count for 'Enki' appears as the numerator of (a), and (b) is possibly related to $\overset{\equiv}{\partial}$ or equations involving 3.68....

The idea of a Mirror Image was mentioned frequently in the Mi book, so here we examine whether or not such a process might be used in an algebraic sense, on the simultaneous equations.

Mi Mathematics Part 2

Let us begin by looking at some simple simultaneous equations in three unknowns. The symbol '⧉', introduced in Part 1, written after the expression in eq.2.8 line 4, identifies the mirror image. Written as in line 5, '⧉' written before the expression, defines the addition of the two mirror image expressions.

2.8

$$4x + 2y + 3z = 19$$

$$2x - y + 2z = 6$$

$$x + y + z = 6$$

$$4x + 2y + 3z⧉ = 3x + 2y + 4z$$

$$⧉4x + 2y + 3z = 7x + 4y + 7z$$

$$7x + 2y + 6z = 31, 7x + 7y + 7z = 42$$

$$(7x + 7y + 7z) - (7x + 2y + 6z) = 5y + z = 11$$

$$4x + 4y + 4z = 24$$

$$(4x + 4y + 4z) - (4x + 2y + 3z) = 2y + z = 5$$

$$(5y + z) - (2y + z) = 3y = 6 \therefore y = 2$$

$$2y + z = 4 + z = 5 \therefore z = 1$$

$$4x + 2y + 3z = 19 = 4x + 4 + 3 = 19$$

$$\therefore 4x = 12 \therefore x = 3$$

Only the coefficients of the LHS are used and it can be clearly seen in this example that the LHS of the first line contains both the second and the third. So, construct the mirror image of the first, then add the mirror image lines together. Although we are left with the same problem as before, the addition seems to have an inviting kind of 'symmetry'. The total of the three lines is similar in structure to ⧉ and the third line is capable of being multiplied by any number uniformly. The number 7 looks like the obvious choice because it will result in a similar pattern. Repeating this procedure but using line 1, the answers then follow by usual substitution. We could have used either line two or line three because both ⧉ would result in just doubling their constants.

The augmented matrix for eq.2.8 is: -

$$\begin{bmatrix} 4 & 2 & 3 & | & 19 \\ 2 & -1 & 2 & | & 6 \\ 1 & 1 & 1 & | & 6 \\ 7 & 2 & 6 & | & 31 \end{bmatrix} \xrightarrow{(7 \times r3) - r4} \begin{bmatrix} 4 & 2 & 3 & | & 19 \\ 2 & -1 & 2 & | & 6 \\ 1 & 1 & 1 & | & 6 \\ 0 & 5 & 1 & | & 11 \end{bmatrix},$$

$$\begin{bmatrix} 4 & 2 & 3 & | & 19 \\ 2 & -1 & 2 & | & 6 \\ 1 & 1 & 1 & | & 6 \\ 0 & 5 & 1 & | & 11 \end{bmatrix} \xrightarrow{(4 \times r3) - r1} \begin{bmatrix} 0 & 2 & 1 & | & 5 \\ 2 & -1 & 2 & | & 6 \\ 1 & 1 & 1 & | & 6 \\ 0 & 5 & 1 & | & 11 \end{bmatrix}$$

'Partial line mirror images' also provide a way to a solution. Now for the equations given to Mi.

2.9

$3a + 4b - 2c = 4, 5a + 2b + 3c = 10, 4a - 3b + 4c = 15$

$\dotplus 3a + 4b - 2c = 3a + 4b - 2c + 2a + 4b - 3c = 5a + 8b - 5c$

$5a + 2b + 3c - (4a - 3b + 4c) = a + 5b - c = -5$

$2 \times (a + 5b - c) = 2a + 10b - 2c = -10$

$3a + 4b - 2c - (2a + 10b - 2c) = a - 6b = 4 - (-10) = 14$

$5 \times (a + 5b - c) = 5a + 25b - 5c = -25$

$5a + 25b - 5c + 5a + 2b + 3c = 10a + 27b - 2c = -25 + 10 = -15$

$10a + 27b - 2c - (2a + 10b - 2c) = 8a + 17b = -5$

$-8 \times (a - 6b) = -8a + 48b = -112$

$-8a + 48b + 8a + 17b = 65b = -117$

$\therefore b = -117/65 = -1.8$

By simple substitution the other results follow. Alternative mirror images are possible, but fractions have been avoided since their $\dotplus$ are not as easy to see. Some agility is required in recognizing such patterns, but this is no different to other methods commonly found in textbooks. Notice that the last two lines of eq.2.9 give the same result as that obtained by eq.2.2, -117.

Section 2

Having introduced a mirror image procedure it becomes necessary to delve a little deeper into this idea. In fact the idea was introduced in Part 1 during the brief discussion on Fibonacci numbers, when we considered numbers directly related to $\overset{\equiv}{\partial}$ – that is 11,22,33 and so on. The first nine twin-numbers have identical $+$, designated here as the alpha mid-bar, α, a subset of $+$, $\alpha \subset +$. Because the number 22 has special significance herein, it will have the special symbol p, where 'p' is short for 'primary', ('p'= primary mid-bar). In this way we can write α_1, α_2, etc. leading to equations such as: -
2.10

$$\frac{p}{6} = \overset{\equiv}{\partial}, \frac{\alpha_n}{3n} = \overset{\equiv}{\partial}, \frac{3n}{\alpha_n} = \frac{1}{\overset{\equiv}{\partial}} = \overset{\equiv}{\partial}^{-1}$$

$n \leq 9$. This leads to a definition of numbers greater than α_9, in the series, in terms of α_n. For example, the last number in this series is 990, equal to $10\alpha_9$. Each hundred has a total of ten numbers with $+$ but only $(\alpha_n)^2$ are exactly devisable by α_1 while the others are not. Next in the series is 1001, and each thousand has a total of ten numbers with $+$ all devisable by α_1. Definitions for higher numbers are formulated similarly though not given here. Is there a use for this group? Let us repeat the Fibonacci sequences mentioned in Part 1: -
2.11

0,1,1,2,3,5,8,13,21,34,55,89,144,233,377

0,11,11,22,33,55,88,143,231,374,605,979,1584,2563,4147

Each nth member of the second sequence can obviously be defined in terms of $\alpha_1 F_n$ of the first, such as $(\alpha_1 F_{10})_1 = (F_{10})_2 = 605$.

Sequential additions (here symbolized as Σ_{+n}) were considered in the Mi book and in F_n a sequential sequence is maintained. For example $\Sigma_{+n}(F_n + F_{n+1}) = \Sigma_{+n}F_{n+2}$.

2.12

$$\sum_{+n}(F_4 + F_5) = \sum_{+n}F_6 = (3+3)+(5+5) = 8+8$$

This is a clear confirmation that Mirror image numbers and sequential figures do have a mathematical significance. However, we will continue with $+$ but only those that have relevance to the Mi book.

Equation 2.13 shows an incredible synchronicity and again illustrates that $+$ have a definite role to play in the general scheme herein: -

2.13

$$+(E1)1696.5 = 1696.5 + 5.6961 = 1702.1961$$

$$+(E2)1699.2 = 1699.2 + 2.9961 = 1702.1961$$

The results are not just very close – they are identical! One wonders if this might be a signal that E1 and E2 should be treated as being the same. Moving on to name counts: -

2.14

$$374 + 473 = 847, \quad \frac{847}{\equiv\partial^2} = 63$$

$$182 + 222 = 404, \quad 404 + 404 = 808$$

In eq.2.14 Norman's full name count is added to its mirror image number and then divided by $\equiv\partial^2$. The result is interesting inasmuch that it is the same as the letter count for BUFORA. However, performing the same procedure on the total count for the author's name does not yield any meaningful result ($126 + \equiv\partial^{-1}$ actually & 'England' + 'Thailand' = 126). However, we need to stop and reflect on this for a moment.

Norman's full count contains all the figures that refer to Norman's name herein. Possible additions to the author's name count come from Lawrencium for obvious reasons. So we add (103+119) to 182 and then add the mirror image of the result. Once again performing a division by $\overline{\overline{\partial}}$ does not reveal anything useful. Looking a little more closely, however, it reveals another synchronicity, because while the numbers 847 and 808 are different they are of the same order. Enter Enki, 847-39 = 808. Still further, with a similar procedure on 847 and using the count of the author's introduction of Mira: -

2.14b

$$\frac{847+41}{37} = \frac{888}{37} = 24, \quad \sqrt{\frac{888}{66}} = 3.668043819$$

There seems no point in dividing 888 by $\overline{\overline{\partial}}$ since three '8's are simply too obvious to ignore. Dividing by Mira's other half, Ceti, gives 24, but then the square root of the division by 'twin' gives a result very close to $\overline{\overline{\partial}}$. The conclusion that we might draw from the above is that Mi may have made use of these connections between Enki, Lawrencium, Mira, $\overline{\overline{\partial}}$, Norman and the author.

With regard to Norman's Chimes experience Σ_L for 'chimes' is 57, 39: -

2.15

$$\overline{+}57 = \overline{+}39 = \overline{+}66 = 132,$$

$$374 - 132 = 242, \frac{242}{\overline{\overline{\partial}}} = 66$$

As a result of using $\overline{+}$ and $\overline{\overline{\partial}}$, 'twin' can be derived, and yet again with $\overline{+}66$ is the same result, 132. As a 'by the way' note: -

NGC1068 + M77 =14+7+3+1+6+8+13+7+7= 66

2.16

$$\frac{374+473}{\overline{\overline{\partial}}} = 231$$

In eq.2.16 Norman's full name-count plus $\overline{+}$, divided by $\overline{\overline{\partial}}$ results in a Fibonacci sequence number. The two numbers not providing mirror image combinations devisable by $\overset{\equiv}{\partial}$ are the author's full name count and 'Lawrencium', but Lawrencium has a special property – radioactive decay. Though Mira Ceti may be in the process of changing, we still call it Mira Ceti. However, Lawrencium was produced from Californium and both belong to the radioactive series (Actinides) so that the name changes as the radioactive decay proceeds. The Actinides finally end up as Lead so we need an extra process (see Notes).

2.17

$103 - 82(\text{Lead}) = 21$ and $119 - 22 = 97$, $21 + 12 = 33$, $97 + 79 = 176$

$$\frac{33 + 176}{\overset{\equiv}{\partial}} = 57(\text{Moon?}) \text{ and } \frac{176 - 33}{\overset{\equiv}{\partial}} = 39$$

One can immediately notice that 82 is 2×41, so the claim about Mira Ceti and Lawrencium being central comes to light yet again.

Now what about the author? Although he is not radioactive (as far as we know), because his name is 'related' to Lawrencium in the obvious way, it would seem reasonable to suppose that the author's name count also requires something extra. Using an analogous process to that which was used for Lawrencium we have: -

2.18

$$182 - (119 + 41) = 22, \ 22 + 22 = 44$$
$$182 - (119 + 37) = 26, \ 26 + 62 = 88$$
$$182 - (103 + 41) = 38, \ 38 + 83 = 121$$
$$182 - (103 + 37) = 42, \ 42 + 24 = 66$$
$$44 + 88 + 121 + 66 = 319$$

Even though the number 319 is devisable by $\overset{\equiv}{\partial}$, the quotient, 87, does not seem to be useful. It is, however, the mirror image of 78, but the number 319 has a much more interesting role to play. The mirror image numbers of both Norman's and the author's individual names are: -

2.19

$78 + 57 = 132$, $76 + 67 = 143$, $142 + 241 = 383$, $81 + 18 = 99$, $= 757$

$81 + 18 = 99$, $79 + 97 = 176$, $22 + 22 = 44$, $= 319$

Now we have two 319's, so, $757 - (2 \times 319) = 119 - $ 'Lawrencium'!
Finally: -
2.20

$$\frac{\mp(374 \times 182)}{182} =$$

$$\frac{68068 + 86086}{182} = 847 = \mp 374$$

There is no simple identity here to cancel out – in fact $86086 = 68068 + (99 \times 182)$, but eq.2.20 does demonstrate the relationship between Norman's and the author's name count using the mirror image process.

<u>Mirror Image theory for $\mp$</u>
Form a generating-function from name counts and equate $\pm$, for example: -
2.21

$$182 = x^2 + 8x + 2 = f, \pm = 2x^2 + 8x + 1$$

$$= \pm - f = x^2 + 0x - 1$$

$$119\pm = 8x^2 + 0x - 8 = 8x^2 = 8$$

$$\therefore x = \pm 1$$

Because we are in $\pm$ the generating function will result in parabolic graphs.
2.22 Proof.

$$x^2 + 8x + 2\pm = 2x^2 + 8x + 1 = 0$$

$$(c - a)x^2 + bx - bx + (a - c) = 0$$

$$= \Delta x^2 - \Delta = 0 \therefore x^2 = \pm 1 \quad \blacksquare$$

Mirror Image theory for +

If the addition of the four digits ≤10 the following rules produce mirror image numbers.

a. The first two digits are repeated.

2.23

$$[(a+d),(b+c),(c+b),(d+a)]$$
$$+1212 = [(1+2),(2+1),(2+1),(1+2)] = 3333$$
$$+4141 = [(4+1),(1+4),(1+4),(4+1)] = 5555$$

b. If the digits are **not** repeated.

2.24

$$[(a+d),(b+c),(c+b),(d+a)]$$
$$+1234 = [(1+4),(2+3),(3+2),(4+1)] = 5555$$

However, as shown in eq.2.23 and 2.24, from + there is no way to determine the original number, except in the one case of 2222.

The indication in eq.2.25 (a & b) is that when forming a generating-function from + and then finding the roots, the pattern seems to be $(x \pm 1)(ax + (a \pm b)x - a)$, depending on whether we add or subtract +. This would infer that any equation having this pattern is the result of + and the one principle root is $x = 1$ or $x = -1$. The other two roots are complex roots, $f + ig$.

2.25a.

$$x^3 + 2x^2 + 3x + 4 = 4x^3 + 3x^2 + 2x + 1 = 5x^3 + 5x^2 + 5x + 5$$

5	5	5	5
+0	−5	0	−5
5	0	5	0

$$= (x+1)(5x^2 + 5) = (x+1)(ax^2 + (a-b)x + a)$$

2.25b.

$$6x^3 + 2x^2 + 6x + 4 = 4x^3 + 6x^2 + 2x + 6 = 2x^3 - 4x^2 + 4x - 2$$

2	−4	4	−2
+0	2	−2	2
2	−2	2	0

$$= (x-1)(2x^2 - 2x + 2) = (x-1)(ax^2 + (a+b)x + a)$$

Trying a different approach, let us take $-(xa + yb + zc) = N$ and compute the values of a, b and c.

Mirror image 1

$$\begin{vmatrix} 4 & 6 & 3 & 182 \\ 8 & 4 & 7 & 374 \\ 4 & 4 & 4 & 222 \end{vmatrix} \rightarrow \begin{vmatrix} -32 & 4 & 40 \\ 16 & 4 & 280 \end{vmatrix} \rightarrow |-192 \quad -9600|$$

$$-192x_3 = -9600 \therefore x_3 = 50, 16x_2 + 200 = 280$$

$$\therefore x_2 = 5, 4x_1 + 20 + 200 = 222 \therefore x_1 = 0.5$$

Mirror image 2

$$\begin{vmatrix} 1 & 6 & 5 & 78 \\ 1 & 3 & 2 & 39 \\ 0 & 4 & 4 & 22 \end{vmatrix} \rightarrow \begin{vmatrix} -3 & -3 & -39 \\ 4 & 4 & 22 \end{vmatrix} \rightarrow |0 \quad -222|$$

Mirror image 3

$$\begin{vmatrix} 5 & 8 & 5 & 144 \\ 1 & 3 & 2 & 39 \\ 0 & 4 & 4 & 22 \end{vmatrix} \rightarrow \begin{vmatrix} 7 & 5 & 51 \\ 4 & 4 & 22 \end{vmatrix} \rightarrow |8 \quad -50|$$

$$8x_3 = -50 \therefore x_3 = -6.25 ; 4x_2 - 25 = 22 \therefore x_2 = 11.75,$$

$$\therefore x_1 = 16.25$$

Mirror image 4

$$\begin{vmatrix} 5 & 8 & 5 & 144 \\ 1 & 6 & 5 & 78 \\ 4 & 4 & 4 & 222 \end{vmatrix} \rightarrow \begin{vmatrix} 22 & 20 & 246 \\ -20 & -16 & -90 \end{vmatrix} \rightarrow \begin{vmatrix} 48 & 2940 \end{vmatrix}$$

$48x_3 = 2940 \therefore x_3 = 61.25$

$-20x_2 - 980 = -90 \therefore x_2 = -44.5, \therefore x_1 = 38.75$

Mirror image 5

$$\begin{vmatrix} 6 & 2 & 5 & 263 \\ 8 & 4 & 7 & 374 \\ 2 & 2 & 2 & 111 \end{vmatrix} \rightarrow \begin{vmatrix} 8 & 2 & 140 \\ 8 & 2 & 140 \end{vmatrix} \rightarrow \begin{vmatrix} 0 & 0 \end{vmatrix}$$

$0x_3 = 0 \therefore x_3 = 0$

$8x_2 + 0 = 140 = \therefore x_2 = 17.5,$

$2x_1 + 35 + 0 = 111 \therefore x_1 = 38$

Mirror image 6

$$\begin{vmatrix} 4 & 6 & 3 & 182 \\ 8 & 4 & 7 & 374 \\ 4 & 0 & 3 & 152 \end{vmatrix} \rightarrow \begin{vmatrix} -32 & 4 & 40 \\ -16 & -4 & -280 \end{vmatrix} \rightarrow \begin{vmatrix} 192 & 9600 \end{vmatrix}$$

$192x_3 = 9600 \therefore x_3 = 50$

$-16x_2 - 200 = -280 = \therefore x_2 = 5,$

$4x_1 + 0 + 150 = 152 \therefore x_1 = 0.5$

Mirror image 7

$$\begin{vmatrix} 9 & 2 & 9 & 118 \\ 7 & 4 & 7 & 423 \\ 6 & 0 & 5 & 253 \end{vmatrix} \rightarrow \begin{vmatrix} 22 & 0 & 2981 \\ -24 & -7 & -767 \end{vmatrix} \rightarrow \begin{vmatrix} -154 & 54670 \end{vmatrix}$$

(Mirror image 7 continued)
$$-154x_3 = 54670 \therefore x_3 = -355$$
$$-24x_2 + 2485 = -767 = \therefore x_2 = 135.5,$$
$$6x_1 + 0 - 1775 = 253 \therefore x_1 = 338$$

The first point to notice in M.i.2 is that although the second set has a det. = 0, coincidentally, part of the meaningless answer is the negative count of 'Lawrencium' + 103. Is there a message here, such as Mira Ceti should not be grouped with Enki and Mi, or it is meaningless to consider -222 etc.? The three digit $+$ in M.i.4, 5 and 6, all show x_i = 55.5 (with the det. not containing a common element), while in M.i.7 a random set of $+$ (not in the Mi book) does not display the same characteristic. Again, is there a message here? (See Epilogue another discussion on $+$)

Section 3

Chimes

One reason why Norman's chimes were chosen as four notes may be due to the number of possible combinations of A to G, $^nC_r = {}^{7!}/_{(7-4)!4!} = {}^{5040}/_{144} = 35$. 144 is the addition of 'Mira' and 'Lawrencium', or the difference between 'Mira Ceti' and 'Lawrencium' + 103. The important synchronicity is that the square root of (Log_n 144 × 5040) is close to $\overline{\overline{\partial}}$. The number 35 is not synchronistic with other material herein with one possible exception on page 227. If we take the chimes as they are CGAD = 3714, DEFD = 4564, BFGC = 2673 and CDEC = 3453, then take away the lowest from the highest in each set we have, 4564-3714 = 850, and 3453-2673 = 780: add the results, 850+780 = 1630: this just happens to be 66 less than the area of the ellipse, 1696. If that is not convincing enough we can even do the reverse. Convert 1696 into note number =1626 =AFBF. Now convert this according to the 8 × 3 (see Mi book) matrix method for the words, = 1323 and add the mirror image, 1323 + 3231 = 4554. This is also the value of $+$(2232 + 2322) for the word 'Twin' whose count is 66. Of course the sequential value for 1696 is 22!

Mi Mathematics Part 2

The Chimes expression was derived from the musical notes originally supplied by Norman, and they appeared to make a very convenient 4×4 matrix. Of course, the determinant of each is 0. Using the 8×3 method mentioned on the previous page: -

Chimes matrix 1

$$\begin{vmatrix} 3 & 1 & 1 & 1 \\ 1 & 2 & 3 & 1 \\ 3 & 1 & 1 & 1 \\ 1 & 2 & 3 & 1 \end{vmatrix} = 0 \quad \begin{vmatrix} 2 & 3 & 1 & 3 \\ 3 & 1 & 2 & 3 \\ 2 & 3 & 1 & 3 \\ 3 & 1 & 2 & 3 \end{vmatrix} = 0,$$

Chimes matrix 2

$$\begin{bmatrix} 3 & 1 & 1 & 1 \\ 1 & 2 & 3 & 1 \\ 3 & 1 & 1 & 1 \\ 1 & 2 & 3 & 1 \end{bmatrix} \times \begin{bmatrix} 2 & 3 & 1 & 3 \\ 3 & 1 & 2 & 3 \\ 2 & 3 & 1 & 3 \\ 3 & 1 & 2 & 3 \end{bmatrix}^T = \begin{bmatrix} 13 & 15 & 13 & 15 \\ 14 & 14 & 14 & 14 \\ 13 & 15 & 13 & 15 \\ 14 & 14 & 14 & 14 \end{bmatrix}$$

$$\sum r = \sum c = 224$$

The addition of all rows or all columns results in the same number, 224. This is synchronistic with day 224, August 12th and whoever, or whatever, sent this message must have intended that 224 be considered as an important number.

Looking at the twenty-four tetrads: -

Tetrad 1

$$\begin{vmatrix} 22 & 24 \\ 41 & 42 \end{vmatrix} \begin{vmatrix} 22 & 24 \\ 68 & 69 \end{vmatrix} \begin{vmatrix} 22 & 24 \\ 77 & 78 \end{vmatrix} \begin{vmatrix} 22 & 24 \\ 181 & 182 \end{vmatrix}$$

$$\begin{vmatrix} 37 & 39 \\ 41 & 42 \end{vmatrix} \begin{vmatrix} 37 & 39 \\ 68 & 69 \end{vmatrix} \begin{vmatrix} 37 & 39 \\ 77 & 78 \end{vmatrix} \begin{vmatrix} 37 & 39 \\ 181 & 182 \end{vmatrix}$$

$$\begin{vmatrix} 39 & 41 \\ 41 & 42 \end{vmatrix} \begin{vmatrix} 39 & 41 \\ 68 & 69 \end{vmatrix} \begin{vmatrix} 39 & 41 \\ 77 & 78 \end{vmatrix} \begin{vmatrix} 39 & 41 \\ 181 & 182 \end{vmatrix}$$

(Tetrad 1 continued on next page)

$$\begin{vmatrix} 45 & 47 \\ 41 & 42 \end{vmatrix} \begin{vmatrix} 45 & 47 \\ 68 & 69 \end{vmatrix} \begin{vmatrix} 45 & 47 \\ 77 & 78 \end{vmatrix} \begin{vmatrix} 45 & 47 \\ 181 & 182 \end{vmatrix}$$

$$\begin{vmatrix} 66 & 68 \\ 41 & 42 \end{vmatrix} \begin{vmatrix} 66 & 68 \\ 68 & 69 \end{vmatrix} \begin{vmatrix} 66 & 68 \\ 77 & 78 \end{vmatrix} \begin{vmatrix} 66 & 68 \\ 181 & 182 \end{vmatrix}$$

$$\begin{vmatrix} 75 & 77 \\ 41 & 42 \end{vmatrix} \begin{vmatrix} 75 & 77 \\ 68 & 69 \end{vmatrix} \begin{vmatrix} 75 & 77 \\ 77 & 78 \end{vmatrix} \begin{vmatrix} 75 & 77 \\ 181 & 182 \end{vmatrix}$$

All of these determinants are negative: -

Tetrad 2

$$Td.1 = -60, Td.2 = -114, Td.3 = -132, Td.4 = -340$$
$$Td.5 = -45, Td.6 = -99, Td.7 = -117, Td.8 = -325$$
$$Td.9 = -43, Td.10 = -97, Td.11 = -115, Td.12 = -323$$
$$Td.13 = -37, Td.14 = -91, Td.15 = -109, Td.16 = -317$$
$$Td.17 = -16, Td.18 = -70, Td.19 = -88, Td.20 = -296$$
$$Td.21 = -7, Td.22 = -61, Td.23 = -79, Td.24 = -287$$

They have a possible connection to the Chimes expression, ^{e}C, because all tetrads when substituted in $^{e}C = 0$ as shown in: -

Tetrad 3

$$(2 \times 37) - (2 \times 39) - (4 \times 77) + (4 \times 78) = 0$$

The first column of tetrad determinants is that which uses the count for 'Mira', so add them together and the result is -208. 224-208 = 16 and 16 numbers make up the tetrads. However the figure of 208 was also used in the calculation of a in the simultaneous equations viz. $^{208}\!/_{65}$. Now $^{208}\!/_{16} = 13$ and the 13th determinant is -37 which is the negative of 'Ceti'.

2.26

2	−2	−4	4	=	2	−2	−4	4	=
22	24	41	42	0	75	77	181	182	0
42	22	24	41	108	182	75	77	181	630
41	42	22	24	6	181	182	75	77	6
24	41	42	22	−114	77	181	182	78	−636

In eq.2.26 each element of a tetrad substitutes (a) to (d) in ^eC, and then the positions are rotated three times. Since all 24 tetrads are described by the same formula, their results follow a similar pattern. The first observation is that all have the second rotation constant of 6. Equation 2.27 is the proof that all the tetrads will have a second rotation constant of 6.

2.27

$$b > a$$
$$2a - 2(a+1) - 4b + 4(b+2) =$$
$$2a - 2a - 2 - 4b + 4b + 8 = 6$$
$$b = a$$
$$2a - 2(a+1) - 4(a+2) + 4(a+4) =$$
$$2a - 2a - 2 - 4a - 8 + 4a + 16 = 6 \quad \blacksquare$$

This also means $^{\equiv}\partial\,(2a - 2(a + 1) - 4b + 4(b + 2)) = 22$ and this result connects ^eC with the count of 'Mi' and $^{\equiv}\partial$.

If we apply the condition that $c \geq b$ then all the tetrads follow the pattern of the matrix (0,2:2,3). The major objection against this restraint is that while it satisfies $^eC = 0$, there is no letter in the English alphabet with a value of 0, or word counts of 2 and 3. Even so, though the objection mentioned is an important one, the matrix in eq.2.28 can remain as a theoretical minimum. The implication here is that any change to matrix 2.28, $^eC = 0$, must be done through matrix addition and not matrix multiplication. (See Notes for the solution set)

2.28

$$\begin{pmatrix} 1 & 1 \\ c & c \end{pmatrix} + \begin{pmatrix} 0 & 2 \\ 2 & 3 \end{pmatrix}, c \geq 1$$

In eq.2.29 the two generating-function alternatives are given for $+^e C$, along with the corresponding roots.

2.29 (Synthetic Division)

$$(2x^3 + 2x^2 + 4x + 4) + = 4x^3 + 4x^2 + 2x + 2$$

$$4x^3 + 4x^2 + 2x + 2 - (2x^3 + 2x^2 + 4x + 4) = 2x^3 + 2x^2 - 2x - 2$$

$$x = 1, \quad \begin{array}{|rrrr|} \hline 2 & 2 & -2 & -2 \\ +0 & 2 & 4 & 2 \\ \hline 2 \nearrow & 4 & 2 & 0 \\ \hline \end{array} = (x-1)(2x^2 + 4x + 2)$$

$$= (x-1)(ax^2 + (a+b)x + a)$$

$$x = -1, \quad \begin{array}{|rrr|} \hline 2 & 4 & 2 \\ +0 & -2 & -2 \\ \hline 2 \nearrow & 2 & 0 \\ \hline \end{array} = (x-1)(x+1)^2 \quad \therefore x = 1; x = -1$$

$$2x^3 - 2x^2 - 4x + 4 = 4x^3 - 4x^2 - 2x + 2 = 6x^3 - 6x^2 - 6x + 6$$

$$x = 1, \quad \begin{array}{|rrrr|} \hline 6 & -6 & -6 & 6 \\ +0 & 6 & 0 & -6 \\ \hline 6 \nearrow & 0 & -6 & 0 \\ \hline \end{array} = (x-1)(6x^2 - 6)$$

$$x = 1, \quad \begin{array}{|rrr|} \hline 6 & 0 & -6 \\ +0 & 6 & 6 \\ \hline 6 \nearrow & 6 & 0 \\ \hline \end{array} = (x-1)^2 (x+1)$$

However, in eq.2.30 we have the other two generating-function alternatives of $^e C$ and the corresponding roots are then used to make an expression in x.

2.30

$$2x^3 - 2x^2 - 4x + 4$$

$$x = 1, \quad \begin{array}{|cccc|} \hline 2 & -2 & -4 & 4 \\ +0 & 2 & 0 & -4 \\ \hline 2 & 0 & -4 & 0 \\ \hline \end{array} = (x-1)(2x^2 - 4)$$

$$x = \sqrt{2}, \quad \begin{array}{|ccc|} \hline 2 & 0 & -4 \\ +0 & 2\sqrt{2} & 4 \\ \hline 2 & 2\sqrt{2} & 0 \\ \hline \end{array} = (x-1)2(x - \sqrt{2})(x + \sqrt{2})$$

$$4x^3 - 4x^2 - 2x + 2$$

$$x = 1, \quad \begin{array}{|cccc|} \hline 4 & -4 & -2 & 2 \\ +0 & 4 & 0 & -2 \\ \hline 4 & 0 & -2 & 0 \\ \hline \end{array} = (x-1)(4x^2 - 2)$$

$$x = \frac{1}{2}\sqrt{2}, \quad \begin{array}{|ccc|} \hline 4 & 0 & -2 \\ +0 & 2\sqrt{2} & 2 \\ \hline 4 & 2\sqrt{2} & 0 \\ \hline \end{array} = (x-1)4\left(x - \frac{1}{2}\sqrt{2}\right)\left(x + \frac{1}{2}\sqrt{2}\right)$$

$$\frac{1}{2}\sqrt{2} = \sin 45°, \left(x - \frac{1}{2}\sqrt{2}\right)(x - \sqrt{2})(x - 1)$$

$$= \left(x^2 - \sqrt{2}x - \frac{1}{2}\sqrt{2}x + 1\right)(x - 1)$$

$$= x^3 - x^2 + x - 1.5\sqrt{2}x^2 + 1.5\sqrt{2}x - 1$$

Equation 2.31 shows the sum of the three simultaneous equations after eq.2.30 root substitution

2.31

$$S_{c1} = 3a + 4b - 2c = 3 + 4\sqrt{2} - 2\left(\tfrac{1}{2}\sqrt{2}\right)$$

$$S_{c2} = 5a + 2b + 3c = 5 + 2\sqrt{2} + 3\left(\tfrac{1}{2}\sqrt{2}\right)$$

$$S_{c3} = 4a - 3b + 4c = 4 - 3\sqrt{2} + 4\left(\tfrac{1}{2}\sqrt{2}\right)$$

$$A = \sqrt[8]{S_i + S_{ci}} = \sqrt[8]{29 + 19.77817459} = 1.625654285,$$

$$\left(\left(\tfrac{1}{2}\sqrt{2}\right) \leftrightarrow \sqrt{2}\right), B = 1.6399361468, \frac{A+B}{2} = 1.6327952156$$

$$\sqrt[3]{S_i + {}^eC} = \sqrt[3]{31} = 3.141380652 \approx \pi$$

The first part of 2.31 might suggest a rectangle of area 1 since this would have an hypotenuse of √2, while the second part might indicate the inscribing circle, radius ½√2. The third part is also suggestive of an object equal to 1, the combination of ^eC with S_i suggesting some area multiplied by 1.623. We are back in the realm of τ – this might infer that the above square is inscribing a circle, so that the area of the larger circle would be 1.621139 of the smaller one, almost exactly $(^4/\pi)^2$. The above results comprise the 'door that opened' mentioned in the Epilogue of the Mi book and in Part 3 we see the conclusion to this interpretation.

The initial problem between ^eC and S_i is that S_i has three unknowns to be found, whereas in the Chimes expression there are four. To find the solution to ^eC we would require further equations, but no such equations have become apparent. It may have been Mi's intention that we substitute a, b and c of ^eC with existing material, so substitute a, b and c of ^eC with the answers from S_i, 3.2, -1.8 and -0.8: '4d' is then the unknown we need to find. The other requirement is that of a final answer or constant but if we make the assumption that Mi was involved, then let ^eC = 22. This would also express the 'twin' idea and what we are looking for is 'd' showing a similar structure, indicating we are on the right track, as it were. In fact d = 2.2, which is $\tfrac{1}{10} \times 22$.

2.32

$$(2 \times 3.2) - (2 \times -1.8) - (4 \times -0.8) + (4 \times 2.2) = 22$$

However, eq.2.32 might raise the criticism that the answer to the original expression was $^{e}C = 2$, and perhaps the above-mentioned justification for using $^{e}C = 22$ needs further support.

2.33

$$(2 \times 3.2) - (2 \times -1.8) - (4 \times -0.8) + (4 \times [-2.8]) = 2$$

We find that $(^{-2.8}\!/_{2.2}) = -\frac{\equiv}{2}\partial$, or, $(^{-2.8}\!/_{2.2})^2 = 1.619834711$. The next thing to do is to insert $^{\equiv}\partial$ with each of a, b and c: -

2.34

$$(2 \times 3.2^{\equiv}\partial) + (-2 \times -1.8^{\equiv}\partial) + (-4 \times -0.8^{\equiv}\partial) + 4d = 22$$

Here, $d = -6.6$ and the idea of 'three' is also expressed because $6.6 = 3 \times 2.2$ and although structurally similar to eq.2.33 the signature of the expression is changed to $+ + + -$.

Issues concerning relevant synchronicities of the English language will be studied in GeoMitry, but what is about to be suggested as being another synchronicity seems a little odd (even to the author). Look at the letters 'b' and 'd'– they are almost images of one another. Could 'b' and 'd' of ^{e}C have any connection to $^{\equiv}\partial$?

2.35

$$\frac{-6.6}{-1.8} = {}^{\equiv}\partial, \frac{(374 \times 22)}{{}^{\equiv}\partial} = 2244, \mathrm{Sq}\frac{(374 \times 22)}{2244} = \frac{14 \times 4}{12} = {}^{\equiv}\partial + 1$$

$$\mathrm{Sq}3.2 = 5, \mathrm{Sq}1.8 = 9, \mathrm{Sq}0.8 = 8$$

$$(5 \times 3.2) + (9 \times -1.8) + (8 \times -0.8) = -6.6$$

The number 2244 is coincidental with the coefficients of ^{e}C but stranger still is the third part of eq.2.35. The sequential addition (Sq) for the values of a, b and c, when multiplied by a, b and c the result is $\Xi = \mathrm{Sq}_i S_i = -6.6$. This synchronicity suggests that symmetry is involved. Substituting in to eq.2.34 we have: -

2.36

$$(2 \times 3.2 \overset{\equiv}{=} \partial) + (-2 \times -1.8 \overset{\equiv}{=} \partial)^* + (-4 \times -0.8 \overset{\equiv}{=} \partial) + 4d =$$

$$((2 \times 3.2) + (-2 \times -1.8) + (-4 \times -0.8)) \overset{\equiv}{=} \partial + 4\Xi = 22$$

– and eq.2.32 can now be expressed as:-

2.37

$$(2 \times 3.2) - (2 \times -1.8) - (4 \times -0.8) - 4\frac{\Xi}{3} = 22$$

What becomes almost visual is that the second term of eq.2.36, '*', is equal to the first three terms of eq.2.37 and that $\Xi = -\frac{1}{2}$ of this. Equation 2.37 also meets Mi's criterion concerning negative numbers.

We can interpret these results as being a connection between the S_i and ^eC, that is $[x \in S_i \rightarrow {}^eC]$. Finally, if we consider ^eC as a diagonal matrix then: -

2.38

$$\begin{pmatrix} 2a & 0 & 0 & 0 \\ 0 & -2b & 0 & 0 \\ 0 & 0 & -4c & 0 \\ 0 & 0 & 0 & 4d \end{pmatrix} = \begin{vmatrix} 2 & 0 & 0 & 0 \\ 0 & -4 & 0 & 0 \\ 0 & 0 & -12 & 0 \\ 0 & 0 & 0 & 16 \end{vmatrix} = 1536 *$$

(* 1536 was introduced on page 25)

Using eq.2.32 the determinant $|{}^eC{}_s| = 648.8064$. This leads to: -

2.39 [$|\int(Ex)|$ = absolute value]

$$2x^4 + 2x^2 - 180 = Ex,$$

$$\therefore \sqrt{\frac{2\left(\left|\int_{-3}^{0}(Ex)\,dx\right| + \left|\int_{0}^{3}(Ex)\,dx\right|\right)}{|{}^eC{}_s|}} = 1.618321065 \approx \tau$$

However using the result of 2.33: -

2.40

$$|2.33| = -825.7536$$

$$\frac{-825.7536}{648.8064} = -\frac{\equiv}{2}\partial$$

This immediately suggests a connection to the rectangle [1696.46 × ($^4/\pi$)], that is $\sqrt{(^{2160}/_{-825.7536})} = -1.617341155$.

That the rectangle 2160 = 1696.46 × ($^4/\pi$), note further that $\sqrt[16]{2160} = 1.61585862$ and $2160/\sqrt{1.61585862} = 1699.223$, which is too close to the calculated figure of eq.1.17 to be ignored. To the first decimal place 2.41 is an identity: -

2.41

$$2\left(\left|\int_{-3}^{0}(Ex)\,dx\right| + \left|\int_{0}^{3}(Ex)\,dx\right|\right) = 2160/\sqrt{1.61585862} = 1699.2$$

In the first part of eq.2.42, the name counts of Mira Ceti and Lawrencium are included but not 103 since it is not a noun: -

2.42

$$41 + 23 + 37 + 18 + 119 + 47 = (222 - 78) + 119 + 22 = 285$$

$$(\mp 374) = 847, 8 \times 4 \times 7 = \left(^{\equiv}\partial - 1\right) \times 3 \times 7 \times 4 =$$

$$\frac{1}{6} \times 1 \times 8 \times 2 \times 3 \times 7 \times 4 = 224, \quad \frac{285}{224} = \sqrt{1.618802}$$

$$\frac{2160 - 2\left(\left|\int_{-3}^{0}(Ex)\,dx\right| + \left|\int_{0}^{3}(Ex)\,dx\right|\right)}{285} = 1.616842$$

The first line of eq.2.42 is intriguing because if it was construed as days, then it would be October 12th, non-leap year. This rather suggests that 182 and 374 are days: 182 would be almost the middle of the year, while 374 would be the 9th of January, very close to the beginning of the second 'crying' session. Since time is inferred, 'time' = 47: -

2.43

$$\sqrt[8]{47} = 1.618125613 \approx \tau, \ \sqrt[12]{\mp(182 + 78)} = 1.618032893 \approx \tau$$

$$\left(\frac{708}{556}\right)^2 = 1.621499922$$

In eq.2.43 the 8th root of the word count for 'time' is close to τ, with the author's name count added to 'Mira Ceti' resulting in almost exactly τ. However, apart from the combined name counts, with that of P. Moon, Norman's name does not show the same pattern, instead it illustrates *two* patterns. Norman's name count appears in the Fibonacci sequence for twinned seeds, and so: -

2.44

$$\frac{374}{63^{\equiv\partial}} = \frac{374}{231} = 1.619047619, \ \frac{374}{63 \times 1.619047619} = {}^{\equiv}\partial,$$

$$\frac{\mp 374}{231} = \frac{847}{231} = {}^{\equiv}\partial, \ \sqrt[64]{374 \times 47 \times 182 \times \tau} \approx \frac{4}{\pi}$$

This clearly demonstrates the dual nature of, and again reinforces the theory that Norman is the connection as mentioned in the Epilogue of the Mi book. The last item of eq.2.44 combines both Norman's and the author's name counts with 'time' and τ, resulting in almost exactly $^4/\pi$.

Section 4

Norman Oliver's recent researches

At about the time the author had the Mi experience Norman became interested in the events that surrounded the experiment involving the USS Eldridge. The study also included certain other experiments that had been carried out at the laboratory at Montauk, Long Island, USA. However, it was not until Norman made an inquiry, that the author began to see that there might be certain points that connected with his own Mi experience analysis.

Mi Mathematics Part 2

Firstly, three men: Edward Cameron, Duncan Cameron and Alfred Bielek – name counts 124, 126 and 90, total 340 – were initially involved in Norman's research. A.B. apparently came into existence at the age of 1 in 1927, the theoretical birth year being the same as Norman's, 1926. Comparing all three names, Edward Cameron, Duncan Cameron and Alfred Bielek with Norman Oliver, the only letter not cancelled out in Norman's name is 'v', which has the value of 22 – Mi or Dale? Agreed that these two coincidences are not enough, but in support is $^{(1926 \times 90)}/_{374} = 463.48$, where, ignoring the decimal part, 463 is equal to $+182$.

Next, Norman's full name minus E.C. and D.C., 374-250 = 124, which is a little confusing to interpret because 124 is also the word count for Omicron Ceti. The inference might be that E.C. should be considered without D.C. or that Mira Ceti was involved somewhere. In fact in turns out to be much more: -
2.45

$$\frac{124 \times 90}{78 \times 39} = 3.668639053$$

By dividing the product of 'E.C.' and 'A.B.' by 'Mira Ceti' and 'Enki' the answer is essentially $\overline{\overline{\partial}}$. The synchronicities now become significant, but there is an anomaly here. In Norman's investigations he found that allegedly E.C. and A.B. were one and the same though from different times. Norman has his own views on this, but we might suggest here, that if this was the case then we might be able to find some numerical connection that would suggest an identity. Either by ordinary methods or by forming generating functions two points become of interest. The generating function of $x^2 + 2x + 4 = 9x + 0$ gives roots such that $\alpha\beta = 4$, and $(1926 \times 124 \times 90)^{0.25} = 68.1$, close to the name count for 'Cetus'. Secondly $(^{(124+90)}/_{2})^{-1} \times 24 \times 60 = (1.0005\overline{\overline{\partial}})^2$ minutes, and this becomes important later. $(124-90)\overline{\overline{\partial}} = 124.666...$

The above three names involve only a single forename and single surname, so using Norman's name similarly, 156 -124 = 32. Using the author's full name count 124 + 90-182 = 32. Using

Norman's two middle names with the combined count of E.C. and D.C., we have 250-218 = 32. Two possible objections here are that a/ we have three names in the author's full name and b/ we have used D.C. Using the author's first and last names, 124 + 90-103 = 111, and Norman's full name, 374-214 = 160. While these two last results are coincidental with other Montauk / USS Eldridge matters yet to be mentioned, whether or not these suggest E.C. = A.B. is debatable, but to be sure, the synchronicities are there.

Moving on, 374 + 250 = 624 = 8 × 78, 1536-374 = 1162, 1536-250 = 1286, 1162 + 1286 = 2448, $\sqrt{(^{2448}/_{182})} = 3.6674242$. $^{(2448-1536-340)}/_{156} = {}^{\equiv}\partial$, $^{(1536-340-374)}/_{224} = 3.669643$. $^{2448}/_{22} = 111 + {}^{1}/{\equiv}\partial$. 111 is the word count for (General) Andrew Hero whose name was used for the original American name for the site of the Montauk laboratory, Fort Hero (see also eq.1.26)

Once again, the inference is that Norman is the essential link between his investigations of Montauk etc. and the author's Mi experience. We then have the questions how and why Norman should be connected? It would seem that someone, or perhaps Mi, knew in advance what was going to happen and therefore made all the possible connections for us to discover now. However, such a situation would have meant that at least the English language was already set up to take into account such connections. This might mean that there could be situations involving the experiences of other people that can be studied similarly. Is our language 'alive' in some way and all our actions determined by it?

In the book *The Philadelphia Experiment* by Charles Berlitz, the unfortunate investigator, Morris Ketchum Jessup, has the word count of 263, while Carl Meredith Allen and Carlos Miguel Allende is 160 and 188 respectively and Carl Meredith Allen also has a signed naval number Z416175. (There is no intention here to discuss the sequence of events that apparently surrounded these three men). The first point to note is 374-111 = 263, while the reverse procedure, using Peter Moon's other name, gives 152 + 111 = 263 and 374-152 = 222 – which might be Lawrencium + 103 or 2 × 111:160 + 103 = 263. The number of the

USS Eldridge (count of 123) was DE173 and the coincidence here is 4 + 5 +173 = 182, but more importantly: -
2.46

$$\frac{182-160}{188-182} = \frac{188+263}{123} = \ ^{\equiv}\partial$$

The arithmetic of 2.46 is surely a sign that 'something is afoot'. Because the identification of the USS Eldridge is a mixture of letters and numbers, it is difficult to form an expression. However, by construing all as numbers we have 4 + 5 + 1 + 7 + 3 + 26 + 4 + 1 + 6 + 1 + 7 + 5 = 70. Using this with a time element 365 (note that the numerator is equal to 22^2, Mi^2?): -
2.47

$$\sqrt[8]{\frac{(365\times3)-(160+188+263)}{70}} = 1.2734105 \approx \frac{4}{\pi}$$

(365×3[names]) $^4\!/\pi$ becomes important in Part 3.

Using eq.2.38 and the trace of the matrix from the sixteen numbers that make up the tetrads we have: -
2.48

$$Tr.\begin{pmatrix} 22 & 41 & 66 & 77 \\ 24 & 42 & 68 & 78 \\ 37 & 45 & 69 & 181 \\ 39 & 47 & 75 & 182 \end{pmatrix} = 315$$

$$\frac{1536\times315}{2160} = 224$$

$$\frac{1536}{224} = \frac{2160}{315} = \frac{a}{b}, \sqrt[4]{\frac{a}{b}} = 1.618213, \left(\frac{a}{b}\right)^2 = 47.02$$

$$\left(\frac{365}{224}\right)^{\frac{8}{3}} = \left(\frac{365}{224}\right)^{\equiv\partial-1} = 3.676655, \frac{\sqrt{45\times173}}{24} = 3.67636$$

$$\sqrt[8]{123\times182\times374} = 7.334255 = 2^{\equiv}\partial + 0.000921787$$

The equations of 2.48 demonstrate multiple synchronicities. The trace of 315 might represent 'Norfolk' + 'Philadelphia' + 'USS Eldridge': 'time', τ, '3' and '8' and time elements – with a result close to $\overline{\overline{\partial}}$ – are all there. The last but one item represents Mi's '....to twenty four' and DE173, with DE = 45, has a result again very close to $\overline{\overline{\partial}}$. Norman's and the author's full names along with 'USS Eldridge', give almost exactly $2\overline{\overline{\partial}}$. However, it would be important to understand what the matrix in eq.2.48, represents, but this discussion must wait for the developments of Part 3.

MKJ died on April 20th 1959, where April 20th is day 110, the word count for name of the author's mother (but see below), so is there a connection between this and items already mentioned? Using the counts so far, plus the counts for Mira Ceti and Lawrencium plus 103 we arrive at a figure of 1959 and $1 + 9 + 5 + 9 = 24$.

2.49

$$188 + 160 + 263 + 374 + 182 + 152$$
$$+124 + 126 + 90 = 1659$$
$$1659 + 78 + 222 = 1959$$

Finding $\mp$ of 188, 305 and 374 we see a 'merry-go-round' of synchronicities.

2.50

$$\mp188 = \mp374 + \mp111 = \mp263 + \mp222$$
$$\mp305 = \mp(182 + 222), \mp374 = \mp124 + \mp250$$
$$\sqrt[8]{\frac{\mp188 + \mp305 + \mp374}{r_\odot}} = 1.617516426 \approx \tau$$

$$(\mp188 + \mp305 + \mp374)^{\overline{\overline{\partial}}} = 365.256 \times 27.34520446$$

The synchronicities in eq.2.50 are so obvious that there is little to be gained in their mention. However, the time element in line 3 is converted to τ via '8' and line 4 shows that $\overline{\overline{\partial}}$ converts other items into time elements, in this case our year and a figure very close to the Moon's sidereal period. $r_\odot = 58.1323$ days.

Finally, we find some peculiar synchronicities with regard to the word counts of the various places involved.

The USS Eldridge allegedly disappeared from the port at Newark, 'Newark' = 72 = ½(144), and is said to have reappeared at the port in Norfolk, 'Norfolk' = 91 = ½(182) – some kind of pointer?

The pseudonym '(Dr.) Franklin Reno' was apparently chosen from a road sign, 'Franklin Reno' = 137 and 'Franklin Reno' + 'Newark' + 'Norfolk' = 'Mira Ceti + Lawrencium 103 = 300. In addition ∓91 + ∓72 = 209 = 91 + 72 + 22 + 24. Perhaps what is more significant: -

2.51

$$\left(\frac{2160}{91} - \frac{1}{2^{\equiv}\partial}\right) \times 72 = 1699.1928 = 2\left(\left|\int_{-3}^{0}(Ex)\,dx\right| + \left|\int_{0}^{3}(Ex)\,dx\right|\right)$$

Equation 2.51 can be expanded differently: -

$$2160 = \mp 95 + \mp 91 + \mp 72 + \mp(160 + 263) + \mp(2160 - 1536)$$

95 = 'Montauk'.

Other issues follow very similar patterns. For example 160 + 188 + 305 + 263 = 916 and $^{\equiv}\partial - \frac{1}{374} = 3.66399287 = 3.664$, $3.664 \times (124 + 126) = 916$. $(916 + 250) \div {}^{\equiv}\partial = 126 + 124 + 68$ (see Notes). Does our 365-day year fit in with the above numbers?

2.52

$$\frac{\left[(365 - 160) + (365 - 188) + (365 - 263)\right]}{(188 - 182)^2}$$

$$= \frac{22^2 \times (39 + {}^{\equiv}\partial)}{1536} = {}^{\equiv}\partial^2$$

Actual time periods seem connected to ${}^{\equiv}\partial^2$. In addition: -

2.53

$$(1943 \times 365.256) + 224 = e^{13.4729},$$

$$(1536 \times 365.256) = e^{13.2374},$$

$$(2160 \times 365.256) = e^{13.578462},$$

$$\frac{e^{13.2374} + e^{13.5785}}{2} = e^{13.408}$$

Also, exp.$^{\equiv}\partial$ = 39.121284 which is close to the word count for 'Enki', with exp.$(^{\equiv}\partial^2)$ / 365.256 = 1889.0814. What is interesting about the year 1889 is that 111 years have elapsed to the time when the author had the Mi experience, the figure mentioned above in connection the site of the Montauk laboratory. This might suggest that the year 1889, and hence $^{\equiv}\partial^2$, is a 'starting point' year. If we consider 111 (years) multiplied by 224(days) then divide by 365.256 the answer is 68.073 (years). 68 = 'Cetus'.

More recently, Norman advised the author that he was again, going to be one of the speakers at an annual UFO conference at Eureka Springs, in the USA. His subject was going to be about another case that he had been studying.

Although there had been cases publicized about contact with aliens from the Pleiades star cluster Norman's case had not been previously publicized. The young lady concerned – Louise – related to Norman her account of her meeting with Pleiadeans. Now, what is to follow is not intended to prove, or disprove, any of the content of Norman's 'contactee' case. Louise could not have known about the author's Mi experience so any synchronicity must come with some surprise, but the coincidence that the author believes is most important is the one that involves Norman. Brief readings of similar accounts by other people do not contain the synchronicities mentioned below.

The count for Louise's real name is 110, the same name count as the author's mother, and is exactly devisable by $^{\equiv}\partial$. The addition 374 +110 = 484 and v484 = 22.

The names of Norman, Louise and the author add up to 666, and one A. Crowley, who was very involved with the Montauk affair, used this number. Louise mentions three 'planet' names Aldina, Argan and Aldera all of which have the same word count as Mira, 41: but the important point here is $3 \times 41 = 123$ which has already been mentioned above as the count for 'USS Eldridge'. Then we have $123 + D + E + 173 + 110 - 374 = 41$.

Using a binary code for the names of the planets such that the letter 'a' is one while all others are zero we have 100001, 10010, 100001. If these were actually binary code numbers in decimal it would be 33,18 and 33, a total of 84.
2.54

$$\left(\frac{33}{84} \times \frac{84}{18} \right) = \frac{33}{18} = \left(\frac{11}{6} \right) = \frac{1}{2} \equiv \partial$$

Notice that the result in brackets has the number of 0's as the numerator, divided by the number of 1's in the binary code.

We must remind ourselves here that even if one is skeptical about any or all of the experiences mentioned, including the author's, we would still have the task of explaining the synchronicities. To disclaim or refuse the existence of the above numbers would be tantamount to disclaiming our own system of arithmetic – though you might get Mi's approval in doing so.

The suggestion therefore is that the author's Mi experience, the Montauk / Philadelphia affair and the 'Louise' contact case are all connected, with Norman as the essential link. With that said we have now completed this section on issues relating to Norman's studies.

<u>Jesus of Nazareth and 'The da Vinci Code'</u>

In the Epilogue of the Mi book there was a brief reference to possible religious implications, though really it was about the possibility that our language had been influenced by other, unknown agencies. In these final paragraphs there is a brief expansion on this point of view.

Mi Mathematics Part 2

In recent times there has been a lot of discussion both in the media and in print, concerning 'The da Vinci Code'. There does appear to be considerable speculation that Mary Magdalene was the wife of Jesus of Nazareth because she apparently performed certain rituals that were, in those days, only used by wives upon their husbands. There is also considerable speculation that the Roman Emperor, Constantine the Great A.D.274-337, manipulated certain ideals so as to combine the Roman religion with that of the evolving Christian movement. Experts say that he may well have destroyed certain writings that included the position of Mary Magdalene being the wife and an apostle of Jesus. This *might* then have led to the idea in later times that only men could be ordained as priests.

Enough of that. What we will examine here, are just one or two sums concerning Leonardo di Ser Piero da Vinci, more commonly known as Leonardo da Vinci.

$\sum$L 'Leonardo di Ser Piero da Vinci' = 264, 'Jesus' = 74, and 'Mary Magdalene' = 119.

The obvious synchronistic count here is 119 since is it also the count for 'Lawrencium'. Next $^{74}/_{12}$ (as in the 12 apostles) × 264 = 22 × 74. Just how does one interpret *that*? Perhaps Jesus met someone with a name that had a count of 22. Even stranger, is that both 'Lawrencium' plus 103 and $^{\equiv}\partial$ are in 22 × 74 = 222 × $2^{\equiv}\partial$. Also: -

$$\sqrt[4]{\frac{(((182+374)22)39)}{264^2}} = 1.617478648 \approx \tau$$

and 374 - 264 = 110. Having said that, the real mystery is – what does $\overline{74} + \overline{+264} = 847 = $ (Norman's name count)374 + 473 mean?

You might argue that we should use the name 'Leonardo da Vinci' since, certainly in our times, this is the name he is known by. Very well then, $\sum$L 'Leonardo da Vinci' = 146. (146 × $\sqrt{\tau}$) - $^{\equiv}\partial$ = 182.05. 374 - 146 - $^{\equiv}\partial$ = 224 + ⅓. ('Leonardo da Vinci' + 'Leonardo di Ser Piero da Vinci') ÷ 2 = 205. Calculating the fourth root, $(^{205}/_{78})^{0.25} = {}^4/\pi$ ($^4/\pi$ + 0.000001377 actually).

Mi Mathematics Part 2

Leonardo da Vinci was obviously an extraordinary man, known for his expertise in Art, Engineering, Science, to name but three topics, and it may also be worth noting that it was Leonardo da Vinci who did the illustrations for the first book known to be published concerning the Golden Ratio in 1509. The author remembers during the days when he (the author) was a member of BUFORA, someone mentioned to him a theory about men like Jesus and Leonardo da Vinci being of alien origin. In view of the sums in the last paragraph but one, perhaps they were one and the same – perhaps a Pleiadean?

At this point, we might be in danger of forming yet another mysterious 'code', a good place to conclude the section.

This completes Part 2 and we have reached the point where we can begin the Generating Access to Time Equations, GATE, proper.

Notes

A possible objection to one of the items on page 56 is that the common name of 'Lead' has been used where the chemical name is Plumbum. In this instance it seemed reasonable to use 'Lead' simply because it is an anagram of 'Dale' and therefore has the same word count as 'Mi'. However, the objection is somewhat softened because many common elements are known, by both lay and scientific communities, using their common names. For example, how often does one hear the names Kalium Chloride or Natrium Chloride? One doesn't, they are only known as Potassium Chloride and Sodium Chloride respectively (though the historical names are represented in any chemical formula, KCl, NaCl). Then there is the count for 'Plumbum', 98, which is not without synchronicity, because 98 is the atomic number of Californium. 98 is also the result of 'Lawrencium' minus the atomic number of Lawrencium plus the atomic number of Lead, $119-103 + 82 = 98$.

The name counts regarding the Montauk Laboratory and the Philadelphia Experiment (from page 76) are used from a larger list found in 'popular' investigative literature, and the Mi book has more details. Those that have been used in this study, seem to be less involved in more 'complicated name arrangements' than other people who were apparently implicated one way or another. On the positive side, having produced synchronicities from such a small number of people is an indication that there is something mysterious here. Perhaps Mi was satisfied with that.

The name 'Mary Magdalene' has a personal connection to the author (although the spelling is different by one vowel), but a discussion here would require approval and obtaining such an approval would be unlikely.

'Muhammad' = 'Jesus' = 74: 'Buddha' = 40: $\sqrt{[\log_n((40\times 74^2)^{\equiv}\partial)]} = 3.6873.$ $(74 + 74 + 40 - ^{74}\!/_{40})^{1/4} = 3.6845.$ Figures very close to these are connected to the 12th of August.

Eigenvectors and eigenvalues for eq. 2.28

$$\begin{pmatrix} 0 & 2 \\ 2 & 3 \end{pmatrix}, \det(\mathbf{A} - \lambda\mathbf{I}) = \begin{vmatrix} 0-\lambda & 2 \\ 2 & 3-\lambda \end{vmatrix} = \lambda^2 - 3\lambda - 4$$

$$\lambda = \frac{3 \pm \sqrt{9+16}}{2}, \lambda = 4, \lambda = -1$$

$$\left[\begin{pmatrix} 0 & 2 \\ 2 & 3 \end{pmatrix} - 4\begin{pmatrix} 1 & 0 \\ 0 & 1 \end{pmatrix}\right]\begin{bmatrix} a \\ b \end{bmatrix} = 0 = \begin{pmatrix} -4 & 2 \\ 2 & -1 \end{pmatrix}\begin{bmatrix} a \\ b \end{bmatrix} = \begin{matrix} -4a & 2b = 0 \\ 2a & -1b = 0 \end{matrix}$$

$$\begin{bmatrix} a \\ b \end{bmatrix} = \begin{bmatrix} 0.5 \\ 1 \end{bmatrix} = \begin{bmatrix} 1 \\ 2 \end{bmatrix}, \begin{pmatrix} -4 & 2 \\ 2 & -1 \end{pmatrix}\begin{bmatrix} 1 \\ 2 \end{bmatrix}$$

&

$$\left[\begin{pmatrix} 0 & 2 \\ 2 & 3 \end{pmatrix} + 1\begin{pmatrix} 1 & 0 \\ 0 & 1 \end{pmatrix}\right]\begin{bmatrix} a \\ b \end{bmatrix} = 0 \therefore \begin{pmatrix} 1 & 2 \\ 2 & 4 \end{pmatrix}\begin{bmatrix} a \\ b \end{bmatrix} = \begin{matrix} a & 2b = 0 \\ 2a & 4b = 0 \end{matrix}$$

$$\begin{bmatrix} a \\ b \end{bmatrix} = \begin{bmatrix} -2 \\ 1 \end{bmatrix} = \begin{pmatrix} 1 & 2 \\ 2 & 4 \end{pmatrix}\begin{bmatrix} -2 \\ 1 \end{bmatrix}$$

$$\therefore \begin{pmatrix} 0 & 2 \\ 2 & 3 \end{pmatrix}\begin{bmatrix} 1 \\ 2 \end{bmatrix} = \begin{bmatrix} 4 \\ 8 \end{bmatrix}, \begin{pmatrix} 0 & 2 \\ 2 & 3 \end{pmatrix}\begin{bmatrix} -2 \\ 1 \end{bmatrix} = \begin{bmatrix} 2 \\ -1 \end{bmatrix}$$

Eigenvector of eigenvalue -1 is (-2, 1), Eigenvector of eigenvalue 4 is (1, 2). The originating equations will be (0a + 2b = 4, 2a + 3b = 8), or, (0a + 2b = -2, 2a + 3b = -1)

Mi Mathematics
Part 3
Generating Access to Time Equations (ᵍₐᵢ)

Section 1

The author suggests that the derivations from page 68 onward, support the theory that it was Mi who was involved with Norman's Chimes Experience and that Norman's researches are connected to $^{\equiv}\partial$. For example : -

3.1

$$\frac{374 \times 22}{2244} = \frac{182 - 160}{188 - 182} = \frac{188 + 263}{123} = \sqrt{\frac{22^2 \times (^{\equiv}\partial + 39)}{1536}} = {}^{\equiv}\partial$$

The 12th of August now became important because the actual time of the Mi encounter gave us very little with which we could study. Our first question is – is day 224 synchronistic with the time of the Mi encounter? A second question would then be – does the time of Norman's Chimes experience also show synchronicities? A third, and fundamental question that we can no longer avoid is – does ^{e}C and S_i combine, giving synchronicities, that allow a conjecture that ^{e}C and S_i *might* form the basis of a theory regarding Mi's ideas about Time?

We start with the Sun's position relative to the Earth on day 224 where the Sun would have another 141 days to go to reach the last day. Here we meet our first synchronicity, because on page 57 of the Mi book the star Mira is introduced: the author's name count minus the count for 'mira' equals 141. Mira is the 15th named object in the constellation of Cetus, so: -

3.2

$$\frac{141 \times 15}{224} \approx 9.442, \frac{141}{15} = 9.4$$

These figures suggest that 9.4 is significant because if '141' were degrees '15' would then also represent the number of degrees in 1 hour of Right Ascension, as mentioned in Part 1. Converting 141 days of arc to degrees of arc we have: -

3.3

$$\frac{360 \times 141}{365 \times 15} \approx 9.271$$

This is a very rough idea of the Sun's R.A on day 224, but it is a little above 1½% less than eq.3.2. To decide about this approach a more accurate computation is required. The basic calculation for the Sun's R.A. is: -

3.4

$$\lambda_\odot = \frac{360}{365.2422}D + \frac{360}{\pi}e\sin\left(\frac{365}{365.2422}D + \varepsilon - \omega\right) + \varepsilon$$

$\lambda_\odot$ is the Sun's ecliptic longitude, D is the number of days from a given epoch, e is the orbital eccentricity, ε and ω are the Sun's ecliptic longitude at the given epoch and ecliptic longitude of perigee respectively. $\lambda_\odot$ must then be converted to R.A., noting also that the Tropical year 365.2422 is used. For the epoch year of 1980: -

3.5

$$\lambda_\odot = \left(\frac{360}{365.2422} \times 224.5\right) +$$

$$\left(\frac{360}{\pi}0.016718\right)\sin\left(\frac{360}{365.2422} \times 224.5 + 278.83354 - 282.596403\right)$$

$+278.83354$

$$= 221.2778261 + \left(\frac{360}{\pi}0.016718\right)\sin\left(217.5149631\right) + 278.83354$$

$$= 221.2778261 + \left(1.915741684 \times -0.608968596\right) + 278.83354$$

$$= 500.1113661 - 1.166626524 = 498.9447396°$$

$$498.9447396 - 360 = 138.9447396$$

We now have to convert this figure to take into account the Earth's inclination (23.441884°) using: -

3.6

$$\tan^{-1}\left[\frac{\sin(138.9447396)\cos(23.441884)}{\cos(138.9447396)}\right]+180=$$

$$180-38.62814807=141.3718519, \frac{141.3718519}{15}=9.42479013$$

The final figure is just under 9.43 hours R.A. However, the above computation does not take into account other small effects and an ephemeris program (see Epilogue) gives just under 9.467 hours R.A. The earlier figures from eq.3.2 are indeed synchronistic with the actual astronomical calculation for the Sun's R.A. on day 224.

Although each year the Sun's R.A. will change it will not be significantly different from 9.4 and the list below shows the Sun's R.A. for the years 1903-2003, to six decimal places. The increase in R.A. values is not sustained, however, and we will discuss this topic later.

Year	R.A.
1903	9.401392
1923	9.411529
1943	9.422149
1963	9.432243
1983	9.442653
2003	9.453129

If we now convert R.A. into seconds of arc we would have for 1943 for example, $3600 \times 9.422149 = 33919.7364$, but $^{\equiv}\partial^8 = 32671.67825$, therefore: -

3.7

$$\sqrt[8]{33919.7364}=3.683889192$$

Although the result, $1.004697052^{\equiv}\partial$, is synchronistic with $^{\equiv}\partial$, and therefore synchronistic with count for 'Mi' also, that it is derived from an astronomical calculation might it be a possible *source* of further synchronicities? Since the author's name count of 182 is close to ½ Earth year (which introduces the dimension of days), divide by the synchronicity of 23 days and combine this with the method at the bottom of the previous page using $\equiv \partial^8$: we have: -

3.8

1. $\sqrt[4]{\dfrac{182-22}{23}} = 1.624044917$

2. $\dfrac{32671.67825}{22^4} = 1.636363636^{-4} \quad \therefore \quad \dfrac{22^4}{1.624044917^4} = 33674.3$

Converting (1) to seconds and using the result in the second part of (2), the answer, 33674.3, is equivalent to just under 9.354 hours. Now, 1.624044917 is suggestive of the Golden Ratio, τ, and τ^4 occurs at R.A. 9.493747159, but this does not happen on day 224 for 1943 or 1983, though 1983 achieves the nearest value of approximately 1.6190. However, 1.624044917 *is* close to $(^4\!/\pi)^2 = 1.621138938$, and therefore is synchronistic with the items concerning $(^4\!/\pi)$ of Part 1. Perhaps more importantly, when the Sun's R.A. for day 224.5 is converted to seconds, using the method of eq.3.8 the result is 1.621059255. The reason for using day 224.5 is that the alleged events surrounding the USS Eldridge would have been closer to noon than during the first seconds of the day.

At the time of the Mi encounter, the Sun's R.A. would have been 18min.52.273secs. = 0.314520277 hours: -

3.9

$$22 \times 0.314520277 = 6.91944611\dot{1} = \sqrt[4]{1.621876693}$$

$$\dfrac{22^4}{6.919446111} = 33854.73291 \equiv 9.404092476$$

These figures are consistent with those previously mentioned and with the second part of eq.3.2. Since Norman seems to have this 'connection' to day 224, we might try a more direct approach. The

Mi Mathematics Part 3
G.A.T.E. ($\overset{a}{G_d}$)

Sun's R.A. on March 3rd 2002 was 22h 56m 24.733s = 22.940203611 hours – minus 9.422149 equals: -
3.10

$$\sqrt{22.940203611 - 9.422149} = 3.676690715$$

The result has an obvious resemblance to $\overset{\equiv}{\partial}$ but is also close to being half way between $\overset{\equiv}{\partial}$ and the result of eq.3.7. However, the result is misleading since it has been calculated from hours and not seconds. We might then try the *obvious* approach where the number of hours, 22, is already 'Mi', so using only the fractional part of 22.940203611: -
3.11

$$\left(\frac{22.940203611 - 22}{0.31452027\dot{7}} \right) \times 3600 \times \left(\pi + \frac{1}{103} \right)$$
$$= 2.989325895 \times 3600 \times 3.151301391 = 33912.96067$$

Although the result of eq.3.11 is about 7 arc seconds different from day 224.5 of year 1943, it loses some credibility because of the term using day 103 and π, though legitimate in their own right, lack a direct reason for being used here. Be that as it may, eq.3.11 does give an indication that the answer is there.

Norman's chimes experience first occurred on March 3rd 2002 at 42 minutes past noon, which is 42 minutes short of 22 days less than two years after the author's entity experience, noon March 25th 2000. Making a calculation based on these figures: -
3.12

$$22 - \frac{42}{60 \times 24} = 21.97083333$$
$$\sqrt{\frac{21.97083333 \times 24 \times 3600}{374^2}} = \sqrt{\frac{1898280}{374^2}} = 3.683905948$$

The result of eq.3.12 gives 33920.97062 arc seconds which is 1.23422 seconds later than the ephemeris figure (1943). What is even more evident is that eq.3.12 tells us that the count for 'Mi' when considered as days, will also be synchronistic. However, When Norman's name count, 374, is divided by √1536 (the determinant of the expanded Chimes expression) the answer is 9.54280379. Perhaps the determinant figure of 1536 may be involved.

3.13

$$\sqrt{\frac{(22\times24\times3600)-1536}{374^2}} = 3.684860626$$

$$\frac{3.684860626^8}{3600} = \frac{33991.35897}{3600} = 9.442044158$$

The result of eq. 3.13 is very close to the Sun's R.A. on day 224.5 1983.

So, if we use the count for 'Mi' and Norman's name count the above results add further support to the theory that it was Mi who was responsible for Norman's Chimes experience. Using the name 'Mi' we might theorize that Mi was involved in the Montauk / Philadelphia Experiment events of 1943 and 1983. Why contact Norman in 2002 and not 2001? :-

3.14 Number of days to = 2002 × 365.256 therefore

a. $\sqrt{\log_n (2002.169863 \times 365.256)} = 3.67458609 \cong {}^{\equiv}\partial$

b. $[(374\times182)/2002]\times[22/(2002-2000)] = 374$

Equation 3.14a is misleading since year 2000 would give a similar result, but b contains all three name counts *and* both years.

We have now achieved an answer, from an astronomical point of view, to the first two questions we asked at the beginning of this section concerning day 224 compared with the time of the Mi encounter, and the time of Norman's Chimes. Having found those synchronicities, we are now ready to tackle the third question concerning the combination of ${}^eC$ and S_i: *might* they provide a basic theory regarding Mi's ideas about Time?

In eq.3.15 below a, b and c from S_i are multiplied by a, b, and c coefficients of ^eC: the results are synchronistic with previous work: -

3.15

1a. $\quad ^eCS_i = 2aa - 2bb - 4cc + 4c$

$= (2 \times 3.2) - (4 \times -1.8) - (12 \times -0.8) + 16 = 39.2$

1b. $\quad \left(^eCS_i \right)^2 = 1536.64 = 1536 = 8^3 \times 3 = 24 \times 8^2, 0.64 = \sqrt{0.8}$

2. $\quad \left(^eCS_i \right)^2 \times 22 = 33806.08$

3. $\quad ^eCS_i \in \theta° \Rightarrow 180° - {}^eCS_i = 140.8° \equiv 33792"$

4. $\quad \log_n 39.2 = 3.668676747 = 1.000548204 \overset{\equiv}{\partial}$

5. $\quad \sqrt{\log_n \left(^eCS_i{}^{"\partial} \right)} = 3.667671569$

6. $\quad \dfrac{\left(^eCS_i \right)^2}{\tau^4} = 224.1927544$

7. $\quad \sqrt{(1699.2 + 8^2)} \overset{\equiv}{\partial} 365.256 = 1536.686172$

8. $\quad \underset{C}{\overset{S}{M}} = \begin{pmatrix} 3 & 4 & -2 & 0 \\ 5 & 2 & 3 & 0 \\ 4 & -3 & 4 & 0 \\ 2 & -2 & -4 & 4 \end{pmatrix}, tr\left(\underset{C}{\overset{S}{M}} \right) = 13, \left| \underset{C}{\overset{S}{M}} \right| = 260$

$\dfrac{tr\left(\underset{C}{\overset{S}{M}} \right)^2 + \left| \underset{C}{\overset{S}{M}} \right|^2}{2} = 33884.5, \dfrac{\left| \underset{C}{\overset{S}{M}} \right| tr\left(eq.2.48 = 315 \right)}{365.256} = 224.2262961$

The significant point about item 8 of eq.3.15 is that it obviously remains true no matter what values the constants have. We can now conclude that ^eC and S_i are the best way to proceed for forming a theory concerning Mi's ideas about Time. Item 1a,

Mi Mathematics Part 3
G.A.T.E. (C$_g$)

(^{c}CS$_i$) and item 8, [^{c}CS$_i$], are respectively type 1 and type 2 of GATE 1, C$_g$1

There might remain a feeling that something is still missing because although the name counts for Norman and the author are present in the above equations they are not in combination with each other. The synchronicities are not hard to find, in fact very straightforward.

Name count

$$182^2 + (2 \times 374) = 33872, 182^2 + +374 = 33971$$

$$\sqrt{\frac{182^2}{374}} = 9.410995958, \left[182^2 + (2 \times 365) = 33854?\right]$$

One criticism of these synchronicities is indicated by (?), that name counts other than Norman's, 400,450 for example, would also be synchronistic with 182 squared. We might answer this criticism by suggesting that since counts of 181 and 183 squared would not produce such synchronicities, 182 squared would be the primary number and that we are looking for the other name count that is at least twice that of the author's. Norman's name is the only one that can be remembered that is long enough, and certainly *is* the **only** one in connection with family and close friends.

One issue that was not addressed earlier, the sixteen 'tetrad' numbers viz: -

22	24		41	42		66	68		77	78
37	39		45	47		69	75		181	182

The question is why these numbers? We will look at this by introducing a new number, the Mi Ratio, M, which is equal to 12. 3.16

$$M = \sqrt{\frac{22 \times 24}{\equiv \partial}} = 12$$

The fact that the Mi ratio is equal to 12 is a mixed blessing as it were. While $M^2 = 144$, is synchronistic with items in the Mi book and herein, it is also coincidental with a great many other topics external to this work (the 'twelve times table', is one that immediately comes to mind). Although there is no intention to debate this here one wonders what relevant issues might be revealed at some later date.

Equation set 3.17 illustrates how the Mi ratio might be used on the sixteen numbers using eq.3.15(1a): -

3.17

$$\left(\left(^eCS_i - 39\right)\frac{24}{22}\right) + \sqrt{M} = 3.682283433$$

$$\left(\left(^eCS_i - 39\right)\frac{78}{77}\right) + \sqrt{M} = 3.666699018$$

$$\left(\left(^eCS_i - 39\right)\frac{182}{181}\right) + \sqrt{M} = 3.66526588$$

By using numbers with a difference of no more than 2, the first line suggests that when figures relating to Mi are used the outcome is synchronistic with day 224, while others are close to $^{\equiv}\partial$. This of course raises the question about $\mathbb{R}$: -

3.18

$$\lim_{b<a,(a,b)\to\infty}\left(\left(^eCS_i - 39\right)\frac{a}{b}\right) + \sqrt{M} \to 3.664101615$$

This procedure does have a kind of 'artificial 'ring' about it since there are fractions that will produce numbers greater than those of interest to us here. On the other hand, we have to remember where eq.3.17 & 3.18 have come from, and as such might be part of some proper Group and we shall revisit this topic in the Epilogue.

Mi Mathematics Part 3
G.A.T.E. (⌬)

Section 2

In this section we will try to develop the ideas of Section 1. We start from the premise that sometime during early August we will have $\sqrt[8]{}$(R.A. secs.) $= \overline{\overline{\partial}}$ (in fact for year 1943 sometime during the first hour of day 219 $\sqrt[8]{}$(R.A. secs.) $= \overline{\overline{\partial}}$). Days 208 and 231 are 99% and 101% of $\overline{\overline{\partial}}$ respectively (these dates vary with other ***3 years). Notice also that 231-208 = 23 days which is synchronistic other items mentioned herein. On Sunday August 12th 1923, at noon the Sun's position is calculated to have been: -

• Ecliptic long. 138° 44' 54.59" lat. -0° 00' 00.48", Apparent R.A. 9h 24m 41.506s Dec.15° 12' 43.47", Apparent longitude 138.742° Total seconds in R.A. = 33881.506.

Using the method of eq.3.8 and dividing 22^4 by 33881.506 we should expect a similar answer, and the result turns out to be 6.913978381. This we know is close to a power of ($^4\!/\pi$) and the answer is: -
3.19

$$\sqrt[4]{\frac{22^4}{33881.506}} = 1.621556197$$

Repeating this procedure we can achieve results for day 224 synchronistic with ($^4\!/\pi$).

• On August 12 Thursday 12h 00m 00.000s 1943, Ecliptic long. 138° 54' 45.04" lat. 0° 00' 00.64", Apparent R.A. 9h 25m 19.735s Dec.15° 09' 39.02", Apparent longitude 138.904°. Total seconds in R.A. = 33919.735.
3.20

$$\sqrt[4]{\frac{22^4}{33919.735}} = 1.621099113$$

• Finally, August 12 Friday 12h 00m 00.000s 1983, Ecliptic long. 139°13' 36.87" lat. 0d 00' 00.63", Apparent R.A. 9h 26m 33.552s

Dec.15° 03' 41.55", Apparent longitude 139.217°. Total seconds in R.A. = 33993.552.

3.21

$$\sqrt[4]{\frac{22^4}{33993.552}} = 1.620218341$$

The results of eq.3.19, 3.20 and 3.21 show a connection to 22 and $(^4\!/\!\pi)^2$ – but $22 = {}^eC_S$ $[d = 2.2]$, therefore: -

3.22 α = R.A.(seconds)

$$\sqrt[4]{\frac{\left({}^eC_{S,d=2.2}\right)^4}{\alpha}} \cong \left(\frac{4}{\pi}\right)^2, \boxdot = \left(\frac{4}{\pi}\right)^4 \Rightarrow \frac{\left({}^eC_{S,d=2.2}\right)^4}{\boxdot} = 33916.402$$

Although eq.3.22 might contain a clue to Mi's four time categories, with root 4, ${}^eC_S$ and powers of 4, it seems certain that $^4\!/\!\pi$ is directly connected to August 12th 1943.

However, $(^4\!/\!\pi)^2$ is 1.001918964τ and therefore implies that τ also has a part to play, perhaps with regard to other numbers herein. For example using eq.3.2 we find: -

3.23

A $\quad \sqrt[4]{\frac{141 \times 15 \times 3600}{224.5^2 \times 22}} = 1.61878576$

B $\quad \sqrt[4]{\frac{141 \times 3600}{22 \times 15 \times 224.5}} = 1.617885684$

With regard to $(^4\!/\!\pi)^2$ and τ eq.3.23 is clearly more synchronistic with τ. Therefore using the figure from eq.3.19 = 33881.506: -

3.24

$$\frac{33881.506}{224.5} = 22 \times (1.618381555)^4$$

We might have used the figures from eq.1.6 ($556^{1/4}\!/3$) because when they are used according to eq.3.22 or eq.3.24 they display a similar relationship. Having established synchronicities with day 224.5 we now turn our attention to the number 22.

As shown in eq.3.22 the count for 'Mi' could be replaced by ^eC_S and while this seems reasonable we must consider the possibility of $^eC = 2 = {^eC_{S(d=-2.8)}}$, using the constants of the original form. This presents us with a dilemma – if Mi 'sent the message' in the first place would it not have suited Mi to be identified with ^eC? Then we might ask – could both ^eC, $d = -2.8$ and $d = 2.2$ be correct?

3.25(See also eq.2.33 & 2.34)

$$^eC_{d=-2.8} + {^eC_{d=2.2}}$$
$$= (4 \times 3.2) - (4 \times -1.8) - (8 \times -0.8) + (4 \times -0.6) = 24$$

This might have a connection to Mi's '…up to twenty four..', and could be considered as adding further support to the idea that Norman's Chimes experience was due to Mi. Therefore eq.3.25 is a synchronicity.

60 is used for both seconds, minutes and Sumerian ideas, where at the end Part 1 it was mentioned that the sexagesimal system was used for their mathematical work.

3.26

$$\left(4 \times \frac{192}{60}\right) - \left(4 \times -\frac{108}{60}\right) - \left(8 \times -\frac{48}{60}\right) + \left(4 \times -\frac{36}{60}\right) = 24$$

$$\left[\left(\frac{M}{3} \times \frac{16M}{5M}\right) - \left(\frac{M}{3} \times -\frac{9M}{5M}\right) - \left(\frac{2M}{3} \times -\frac{4M}{5M}\right) + \left(\frac{M}{3} \times -\frac{3M}{5M}\right) = 2M\right]$$

That the numerators are multiples of 12, considered with the Fibonacci sequence (seed numbers $F_0 = 0$, F_1 and $F_2 = 12$) show some synchronicities. For example, from the Mi book M77 = NGC1068 and $F_{11} = 1068$. With the numerators of eq.3.26, i. $\frac{1}{12}36 \times 36 = 108$; ii. $\frac{1}{12}48 \times 48 = 192$; iii. 192-108 = 36 + 48; iv. 192 + 108 = 300 = ('Lawrencium' + 103 + 'Mira Ceti'); v. 192-48 = 144 = ('Lawrencium' 103 - 'Mira Ceti') or the 'glue' number from the 'reaction chamber' and vi. 2 × (108 - 36) = 144. The reduced size item in brackets shows how the whole formula can be expressed in terms of the Mi ratio.

We might conclude at this point that eq.3.25 is the one we seek. It incorporates the unknowns from S_i equations and °C, the count for 'Mi' and 'up to 24', what more could we want? The previous initial guess of 3.680827815, or a figure close to the Sun-calculator computation for day 224.5, would certainly add credence to eq.3.25. Using the numerators of eq.3.26 alone and with part of the Sun-calculator program we find: -

3.27

$$\sqrt{(192 \times 108) - (36 \times 48)} = 137.8695035,$$

$$\sqrt[8]{\left(\frac{\tan^{-1}\left(\tan(137.8695035)\cos 23.441884\right) + 180}{15} \right) \times 3600}$$

$$= 3.680552579$$

($\tan(\theta)$ is substituted for the definition on page 84)
Before conversion, the figure 137.8695035 gives 3.672484163 ≈ $\overset{\equiv}{\partial}$. Note also, the circumference of a circle divided by τ gives a result of $360 - (^{360}/\tau)$ = 137.5, equivalent to 3.671252362. These synchronicities allow us to conclude that equation 3.25 is G²2.

We make a short digression here. °C from Norman's Chimes experience, the Chimes sound was produced electronically, we might, therefore, consider the idea of both electromagnetic and mechanical waves. For electromagnetic waves the ratio of the frequencies to the wavelength is: - (both Metric and Imperial systems)

3.28d.1

$$f = \frac{c}{\lambda} \therefore \frac{29979245800}{1983} = 1511812698, \frac{29979245800}{1943} =$$

$$1542935965, \left(\frac{1542935965}{1511812698}\right)^{64} = \left(\frac{1983}{1943}\right)^{64} = 3.68463498$$

Equation 3.28d.1 shows that the ratios are almost inversely equivalent. Ratios like $^{1980}/_{1940}$, $^{1985}/_{1945}$ go outside acceptable figures.

Next, consider a standing wave of the first harmonic. At roughly sea level, air temperature of 20°C, the speed of sound is about 343m/s, so in an open-ended pipe of $\overline{\overline{\partial}}$ meters length: -
3.28d.2

$$\frac{1 \times 343}{2^{\overline{\overline{\partial}}}} = 1.617145463^8 \cong \tau^8$$

The *eighth* harmonic is interesting because the resulting frequency is 374.181818..., where the integer is the same as Norman's full name count. A frequency, in the 4th harmonic, of +374 is the result of using a pipe exactly $_2\overline{\overline{\partial}}{}^2$ m long. Various combinations of the author's name count do not appear to give any synchronicity, which, again, might add support to the theory that Mi chose Norman for the Chimes experience. So ends this short digression.

We should also require some form of eq.3.25 to be equal to zero. If we return to the very early stages of this study, then by using Norman's, the author's, Lawrencium and Mira Ceti name counts we can make generating functions with the individual digits of the name counts as the coefficients for 3.2, -1.8, -0.8. We have a problem, because there are four items and three of them, 182, 222, 374 suggest a 3×3 matrix, while 78 presents the problem. However, by forming the matrix in ascending value we find that the matrix automatically solves the problem for us because the diagonal, 124, is Mira Ceti's official name count, Omicron Ceti.
3.29

$$A_1 = \begin{bmatrix} 1 & 8 & 2 & | & -12.8 \\ 2 & 2 & 2 & | & 1.2 \\ 3 & 7 & 4 & | & -6.2 \end{bmatrix}$$

The row representing Lawrencium gives a positive result of 1.2 so

that we have: -
3.30(See also Tetrad 3 in Part 2)
$$2a + 2b + 2c - 1.2 = 2a + 2b + 2c + 2d = 0$$
$$\therefore d = -0.6$$

The value of d is precisely the value of d in eq.3.25 with the coefficients adding up to 8. So finally we have: -
3.31
$$a + b + c + d = 0$$

Since 3.31 can be expressed as $1a$ etc., the coefficients of the simultaneous equation entries are 111, exactly the name count for Andrew Hero, whose name was used for the original site of the Montauk Laboratory. So, eq.3.31 is $G_3^0$3.

A peculiar thing happens if we form another set of simultaneous equations using 222, 182 and 78, but with the same 0 values: -
$$2a + 2b + 2c = 4$$
$$1a + 8b + 2c = 10$$
$$0a + 7b + 8c = 15$$

The solution set is (0,1,1). (This happens with other situations but we are not discussing matrix algebra in general). However, since the 'a' column = 0, when we convert back to numbers we have 22 + 82 + 78 = 182, precisely the author's full name count.

Section 3

$G_3^0$3 has an actual signature of (+ - - -) and as such cannot represent, directly, an equation in Gravity. It could, on the other hand, represent 'particles' which are charged in some way as negative and positive. However, as every Physicist knows, one of the laws exhibited by charged particles is the electrical counterpart of the inverse square law for planetary gravitation, viz.: -

3.32

$$F = k\frac{|q_1||q_2|}{r^2}$$

Just as G represents the Gravitational Constant, so k represents an electrical constant, with q_1 and q_2 representing the charges of particles 1 & 2. Equation 3.32 is Coulomb's Law. However, this is where the similarity with the Gravitational counterpart, ends. An example will show why.

    Consider two free positive charges, say protons, approaching each other. As they get closer the force of the positive field from each proton reacts against the other and eventually the two protons repel each other. Similar situations arise for electrons. In an atom of Iron there are 26 protons (plus neutrons) in the nucleus surrounded with the orbiting electrons. The electrons remain confined because of the proton-electron attraction, and although the are also neutrons in the nucleus with the protons, the protons are still in very close proximity. What prevents the nucleus from 'exploding' apart due to proton-proton repulsion? Suppose we have two protons in a nucleus separated by 4×10^{-15}m, what is the magnitude of the repulsive electrostatic force between them?

3.33

$$F = k\frac{|q_1||q_2|}{r^2}, F = \frac{1}{4\pi\varepsilon_0}\frac{e^2}{r^2} = \frac{\left(8.99\times10^9\right)\times\left(1.60\times10^{-19}\right)^2}{\left(4\times10^{-15}\right)^2} =$$

$14.384N$

$$F = G\frac{|m_1||m_2|}{r^2} = \frac{\left(6.67\times10^{-11}\right)\times\left(1.67\times10^{-27}\right)^2}{\left(4\times10^{-15}\right)^2} =$$

$1.163\times10^{-35}\,N \therefore F_e = 1.2368013\times10^{36}\,F_G$

The repulsion force between two protons in such a nucleus is greater than the gravitational force on the surface of planet Earth, and also approximately 1.2368 million-million-million-million-million-million times greater than the gravitational attraction between the two protons. It should be noted that eq.3.33 is an 'ideal' situation between two protons in the nucleus and not necessarily the actual reality. It was questions not dissimilar to this that led to theoretical research into 'String theory', because at even smaller distances it seems that a similar situation exists within a proton itself. According to modern theory protons are made of three Quarks, and the quarks apparently cannot be separated because of a 'gluon force'. As shown above, if the force holding protons together cannot be explained by gravity it is highly improbable that the force holding quarks together will be gravity. String theorists interpret some experimental results differently to those who maintain a 'particle' standpoint and our present level of technology is inadequate in providing further experimental results that might resolve the issue.

String theory does have a resemblance to classical string theory (musical instruments, tension of ropes etc.), hence the name, so we might use such theories here. For example, a periodic function with a period T, an angular velocity ω and frequency f then: -

3.34

$$T = 2\pi/\omega, f = 1/_T, \omega = 2\pi f$$

Now, it is certainly true that as the Earth moves around the Sun it has both a period and an angular velocity, but whether it produces a frequency is open to debate. On the other hand, the Earth doesn't just move through empty space since there is a lot of radiation of various forms that continually bombard it. While the Earth's magnetic field and atmosphere protect us on the surface, there must be some 'noise' produced by the protective fields and the bombardment. The 'noise' is not likely to be constant and it may possess a certain periodic change.

Let us suppose that we are moving through (Mi) Time at a rate of $^{=\partial}/4 = {}^{22}/_{24}$, if we produced a 'noise' what would f and T be?

3.35

$$T = \frac{2\pi}{\omega} = \frac{2\pi}{0.91666} = 6.854383971 = 1.000041143\tau^4$$

$$f = \frac{1}{T} = 0.145892031 = 0.618027631^4$$

The period turns out to be very close to the fourth power of the Golden Ratio and the frequency similarly so for the Golden Ratio's inverse, 0.618033988. Now let us translate the period T into the length of pipe used in eq.d2 of the previous section.
3.36

$$\frac{343}{6.854383971} = 50.04096669 = 3.685037375^3$$

If we used the figure for day 224.5 of 1983 the denominator would be 6.855204514. We now combine the two expressions: -
3.37

$$\frac{343}{T} = \frac{343\omega}{2\pi} = \frac{343 \times 0.91666}{2\pi} = 50.04096669 = 3.685037375^3$$

The figures are so synchronistic that we might be inclined to shout 'eureka', but let us examine what we have done. Firstly, transferring the period T to the harmonic equation is not really legitimate, even though we might consider arguing that the 'length' of period T is analogous to the length of a pipe. Secondly, the harmonic equation does take into account the speed of sound at around sea level and at a certain temperature. Therefore we would need to take into account the general expression for all heights and temperatures, but we are not yet ready for such general expressions. What we need to do is to derive the number 343 from material in this work so that we end up with the same structure as the harmonic equation but derived from different sources and therefore not of the same dimensions. If Mi was involved in the

Chimes experience then this may be precisely what Mi intended us to do.

We have $343 + 22 = 365$, a synchronicity in itself and which looks very tempting since we couldn't get any closer to Earth's year. However, the Sun's R.A. on 12th of August, is a specific point in time that has interested us, so perhaps this is the route that we should study.

3.38

$$1. \quad 182 - 41 = 141, 141 + 343 = 484 = 22^2$$

$$2. \quad 119 + 224 = 343, 374 - 343 = 31$$

$$3. \quad 110 + 31 = 141, 484 - 110 = 374$$

$$\therefore (374 - 343) + (22^2 - 374) = 374 - (110 + 123) = 141$$

$$4. \quad \therefore \frac{(119 + 224)\omega}{2\pi} = \frac{\left(22^2 - (182 - 41)\right)\omega}{2\pi}$$

$$= \frac{\left(22^2 - ((374 - (119 + 224) + (22^2 - 374)))\right)\omega}{2\pi} =$$

$$\frac{343 \times 0.91666\dot{6}}{2\pi} = 50.04096669 = 3.685037375^3$$

Equation 3.38 contains the counts for 'Lawrencium', 'Mira', 'Mi', day 224, 'USS Eldridge', 141 from eq.3.2 (Sun's R.A. in degrees to the nearest integer), both Norman's and the author's full name counts and Norman's contactee case – all are there.

Now let us step up a gear or two, well a few billion billionths of a gear actually, and return to lengths of eq.3.33, much shorter in fact – the Planck length of 1.616×10^{-33}cm. Replace T with 1.616×10^{-33} in eq.3.37 and multiply by the rate $^{=\partial}\!/_4$ mentioned on previous page but one.

3.39

$$\frac{343 \times 0.91666\dot{6}}{1.616 \times 10^{-33}} = 1.9456476 \times 10^{35}$$

Now reduce this number an nth root that is a multiple of 8, the 16th root is: -

3.40

$$\sqrt[16]{1.9456476 \times 10^{35}} = 160.5338099 \text{ but } {}^{\equiv}\partial^4 \div \sqrt{{}_2^{\equiv}\partial} = 160.2204866$$

$$\& \left({}^{\equiv}\partial^4 \div 160.5338099 \right)^4 = 1.607225582, \therefore \text{ try } \tau^4$$

$$\sqrt[64]{1.9456476 \times 10^{35} \times \tau^4} = 3.668202949 \approx {}^{\equiv}\partial$$

Now compute the 8^2 (or the 'Eldridge') root of the figure from eq.3.33: -

3.41

$$\sqrt[64]{1.2368013 \times 10^{36}} = 3.663887975$$

The inference here is that billions upon billions of 'something' at the Planck length (or perhaps sub-Planck length) has an energy of, or is moving / vibrating, at a rate according to some Law which seems to involve ${}^{\equiv}\partial$.

We have now confirmed that ${}^{\equiv}\partial$ is involved at both Quantum and Macro levels, though it is not easy to see where this is leading us, except that ${}^{\equiv}\partial$ is perhaps all around us.

We return to item 5 of eq.3.15 and notice the Log_e is used, so let us compute the reverse for eq.3.40: -

3.42

$$\left(e^{\left(\sqrt[64]{1.9456476 \times 10^{35} \times \tau^4} \right)} \right)^2 = \left(e^{3.668202949} \right)^2 = 1535.184577$$

$$\therefore \left(e^{3.668202949} \right) = 39.18143153 \approx 39.2$$

$$[{}^{e}CS_i = 2aa - 2bb - 4cc + 4c = 39.2]$$

3.43

$$\sqrt[4]{\frac{e^i}{{}^{\equiv}\partial} - \frac{{}^{\equiv}\partial}{e^i}}$$

3.43 continued

$$\sqrt[4]{\dfrac{\overline{e^{3.2}+e^{-1.8}+e^{-0.8}+e^{-0.6}}}{\stackrel{\equiv}{\partial}}-\dfrac{\stackrel{\equiv}{\partial}}{e^{3.2}+e^{-1.8}+e^{-0.8}+e^{-0.6}}}$$

$$=\sqrt[4]{6.8652975}=1.618694311$$

The idea of eq.3.43 is simple in that we have just the constants from eq.3.25 & 3.30, root 4 to represent 4 time categories, and of course $\stackrel{\equiv}{\partial}$, and the result is synchronistic with τ. Next we include a true time component and the count for 'Mi': -

3.44

1. $\quad \sqrt[4]{\dfrac{365.256}{e^i}}-2\stackrel{\equiv}{\partial}=1.619630369$

$\therefore \sqrt[4]{\dfrac{365.256}{e^i}}-2\stackrel{\equiv}{\partial}\approx 0.5\left(\left(\dfrac{4}{\pi}\right)^2+\tau\right)[=1.619586464]$

2. $\quad \left(\dfrac{\left(e^{3.2}-e^{-1.8}-e^{-0.8}-e^{-0.6}\right)}{22}\right)^8=1.620888228$

3. $\quad \left(e^{3.2}-e^{-1.8}-e^{-0.8}-e^{-0.6}\right)\stackrel{\equiv}{\partial}\times 1.620888228=138.8885081$

$$\left.\begin{array}{l}180°+\tan^{-1}\left(\tan(138.8879984)\cos(23.441884)\right)=\\ 141.316477\equiv 9.25'16''\equiv 3.683837847\end{array}\right\}$$

The result of 3.44 (1) is almost exactly half between the average of the Golden Ratio and $(^4\!/\pi)^2$, perhaps suggesting both Geometrical and Sequential properties while the result of (2) is closer to $(^4\!/\pi)^2$. The result of (3) is synchronistic with the number of degrees R.A. for the Sun on day 224.5 and the correction in braces shows the value of the would-be R.A. (only 4secs different to year 1943. $-e^{-x}$ will be derived later). Now let us take a bold step and combine both the 'converted' Chimes expression (using the simultaneous equation substitutions) with the original version: -

3.45

$$\sqrt[3]{2e^{3.2} - 2e^{-1.8} - 4e^{-0.8} + 4e^{-0.6}} = 3.662598444 \cong \,^{\equiv}\partial$$

Then with the full, expanded version, (2×1- 2×2 - 4×3 + 4×4): -

3.46

1. $\sqrt{\left(2e^{3.2}\right)^2 + \left(-4e^{-1.8}\right)^2 + \left(-12e^{-0.8}\right)^2 + \left(16e^{-0.6}\right)^2} =$

$50.13976613 = (3.68740991)^3$

2. $\sqrt[4]{\dfrac{\left(2e^{3.2}\right)^2 + \left(-4e^{-1.8}\right)^2 + \left(-12e^{-0.8}\right)^2 + \left(16e^{-0.6}\right)^2}{365.256}}$

$= 1.619726965$ [note 1.619726965 days $\approx (374.1)^2$ secs.

3. $\sqrt{\dfrac{365.256 \times 22^4}{\left(2e^{3.2}\right)^2 + \left(-4e^{-1.8}\right)^2 + \left(-12e^{-0.8}\right)^2 + \left(16e^{-0.6}\right)^2}}$

$= 34034.82126$

4. $\sqrt[4]{\,^{\equiv}\partial\left(\sqrt{\left(2e^{3.2}\right)^2 + \left(-4e^{-1.8}\right)^2 + \left(-12e^{-0.8}\right)^2 + \left(16e^{-0.6}\right)^2}\right)}$

$= 3.68225138$

Equation 3.46 uses the equivalent of the magnitude of a 4-D vector and results (1), (3) & (4) are synchronistic with day 224, while (2) exhibits a similarity to eq.3.44 (1). Equations 3.42 to 3.46 therefore suggest considerations from other mathematical standpoints involving *e* and this is the subject of Section 4.

Notes section 1, 2 & 3

Group Theory (page 90) is another of those topics that has been brought forward from 'Higher Mathematics' and introductory concepts are taught sometimes at pre-college level.

Mi Mathematics Part 3
G.A.T.E. (G)

Group Theory might be seen as an extension of Set Theory but delves more deeply into the effect that one group might have on another group and also the interaction of group members between themselves. In a non-mathematical sense it is easy to see what this means. For example, say that one particular small group of people has the ability to affect the result of an election of some candidate to Parliament. What happens to that small group from outside and how they behave towards one another becomes crucial to the candidate. If someone else wanted to diminish the affect of the group, there might be several different ways this could be achieved. This would constitute a 'permutation' on that group, and hence, mathematically, we also have permutation groups.

Each mathematical group has a name and there are a large number of groups, but what may be of concern to us here is the process of +, and as already mentioned, we shall revisit this subject briefly in the Epilogue. However, it may that there is a certain type of symmetry group involved with +, although at first sight the numbers do not suggest this. The symmetry may be found in a geometrical equivalent but this discussion will have to wait for the next book.

The 'speed of sound' is another item that seems to vary depending on the source one consults, even though there is a definite formula for its calculation. The reason for apparent differences is that various types of equipment have been used to ascertain the speed of sound in air. The figure used in this work, 343m/s, is partly due to the range found in various sources, 342-344, but mostly because memory suggests 343.2. However, 343 is the figure quoted in the textbook, Fundamentals of Physics by Halliday, Resnick and Walker, Wiley International Edition, 2001 ISBN 0471392227 which was purchased by the author to replace books lost due to the flooding in Thailand as mentioned in the Mi book. One Internet source, 'Wikipedia, the free encyclopedia' quotes T_{20} is 293.15 K = 20°C (= 68°F), giving a value of 343.4 m·s^{-1} (= 1126.6 ft/s) = 1236 km·h^{-1} (= 768.2 mph). The general formula for the speed of sound in gases is: -

$$\sqrt{\gamma \times R\left(\varphi + 273.15\right)} = \sqrt{\gamma \times R \times 273.15} \times \sqrt{\left(1 + \frac{\varphi}{273.15}\right)}$$

where γ is the adiabatic constant, 1.4 for air, R = 287.053072 the gas constant for air, T is 273.15 Kelvin plus φ Celsius. Using these figures directly gives just under 343.234, but since a Taylor expansion is used, the result will be a little higher.

    Note also that the formula is in metric units and not fps units, but $^{\equiv}\partial$ was given as meters and if conversion is desired one must use the appropriate factor. However, one might suggest that the resulting number is not synchronistic, because it isn't directly related to $^{\equiv}\partial$. True, but it does produce another intriguing synchronicity, $^{375.19}\!/_{8.0216}$, which is very close to $^{375}\!/_{8}$. To put it another way $^{374.18}\!/_{8}$ is almost an identity and uses an eight and Norman's full name count plus. There is more. Convert meters to inches and use the expanded form of ^{e}C the answer is very close $^{\equiv}\partial$ and we have: -

$$\frac{\left(\dfrac{1760}{1609} \times 36\right)^{2} - 1536}{4} = 3.666486025 \approx {}^{\equiv}\partial$$

There is 'someone else' lurking in the shadows, as it were, because: -

$$\frac{1536}{36} \times \frac{1609}{1760} = (39 + {}^{\equiv}\partial) \times \frac{1609}{1760} = 39.006 \quad \text{Enki?}$$

Mi Mathematics Part 3
G.A.T.E. (♀)

Section 4

In the Notes to this section there are two lists and two graphs that cover the years 1793 to 2103 at ten-year intervals. List 1 and graph 1 correspond to the eighth root of the Sun's R.A. results in total arc seconds, for day 224.5, while List 2 and graph 2 are figures for the same years but produced from 22 divided by the fourth root of R.A. in arc seconds. For example, for the year 1943 the results are 3.683889173 and 1.621099113 respectively. There are several mathematical models that describe an alternate year pattern among which are those involving power series or exponential series. For example the Weibull model: -

$$a - be^{-cx^d}$$

Although correlation figures are very close to 1 there seems little point in pursuing this path since the astronomical programs provide us with the correct information. However: -

$$J_1(x) = \frac{x}{2} - \frac{x^3}{(1!2!)2^3} + \frac{x^5}{(2!3!)2^5} - \frac{x^7}{(3!4!)2^7} + \frac{x^9}{(4!5!)2^9} \cdots$$

$$\frac{J_1(\tau)}{J_1(L1_{1943})} = \frac{0.57161862}{0.060508129} = 9.446972323$$

Using τ and List 1 for 1943, ($L1_{1943}$), in the power series for the Bessel function of the first kind, the result is comparable to the Sun's R.A. (hours) for day 224. (Remember that $J_1 = {}^d/_{dx}[J_0]$) Let us take this path and see where it leads.

We begin with simple factorials. Use the digits in both Norman's full name count and the author's to compute ($n!$). With the exception of the second part of eq.3.47 (2a) below, results are synchronistic with both $\overline{\overline{\partial}}$ and day 224 establishing factorial synchronicities.

3.47

1. $374 = n_1! + n_2! + n_3! = 3! + 7! + 4! = 5070$

$$\sqrt{\frac{5070}{374}} = 3.681867696$$

2a. $182 = 1! + 8! + 2! = 40323, \sqrt{\frac{40323}{182}} = 14.88472187,$

2b. $\dfrac{40323 \times 365.256}{182 \times 360} = 224.7896473$

3. $\sqrt[8]{40323 - 5070 - (365.256 \equiv \partial)} = 3.683807617$

4. $\sqrt{\log_n (n_1! \times n_2! \times n_3!)} = \sqrt{\log_n (3! \times 7! \times 4!)} = 3.673550688$

5. $\dfrac{3! \times 7! \times 4!}{(3! + 7! + 4!) \times 39} = 3.670459718,$

6. $\sqrt{\log_n \left[(3! \times 7! \times 4!) + (3! + 7! + 4!) + (1! + 8! + 2!) \right]}$

$= 3.681798756$

7. $\sqrt{2(3! + 7! + 4!) + (1! + 8! + 2!)} = 224.6397115$

The final expressions of eq.3.47 might suggest using $[(n-1)!]$, but with one *possible* exception no synchronicities are revealed. The exception is this. Using Norman's name count (n_1-1) (n_2-1) (n_3-1) = 263 which is the name count for the unfortunate investigator of the affairs concerning the Philadelphia Experiment, MKJ. The synchronicities are: -

3.48

$$2! + 6! + 3! = 728, 2! \times 6! \times 3! = 8640, \frac{8640 \times 182}{728} = 2160$$

$$\frac{728}{182} = 4, \sqrt[16]{728\pi} = 1.621642352, \sqrt{\log_n \left(\frac{8640 \times 182}{2} \right)} = 3.684429$$

Mi Mathematics Part 3
G.A.T.E. ($\frac{G}{d}$)

There are two possible interpretations to the somewhat peculiar synchronicities of eq.3.48 – either they are a signal that this is as far as we can go on this route or, when considered with eq.3.47, are perhaps intermediate to something more elaborate. (224)! gives a curious result, 28, curious because $\underline{8} \times 28 = 224$. Although there are one or two others to add to eq.3.47 we will continue looking for synchronicities in e.

The Gamma function is defined by: -

$$\Gamma(x) = \int_0^\infty t^{x-1} e^{-t} dt$$

For $\Gamma(x+1)$ using integration by parts: -

$$\int t^x e^{-t} = f(x)g'(t) + f'(x)g(t)$$

$$\Gamma(x+1) = \int_0^\infty t^x e^{-t} dt = \left[-t^x e^{-t} \right]_0^\infty + x \int_0^\infty t^{x-1} e^{-t} dt$$

$$= x\Gamma(x), x > 0$$

For positive integers $x = n \geq 1$: -

$$\Gamma(n+1) = n\Gamma(n) = n(n-1)\Gamma(n-1)..... = n!\Gamma(1),$$

$$\Gamma(1) = \int_0^\infty e^{-t} dt = 1 \therefore \Gamma(n+1) = n!$$

Unlike the ordinary factorial $n!$ that uses only nonnegative integers, the gamma function, $\Gamma(x)$, can be used as one method of solution to certain types of Integral equations, where x may be an integer or fraction, negative or positive. However, the gamma function is more suited to equations involving small values of t and x, so first we shall evaluate the gamma functions of the familiar constants $\Gamma(-1.8)$, $\Gamma(-0.8)$, $\Gamma(-0.6)$ and $\Gamma(3.2)$.

3.49

$$\Gamma(3.2) = (2.2)\Gamma(2.2) = (1.2)(2.2)\Gamma(1.2) = 2.423965474$$

$$(x_1 = 2.2, x_2 = 1.2, x_3 = 0)$$

$$\Gamma(-1.8) = \left(\frac{1}{-1.8}\right)\Gamma(-0.8) = \left(\frac{1}{-1.8}\right)\left(\frac{1}{-0.8}\right)\Gamma(0.2)$$

$$= \left(\frac{1}{-1.8}\right)\left(\frac{1}{-0.8}\right)\left(\frac{1}{0.2}\right)\Gamma(1.2) = 3.188085903$$

$$\Gamma(-0.8) = \left(\frac{1}{-0.8}\right)\Gamma(0.2) = \left(\frac{1}{0.2}\right)\left(\frac{1}{-0.8}\right)\Gamma(1.2) = -5.73855463$$

$$\Gamma(-0.6) = \left(\frac{1}{-0.6}\right)\Gamma(0.4) = \left(\frac{1}{0.4}\right)\left(\frac{1}{-0.6}\right)\Gamma(1.4) = -3.69693258$$

$$\Gamma(1.2) = 0.91816874, \Gamma(1.4) = 0.88726382$$

The first obvious 'peculiarity' is that $\Gamma(-1.8)$, $\Gamma(-0.8)$, and $\Gamma(3.2)$ have the same final $\Gamma(1.2)$, which, from a list of one hundred values in the Gamma function tables, and that they all came from the same source, is surely a synchronicity.

Table 1

	x_1	x_2	x_3	$\Gamma(x)$ table	$\prod x_n \, \Gamma(x)$
-1.8	-0.55556	-1.25	5	0.91816874	3.188085903
-0.8	-1.25	5	0	0.91816874	0
-0.6	-1.66667	2.5	0	0.88726382	0
3.2	2.2	1.2	0	0.91816874	0
Total	-1.27222	7.45	5	3.64177004	3.188085903

Although at this stage Table 1 is does not seem very useful there is one obvious synchronicity: $-1.27222^2 = 1.6185437428$ which is close to the value of τ. The fourth total of 3.64177004 looks inviting as it is approaching $\overset{=}{\partial}$ but what is not quite so obvious is $3.188085903 - 1.27222 = 1.915865903$, $1.915865903^2 =$

3.670542158 and 3.670542158 + 3.64177004 = 3.656141099. Another curious result is $((x_3)^{-2} + 3.64177004)^8 \div 3600 = 9.378875573$. So perhaps there are some hidden pointers here but due to the nature of the Gamma function it was never going to be a straightforward case of finding any synchronicity.

The major criticism here is that $\Gamma(x)$ is not just a list of figures for us to play around with but are used in solving certain types of equations. However, the synchronicities might indicate that we should examine the function $y = t^{x-1}e^{-t}$. There is not much point in considering infinity since infinity would just about cover all synchronicities.

Let us say $t = \tau$ and $x = \{3.2, -1.8, -0.8, -0.6\}$ and plot x against $(t^{x-1}e^{-t})$, but because of the large interval between -0.6 and 3.2 we can use the intermediate of eq.3.49 viz. 0.4, 1.2 and 2.2. The x values are $\{3.2, 2.2, 1.2, 0.4, -0.6, -0.8, -1.8\}$, and the y values are 0.57157, 0.35325, 0.21832, 0.14856, 0.091816, 0.083391 and 0.051539. The graph (Graph 1) is shown below.
Graph 1

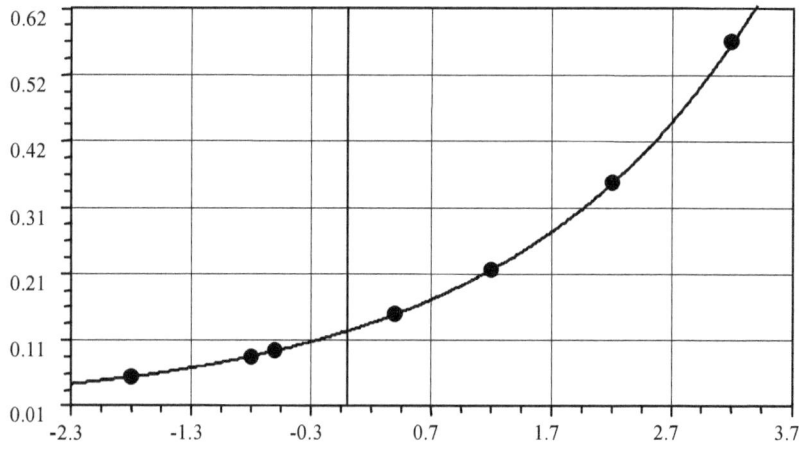

Mi Mathematics Part 3
G.A.T.E. ($\mathcal{G}_{\partial}$)

The first two best-fit graphs had the following details.

1.Exponential Fit: $y = ae^{bx}$

Coefficient Data: $a = 0.12254877$: $b = 0.48121185$

Standard error: 0.00000050. Correlation coefficient: 1

2.Modified Power: $y = ab^{x}$

Coefficient Data: $a = 0.12254877$: $b = 1.618034$

Standard error: 0.00000050. Correlation coefficient: 1

Table 2 below is a comparison table, between the accurate values of $y = t^{x-1}e^{-t}$ (input values) for values in between the original x values and the computer program calculation for those values, corresponding to ae^{bx} and ab^{x}. Evidently $t^{x-1}e^{-t} = ae^{bx} = ab^{x}$.

Table 2

x	$y = t^{x-1}e^{-t}$	ae^{bx}	ab^{x}
-1.3	0.0655579	0.0655579	0.0655579
-0.5	0.0963419	0.0963419	0.0963419
0.6	0.1635693	0.163569	0.163569
1.8	0.291398	0.291398	0.291398
2.7	0.4493407	0.449341	0.449341

As τ was used in $y = t^{x-1}e^{-t}$ the coefficient 'b' in ab^{x}, could not be claimed as a synchronicity but the aim should be to see if $^{\equiv}\partial$ can be calculated, with a condition that it is not too far removed from the figures obtained. A clue comes from $^{\tau}\!/\!_{\partial} = 0.4412727\ldots$

3.50

$$\frac{b_2}{b_1} = 3.362415119 \therefore \sqrt{\frac{b_2}{b_1}} \cong \frac{1}{2}{}^{\equiv}\partial \therefore 2\sqrt{\frac{1.618034}{0.48121185}}$$

$$= 3.667377875 = 1.000194{}^{\equiv}\partial = {}^{\equiv}\partial_b$$

$$\frac{1}{1-\left(a{}^{\equiv}\partial_b b_2\right)} = 3.665652932 = 0.999724{}^{\equiv}\partial,$$

$$\frac{{}^{\equiv}\partial_b + \left(1-\left(a{}^{\equiv}\partial_b b_2\right)\right)^{-1}}{2} = 3.666515404 \approx {}^{\equiv}\partial$$

So the results are synchronistic with $\overset{=}{\partial}$ and easy to find. Now we ask, are we able to derive some familiar synchronicity from using $y = t^{x-1}e^{-t}$ but with $t = \overset{=}{\partial}$? The y values are 0.000672398, 0.00246546, 0.00319707, 0.0117226, 0.0331468, 0.121538 and 0.44564.
Details of Graph 2 below.
As before, the first two best-fit graphs had the following details.
1.Exponential Fit: $y = ae^{bx}$
Coefficient Data: $a = 0.0069713097$: $b = 1.2992838$
2.Modified Power: $y = ab^x$.
Coefficient Data: $a = 0.0069713097$: $b = 3.6666698$
Standard error: 0.00000005. Correlation coefficient: 1

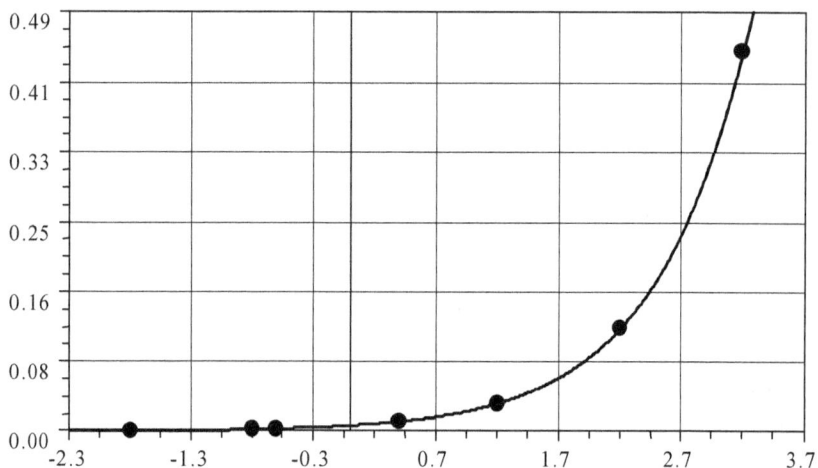

3.51

$$\sqrt[4]{\left(a^{-1}b_3\right)} - a = 3.68788379236$$

Once again the synchronicity is revealed without complication and is synchronistic with the values obtained for the Sun's R.A. on day 224.

We now complete the picture by reducing ab^x and ae^{bx} to a linear law using $\text{Log}_{10}y = \text{Log}_{10}a + x\,\text{Log}_{10}b$ and $\text{Log}_n y = \text{Log}_n a + bx$ respectively.

Graph 3 ab^x: $a = 0.12254877$, $b = 1.618034$

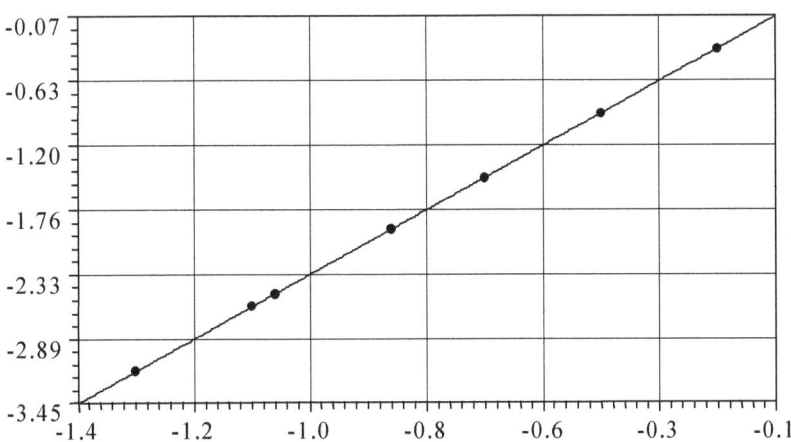

The details of Graph 3 are:

Linear Fit: $y = a + bx$

Coefficient Data: $a = 0.30490084$: $b = 2.7000235$

Standard Error: 0.0000062. Correlation Coefficient: 1

X values: -1.28787,-1.07888,-1.03708,-0.828096,-0.660906, -0.451918,-0.242931

Y values: -3.17237,-2.6081,-2.49525,-1.93098,-1.47956,-0.915288, -0.351016

3.52

$$\tan^{-1}\left(\tan\left(\frac{365.256}{2.7000235} + {}^{\equiv}\partial\right)\cos\left(23.441884\right)\right) + 180 =$$

141.3725901

This figure is synchronistic with the Sun's R.A. (9hr.25′ 29″) on day 224 and as ${}^{\equiv}\partial$ appears in the equation with a time value, this is further support for the conjecture that $\overset{\equiv}{\partial}$ is involved with time. However, a more direct method might be: -

3.53

$$\left[\left(\frac{365.256}{2.7000235}\right) \times 224.5\right] + \left[365.256 \times \left(\overset{\equiv}{\partial}{}^2 - \overset{\equiv}{\partial}\right)\right] =$$

$$33941.48767, \frac{33941.48767}{3600} = 9.428191019, \sqrt[8]{33941.48767} =$$

3.684184399

Although the dimension is days and not seconds, the figures are synchronistic to the Sun's R.A. (9hr. 25′ 42″) on day 224.
Graph 4 ab^x: $a = 0.00697131(0.0069713097)$, $b = 3.6666698$

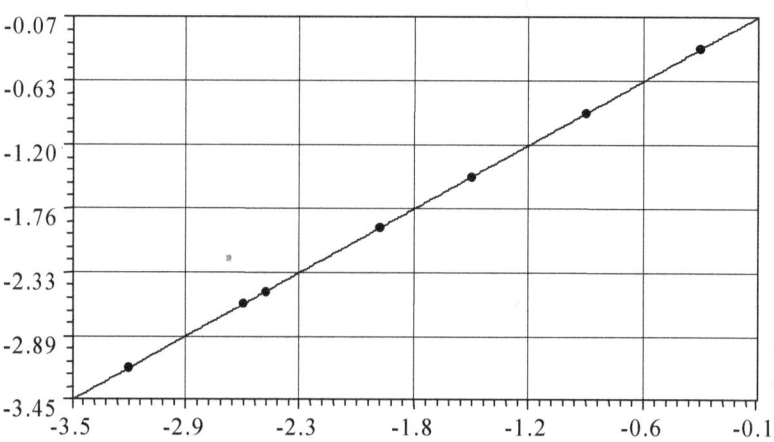

X values: -3.17237,-2.6081,-2.49525,-1.93098,-1.47956,-0.915288, -0.351016
Y values: -3.17237,-2.6081,-2.49525,-1.93098,-1.47956,-0.915288, -0.351016
Linear Fit: $y = a + bx$
Coefficient Data: $a = 0$: $b = 1$. Standard Error: 0.0000000
Correlation Coefficient: 1.0000000

Graph 5 ae^{bx} : $a = 0.12254877$, $b = 0.48121185$

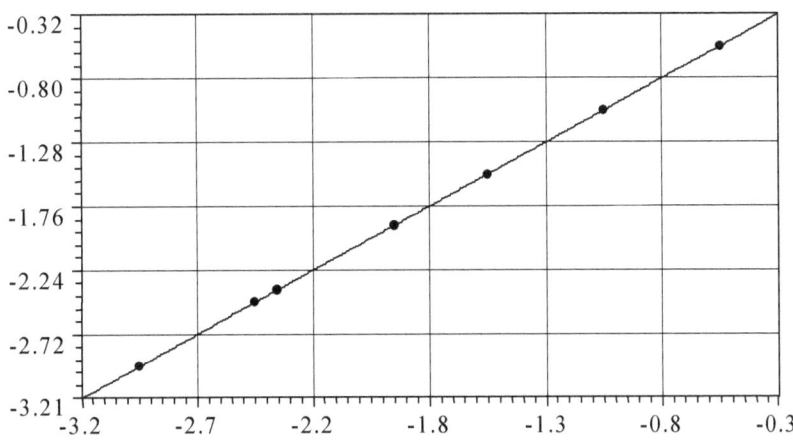

X values: -2.96543,-2.48422,-2.38973,-1.90676,-1.51792,-1.04058,
-0.559368
Y values: -2.96542,-2.48421,-2.38797,-1.90677,-1.52179,-1.04058,
-0.559368
Linear Fit: $y = a + bx$:
Coefficient Data: $a = -0.0012355282$: $b = 0.99949103$
Standard Error: 0.0018086. Correlation Coefficient: 0.9999981
    (The coefficients, a & b, of this graph are interesting for perhaps just one possibility: -

$$\frac{0.99949103}{-0.001235528} = -808.9586234, -\sqrt{\frac{808.9586234}{60}} = -3.671871964$$

The dimension here would seem to be minutes or hours where in the former, one is reminded of 806 seconds which, two or three decades ago, was used in rocket orbital calculations. However, the figure is in the negative and therefore might imply a reverse orbit.)

115

Graph 6 ae^{bx} :a = 0.00697131(0.0069713097), b =

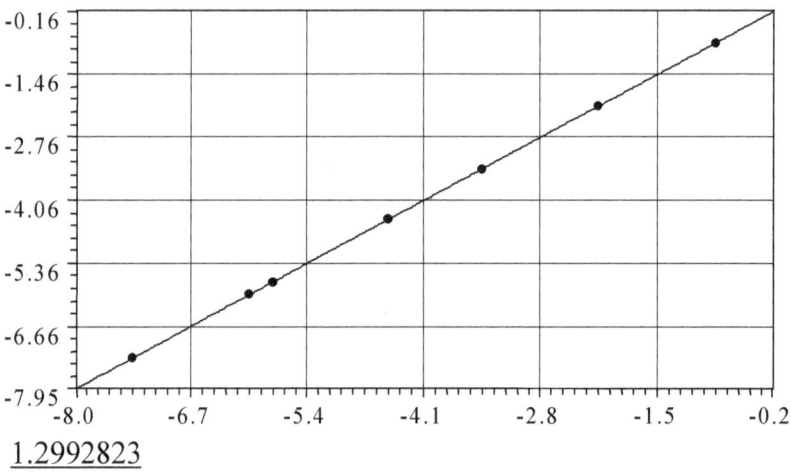

1.2992823

X values: -7.30466,-6.00538,-5.74552,-4.44624,-3.40681,-2.10753 -0.808244
Y values: -7.30466,-6.00538,-5.74552,-4.44624,-3.40681,-2.10753, -0.808244
Linear Fit: $y = a + bx$
Coefficient Data: $a = 0$: $b = 1$
Standard Error: 0.0000000. Correlation Coefficient: 1

~~~~~~~~~~

With the Linear Graphs 3-6 we have proved that ae^{bx} and ab^x do exhibit the property of being a Law in our present context. However, ae^{bx} is perhaps more important because it is confirmation that e should be in any formulation of Mi's ideas.

We now move on to other exponential ideas.

The exponential form of $^{\|e\|}C_{Se^i}$, is reminiscent of various mathematical entities, but the one we will explore here is likely to meet with much disapproval from Mi, that is, should Mi be 'tuning in'. The Complex variable is regarded as a generalization of Real numbers where the complex number z is defined as an ordered pair of real numbers (x, y) and an *imaginary* number $i = \sqrt{-1}$. Mi stated that negative numbers don't exist so no doubt $\sqrt{-1}$ would probably cause the equivalent of a heavy sigh of disbelief. Be that as it may, Mi must realize that there is no mystery here since $\sqrt{-1}$ was invented to solve equations like $x^2 + 1 = 0^+$. Let us just briefly revise one example.

Example 1 express $z = 4 + i3$ in mod-arg. form

$$r = \sqrt{\left(4^2 + 3^2\right)} = 5; \tan\theta = \frac{3}{4} = 0.75, \tan^{-1}(0.75) = 36.86989765^0$$

$$= 5(\cos 36.86989765^0 + i\sin 36.86989765^0)$$

$$= 5\underline{/\theta} = 5e^{i(36.86989765^0)} = 5\exp(i36.86989765^0)$$

In this very elementary example we can see a similarity with the form of the constituents of $^{\|e\|}C_Se^i$, but in the present form we are considering strictly a 2-D situation. In Ke^x, $x = \theta$ and equating tan θ, $\frac{g}{h}$ with $\sqrt{(g^2 + h^2)} = K$.

3.54

$$2\left(\cos 3.2 + i\sin 3.2\right) = 1.996881528 + 0.11164301$$

$$\sqrt{\left(1.996881528\right)^2 + \left(0.11164301\right)^2} = 2$$

$$-4\left(\cos-1.8 + i\sin-1.8\right) = 3.998026241 + \left(-0.125643036\right)$$

$$-\sqrt{\left(3.998026241\right)^2 + \left(-0.125643036\right)^2} = -4$$

$$-12\left(\cos-0.8 + i\sin-0.8\right) = 11.99883029 + \left(-0.167546164\right)$$

$$-\sqrt{\left(11.99883029\right)^2 + \left(-0.167546164\right)^2} = -12$$

$$16\left(\cos-0.6 + i\sin-0.6\right) = 15.99912271 + \left(-0.167548545\right)$$

$$\sqrt{\left(15.99912271\right)^2 + \left(-0.167548545\right)^2} = 16$$

Obviously one would not be surprised to see that the best-fit graph of the (x, y) coordinates is sinusoidal and this is in fact the case when using the CurveFit 1.3 program. The details are: $y = a + (b\cos(cx+d))$, where a =-0.17745189, b=0.3473883, c = 3.5562262 and d=-0.23042739. The error and correlation are 0 and 1 respectively. Maintaining that any synchronicity, if present, should be close at hand, the first one is so simple we might doubt its validity: -

3.55

$$\frac{\pi\tau^{\equiv}\partial}{abcd} - {}^{\equiv}\partial = 365.302$$

Clearly a synchronicity with the Earth's year. We would very fortunate if there was a synchronicity with day 224 so let us return to a couple of examples from Part 2.

3.56

$$\frac{\left[\frac{1}{2}\left(\frac{124\times90}{78\times39}\right)\right]^4}{abcd} = 224.12, \sqrt{\frac{2448}{3600abcd}} = 3.668975478$$

The first equation in 3.56 uses eq.2.45 while the number 2448 is taken from the page following eq.2.45. When using the coefficient data from the curve fit program, the synchronicities not only concern the 12th of August and ${}^{\equiv}\partial$ but again connect ${}^{\equiv}\partial$ with a time element.

If we decide that the coefficients of ${}^{e}C$, 2, -4, -12 and 16 are radii of circles, calculating their separate areas and adding: -

3.57

$$\left(2^2 + 4^2 + 12^2 + 16^2\right)\pi = 1319.468915$$

$$\frac{1319.468915}{360} = 3.665191429, \frac{1319.468915}{\left(3.683889173\right)^2 \times 60} \cong \left(\frac{4}{\pi}\right)^2$$

While the first part of eq.3.57 is synchronistic with ${}^{\equiv}\partial$, the denominator in the second part is the figure for day 224.5, 1943 and the answer is close $({}^4\!/\pi)^2$. We can go further and confirm that ${}^{e}C$ from Norman's Chimes experience is synchronistic.

3.58

$$\left(365.256 - \frac{1319.468915\pi}{180}\right) = \psi$$

and 3.58b

$$\left(\left(\frac{1319.468915}{\psi} - \left(\overset{\equiv}{\partial} - \psi^{-1}\right)\right) + 39\right)^2 = 1535.996669$$

Since $\left|{}^{\circ}C\right|$ is 1536, we can consider the synchronicity established. The other synchronicity in eq.3.58 is that $\psi = 342.2269231$, where day 342 is the author's birthday, which means the negative part of ψ is equal to day 23, a synchronicity already found in the Mi book. The count for 'Mi' is also synchronistic: -

3.59

$$\sqrt[8]{\left(22 + \overset{\equiv}{\partial}\right) \times 1319.468915} = 3.683164187$$

This is within the limits of List 1 and therefore consistent with the Sun's R.A. on day 224.5.

We can now search for circular synchronicities, firstly by investigating the circumference of the circles with the ${}^{\circ}C$ radii.

3.60

1. $\sqrt[4]{\dfrac{\pi 4}{0.5 \overset{\equiv}{=} \partial}} = 1.61805063159354 = O_\tau$, 2. $\sqrt[4]{\dfrac{\pi 8}{\overset{\equiv}{=}\partial}} = O_\tau$

3. $\sqrt[4]{\dfrac{\pi 24}{3 \overset{\equiv}{=} \partial}} = O_\tau$ 4. $\sqrt[4]{\dfrac{\pi 32}{4 \overset{\equiv}{=} \partial}} = O_\tau$

$O_\tau = 1.00001028584304\tau$

If we use τ then we have $3.666817526 = 1.000041143\overset{\equiv}{\partial}$.

Equation 3.60 contains steps to another discovery because it doesn't take a genius to notice that the coefficient of $\overset{\equiv}{\partial}$ is ⅛ of $2r$. Perhaps we now see the importance of the '8 syndrome'

mentioned throughout the Mi book. The procedure of eq.3.60 is true for all r. Proof: -
3.61

$$\sqrt[4]{\frac{\pi 2r}{x \overline{\equiv} \partial}} = 1.618050632 = \frac{\pi D}{x \overline{\equiv} \partial} = (1.618050632)^4 \approx \tau^4$$

$$\frac{\pi}{(1.618050632)^4 \overline{\equiv} \partial} = \frac{x}{D} = \frac{1}{8} \therefore x = \frac{D}{8}$$

$$\frac{\pi}{(1.618050632)^4 \overline{\equiv} \partial} = O_{\underline{\equiv}} \therefore \frac{1}{O_{\underline{\equiv}}} = 8$$

The ratio in the LHS of the second line will be known as the Oliver Ratio, since, as mentioned in the Mi book, Norman's Chimes experience was instrumental in developing a theory on Mi's ideas. The Oliver Ratio, symbolized as $O_{\underline{\equiv}}$, also reminds us that $\overline{\equiv}\partial$ is contained within it.

Having introduced the idea of Complex Numbers we might find that we could extend some previous ideas a little further. The number 16 has appeared a few times and since this is the square of 4, what would be the four fourth roots of -16?
3.62

$$\arg(-1) = \arg(-16) = 180° \therefore$$

$$z = 16(\cos\theta + i\sin\theta) = 16(\cos 180° + i\sin 180°)$$

$$w = \sqrt[4]{16}\left(\frac{\cos 180° + k360°}{4} + \frac{i\sin 180° + k360°}{4}\right) =$$

$$2\left(\cos(45° + k90°) + (i\sin(45° + k90°)\right), k = 0,1,2,3$$

So r = 2: the angle is 45°: each of the four points is an apex of a square, which itself is bisected by the (x, y) axes with sides √2 inscribed in a circle with radius 2. We shall see that this is synchronistic with items yet to be derived.

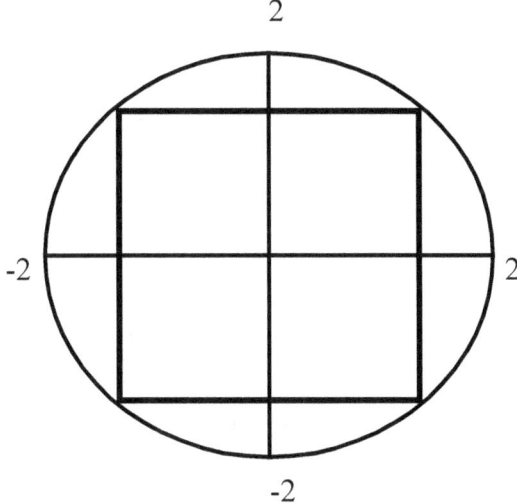

If Mi was to view these as 'active & passive ' time categories *we* could describe them as the above mentioned roots: -

$$k = 0, \ w_1 = \sqrt{2}(1+i)$$
$$k = 1, \ w_1 = \sqrt{2}(-1+i)$$
$$k = 2, \ w_1 = \sqrt{2}(-1-i)$$
$$k = 3, \ w_1 = \sqrt{2}(1-i)$$

We have a possible synchronicity with '8' in the above diagram if we consider $4 \times \|2\|$ but we could also have an external '8' synchronicity. If the above radius 2 circle becomes an inscribed circle with the resulting square area of 16, then the inscribing circle would have an area of area 8π.

Returning to exponential ideas there may be yet another interpretation of e^i. Suppose that the indexes 3.2, -1.8, -0.8 and -0.6 represent rotations about a fixed point (mod.360°) so that 3.2 × 360° = 72°, -1.8 = -0.8 = -288° = 72°, -0.6 = -216° = 144° = 2 × 72°. Once again we are shown the fact that 3.2, -1.8, and -0.8 come from the same source and though this may have been intended during the course that the author attended many years ago, - 0.6 from the Chimes expression could not have been anticipated by anyone. The most obvious synchronicity here is with the 'reaction chambers' on pages 79 and 83 of the Mi book. We also have to remind ourselves of the synchronicity that $144^{\overline{\overline{\partial}}} = 22 \times 24$, which just about sums up Mi and demonstrates again that $\overline{\overline{\partial}}$ is a 'conversion factor'.

The two previous paragraphs show that there is a need for a Geometrical approach to Mi's ideas, but this, however, would be outside the scope of this present work because here we are considering Numerical Synchronicities, so we move on in search of further equations of the four time categories.

If we were to suggest that: -

1a

$$\left(e^{3.2} + e^{-1.8} + e^{-0.8} + e^{-0.6}\right) = \bigcup_{1}^{4} \mathbb{T}$$

describes some Mi Time Equation, MTE, we would have to show that in the limit, it reflects exactly what we experience in everyday life – anything less will not do. That is to say that any equations we use to compute some time dependent situation, must give results consistent with our experience, when MTE is included. Inspection of eq.1a does not fulfil this criteria, but perhaps some simple examples might lead the way to a more consistent equation.

A rocket shoots straight up at an initial velocity 128 feet per second (39.0144m/s) We want to know what its height is after 1 second, the velocity at that time and when does it reach its maximum height. The equation for this is s $= s_0 + v_0$ -16t^2: -

1b

$$s = s_0 + v_0 t - 16t^2, s_0 = 0, t = 1 \therefore s = 128t - 16t^2 = 112$$

$$\therefore \frac{ds}{dt} = 128 - 32t = 96 \therefore s_m = \frac{ds}{dt} = 0, \frac{ds}{dt} = 128 - 32t = 0 \therefore t = 4$$

We require that the example above remains true when using the four time categories. Let us use $t = 1$. We already know that from equations 3.31 and 3.32 that $3.2 -1.8 -0.8 -0.6 = 0$, therefore:

1c

$$\prod_{i=a}^{i=d} e^i = e^{3.2} e^{-1.8} e^{-0.8} e^{-0.6} = e^{3.2-1.8-0.8-0.6} = e^0 = 1, \quad \frac{de^0}{dx} = e^0$$

So, multiplying Example 2 by e^0 would not affect the results. Now differentiate each e^i separately, which is only legitimate if all are indeed separate before some cause to combine we have: -

1d

$$\frac{d}{di} e^i = e^{3.2}, \frac{d}{di} e^{-i} = -e^{-i}$$

$$= e^{3.2}, -e^{-1.8}, -e^{-0.8}, -e^{-0.6}$$

$$e^{3.2}\left(-e^{-1.8}\right)\left(-e^{-0.8}\right)\left(-e^{-0.6}\right) = -e^{3.2-1.8-0.8-0.6} = -1$$

The differentials show quite clearly that the individual gradients multiplied together give the exact reverse of eq.1c and as such would give a negative Time when applied to our view of Time. Though mathematically correct we should still apply the usual constraint that differentials of 1d should display a synchronicity when used with other numbers given herein. Equation 1e, * and ** are –

1e(eq.3.44 page 102)

$$\left(\frac{\left(e^{3.2} - e^{-1.8} - e^{-0.8} - e^{-0.6}\right)}{22}\right)^8 = 1.620888228,$$

$$\left(e^{3.2} - e^{-1.8} - e^{-0.8} - e^{-0.6}\right) \equiv \partial \times 1.620888228 = 138.8885081$$

$$\left(\frac{22^4}{1.620888228^4} = 33937.39\right) *, \left\{ \begin{array}{l} 180°+\tan^{-1}(\tan(138.8879984)\cos(23.441884))= \\ 141.316477 \equiv 9.25'16" \equiv 3.683837847 \end{array} \right\} **$$

– synchronistic with previous figures for τ and the Sun's R.A. for day 224. What we have deduced in recent pages is based on all the prior synchronicities so now we can say: -

GATE 4, $\mathcal{G}$4

$$\prod_{i=a}^{i=d} e^i = e^{3.2} e^{-1.8} e^{-0.8} e^{-0.6} = e^{3.2-1.8-0.8-0.6} = e^0 = 1,$$

$$\frac{d}{di} e^i = e^i, \frac{d}{di} e^{-i} = -e^{-i}$$

$$= e^{3.2} \left(-e^{-1.8}\right)\left(-e^{-0.8}\right)\left(-e^{-0.6}\right) = -e^{3.2-1.8-0.8-0.6} = -1$$

▶ $\mathcal{G}$4, are the candidates for the Components of the Four Mi Time Categories, with their Reversal ◀

$\mathcal{G}$4, on the one hand, could be regarded as definite progress concerning an interpretation of Mi's ideas. On the other hand, it would be premature to claim that it solves the problem of Time Travel <u>in the Mi context</u> (TTM) but at least we have a theory based on the synchronicities.

As a prelude to other ideas to be developed in Part 4 we note the following equations.

3.63

a $\quad \sqrt[3]{2e^{3.2} - 2e^{-1.8} - 4e^{-0.8} + 4e^{-0.6}} = 3.662598444 \cong {}^{\equiv}\partial$

b $\quad \sqrt{\left(e^{3.2}\right)^2 + \left(e^{-1.8}\right)^2 + \left(e^{-0.8}\right)^2 + \left(e^{-0.6}\right)^2} = e^{3.2} + 0.01081$

c $\quad \sqrt{\left(2e^{3.2}\right)^2 + \left(-2e^{-1.8}\right)^2 + \left(-4e^{-0.8}\right)^2 + \left(4e^{-0.6}\right)^2} =$

49.14813219 = (3.66298949)³

1. $\sqrt{\left(2e^{3.2}\right)^2 + \left(-4e^{-1.8}\right)^2 + \left(-12e^{-0.8}\right)^2 + \left(16e^{-0.6}\right)^2} =$

50.13976613 = (3.68740991)³

3.63 continued

2. $\sqrt[4]{\dfrac{\left(2e^{3.2}\right)^2 + \left(-4e^{-1.8}\right)^2 + \left(-12e^{-0.8}\right)^2 + \left(16e^{-0.6}\right)^2}{365.256}} = 1.619726965$

3. $\left(\text{using the previous format of } \sqrt[4]{\dfrac{\left(^{e}C_{s,d=2.2}\right)^4}{\alpha}}\right),$

$\dfrac{365.256 \times 22^4}{\left(2e^{3.2}\right)^2 + \left(-4e^{-1.8}\right)^2 + \left(-12e^{-0.8}\right)^2 + \left(16e^{-0.6}\right)^2} = 34034.82126$

The first part of eq.3.63(a) needs no explanation, 3.63(b) might be a coordinate equal to $e^{3.2}$ and would, of course, be the dominant one as far as proportions are concerned, being more than $148 \times e^{-1.8}$ and greater than $44 \times e^{-0.6}$ so hardly a synchronicity. 3.63(c) is approximately 3.63(a): 3.63(1) is the expanded form of ^{e}C and the result is synchronistic with Sun's R.A. for day 224: 3.63(2) is synchronistic with τ and our year: 3.63(3) is synchronistic with the earlier equations being equivalent to about 9h.27¼m but the dimension is days / Mi, whatever that means. Nevertheless the result is a synchronicity.

    The next equation set continues with computations similar to the above but with the addition of $^{\equiv}\partial$, showing that $^{\equiv}\partial$ has 'transformation' properties. First we use a type of reverse element to eq.3.63(3): -

3.64

$\sqrt[4]{365.256} \times 22$

$\left(\dfrac{\sqrt[4]{365.256} \times 22}{\sqrt{\left(2e^{3.2}\right)^2 + \left(-4e^{-1.8}\right)^2 + \left(-12e^{-0.8}\right)^2 + \left(16e^{-0.6}\right)^2}}\right)^2 =$

(equation 3.64 continued on the next page)

$$\frac{\sqrt{365.256} \times 22^2}{\left(2e^{3.2}\right)^2 + \left(-4e^{-1.8}\right)^2 + \left(-12e^{-0.8}\right)^2 + \left(16e^{-0.6}\right)^2} = 3.67942058$$

$$\therefore \sqrt{365.256} \times 22^2 =$$

$$3.67942058\left[\left(2e^{3.2}\right)^2 + \left(-4e^{-1.8}\right)^2 + \left(-12e^{-0.8}\right)^2 + \left(16e^{-0.6}\right)^2\right]$$

$$\left(3.67942058 \equiv \partial\left[\left(2e^{3.2}\right)^2 + \left(-4e^{-1.8}\right)^2 + \left(-12e^{-0.8}\right)^2 + \left(16e^{-0.6}\right)^2\right]\right)$$

$$\equiv 9.25'17''$$

If the final figure was in seconds it would be equivalent to the Sun's R.A. of about 9hr.25min.17secs, a little less than 3 arc secs. for the year 1943. There is a somewhat intriguing synchronicity here with the catalogue number for M77, NGC 1068. If we were to use $22 + \frac{1}{1068}$ in eq.3.64 we would find an equivalent R.A. of 9hr.25min.19.73secs, almost exactly that for day 224.5, year 1943.

We might conjecture that since the result of eq.3.64 involves the count for 'Mi' it might represent a basic formulation of the Mi environment as compared to our year. However: -
3.65

$$\sqrt[4]{\equiv \partial\left(\sqrt{\left(2e^{3.2}\right)^2 + \left(-4e^{-1.8}\right)^2 + \left(-12e^{-0.8}\right)^2 + \left(16e^{-0.6}\right)^2}\right)}$$

$$= 3.68225138$$

Equation 3.65 has not been simplified because it shows clearly that multiplying the equivalent of a resultant 4-vector by $\overset{\equiv}{\partial}$ then taking the 4th root, gives a figure that is synchronistic with day 224.5, being equivalent to the Sun's R.A. of 9h.23m.19s. This figure is approximately 2 minutes prior to the figure obtained previously for the year 1943 – but it is even closer to day 224.0 on which the Sun's R.A. is calculated as 9h.23m.27.3s, a difference of a little over *eight* arc seconds. We can theorize that the equations of this section could be the reason for the synchronicities found with the

Montauk / Philadelphia affairs and that $\overset{\equiv}{\partial}$ is clearly established in its role with Time. Therefore eq.3.64 and 3.65 are ♑5.

The synchronicities might suggest that $\sqrt{(\sum({}^{e}Ce^{i})^{2})}$ is a resultant 4-d vector which can be converted to day 224 of our year. However, perhaps to Mi such a figure might *not* represent day 224, and the zero elements considered previously might imply that day 224 could be 'day' 0 as far as Mi is concerned. If that were the case some intriguing new ideas come in to play. For example, the author's birthday would be on day 118, but Norman's would be day 342, which is the author's birthday in our year. Day 118 would be the 28th April and 28th April in our year is, mysteriously enough, *eight* days after M.K.Jessup's death. There are also some numerical synchronicities: -

3.66

$$\sqrt[8]{(118 \times 224)\overset{\equiv}{_{2}\partial}} = 3.680088, \sqrt[8]{(118 \times 141 \times 2)} = 3.675076548,$$

$$\sqrt[8]{\frac{(118+141)^{2}}{2}} = 3.67871541$$

However, what is more significant is this. It was on March 25th 2000 when the Mi entity was encountered, day 85, to Mi = day 226, or 139 days to end of the year. Convert 139 to degrees on the circle, approximately 137°, which compares with $\sqrt{({}^{360}/_{137.5})}°$ this being one of the geometrical equivalents of τ. More specifically, the synchronicity is related to the Sun's R.A. in arc seconds for day 224, year 1943: -

3.67

$$\sqrt{\frac{360}{137}} = 1.621029681 \approx \sqrt[4]{\frac{22^{4}}{33919.735}} = 1.621099113$$

These synchronicities therefore suggest that it is possible that the connection between our year and the Mi 'year', or perhaps more generally, our universe and the Mi domain, is τ, or a multiple thereof. A diagram of the theoretical point of connection is now possible, although this does raise further questions.

Figure U⊂ **M**

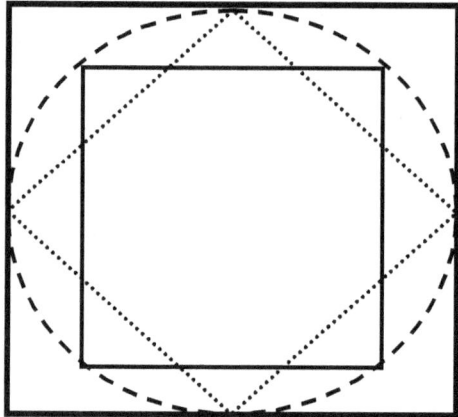

Figure U⊂**M** is an ideal 2-D representation. If the smaller inscribed square represents, say, our Time, as it rotates on a central axis (the inscribed diamond) it describes a circle. If the outer square is rotating at a different rate to that of the inscribed square, the apexes of the inscribed square will, at some point, coincide with the sides of the outer square creating *four* connections. If this were the case then a particle on the outer perimeter would need to have a velocity of $^4\!/\pi$ greater than that of a particle on the circle, to remain synchronous.

3.68

$$R_c = \frac{1}{2}\sqrt{x^2 + y^2} \;\therefore A_c = \pi\left(\frac{1}{2}\sqrt{x^2 + y^2}\right)^2$$

$$A_\square = \frac{4}{\pi}\pi\left(\frac{1}{2}\sqrt{x^2 + y^2}\right)^2 = 4\left(\frac{1}{2}\sqrt{x^2 + y^2}\right)^2 =$$

$$x^2 + y^2 = 2A_\square, \frac{A_\square}{A_c} = \frac{4}{\pi} \;\therefore A_\square = \frac{4A_c}{2\pi}$$

Equation 3.68 shows the relationship between the outer square, '$A_\square$' with a rectangle subscript, and the inner square, '$A_\square$' with a smaller rectangle subscript, and the area of the inscribed circle, A_c. This means that the area of the outer will be twice that of the inner square. Could this be part of the meaning for 'twin' or the resultant 2 of ^eC? Furthermore, if the sides of the inner square are <u>two</u> units then the outer square has an area of <u>eight</u> units. It is not hard to see that if such a situation existed movement from one to the other would be theoretically possible. Figure $U \subset M$ highlights, once again, the need for a geometrical approach. It is, however, unlikely that such a situation is going to be achieved easily. For example, there may not be a common center of revolution, or, other forces may affect the rate of movement, to mention but two possibilities.

Notes

On page 127 it was assumed that Mi's system 'lagged behind' ours, that is, that day 226 was in the 365 day period. Perhaps a better idea would have been to maintain a 365.256 day period so that 139.256 would result in a figure almost exactly halfway between τ and 1.621099113.

Because the Earth's orbit around the Sun is almost a circle and that the period is not that far out from 360° it follows that some computations on one system will reflect a similar result on the other. For example, if we choose the radius as being equal to 58.1323° and an arc of 224.5° then 224.5-180 = 44.5. The Sine^{-1} of the angle is Sine^{-1} ($^{44.5}/_{58.1323}$) = 49.95107253° = $(3.682829437)^3$.

[†] Leonhard Euler apparently considered equations that others of his time tried to avoid. Although there is no real solution to the equation $x^2 + 1 = 0$, the 'invented' solution led the way to solving many other real equations.

Lists and graphs begin on the next page.

Mi Mathematics Part 3
G.A.T.E. Notes

Below is List 1 for years 1693 to 2103, day 224.5, with the corresponding eighth root of the calculated Right Ascension results converted to total seconds. The average is 3.685779931.

List 1

1693	3.688312649	1903	3.682870195
1703	3.683938274	1913	3.68467259
1713	3.685744327	1923	3.683369929
1723	3.684455819	1933	3.685158116
1733	3.686244408	1943	3.683889173
1743	3.684942941	1953	3.685696395
1753	3.686755196	1963	3.684382299
1763	3.685476905	1973	3.686197428
1773	3.687237943	1983	3.684890342
1783	3.685984177	1993	3.68669523
1793	3.687737876	2003	3.685401118
1803	3.683411239	2013	3.68719928
1813	3.6851717	2023	3.685917781
1823	3.683938994	2033	3.687702889
1833	3.685685287	2043	3.686429358
1843	3.684439423	2053	3.688185981
1853	3.686188209	2063	3.68692852
1863	3.684942155	2073	3.688707535
1873	3.686691111	2083	3.687456053
1883	3.685459999	2093	3.687664988
1893	3.687212528	2103	3.683370745

List 2 uses the formula from eq.3.22 values, approximating the Fibonacci sequence numbers, plotted against the years 1693 to 2103. The average is 1.619437116

Equation 3.22 where α = R.A. in seconds.

$$\sqrt[4]{\frac{\left(^{e}C_{s,d=2.2}\right)^{4}}{\alpha}}$$

List 2

1693	1.617213004	1903	1.62199629
1703	1.6210559	1913	1.620409846
1713	1.619467621	1923	1.621556197
1723	1.620600522	1933	1.619982891
1733	1.619028252	1943	1.621099113
1743	1.620172088	1953	1.619509744
1753	1.618579661	1963	1.620665199
1763	1.61970265	1973	1.619069521
1773	1.618155868	1983	1.620218341
1783	1.619256867	1993	1.618632316
1793	1.617717162	2003	1.619769267
1803	1.621519826	2013	1.618189803
1813	1.619970948	2023	1.619315205
1823	1.621055267	2033	1.617747859
1833	1.619519505	2043	1.618865802
1843	1.620614945	2053	1.61732409
1853	1.619077619	2063	1.618427484
1863	1.620172779	2073	1.616866768
1873	1.618635932	2083	1.617964448
1883	1.619717509	2093	1.617781113
1893	1.618178175	2103	1.621555479

The next page shows the graph of Lists 1 and 2 in two halves.

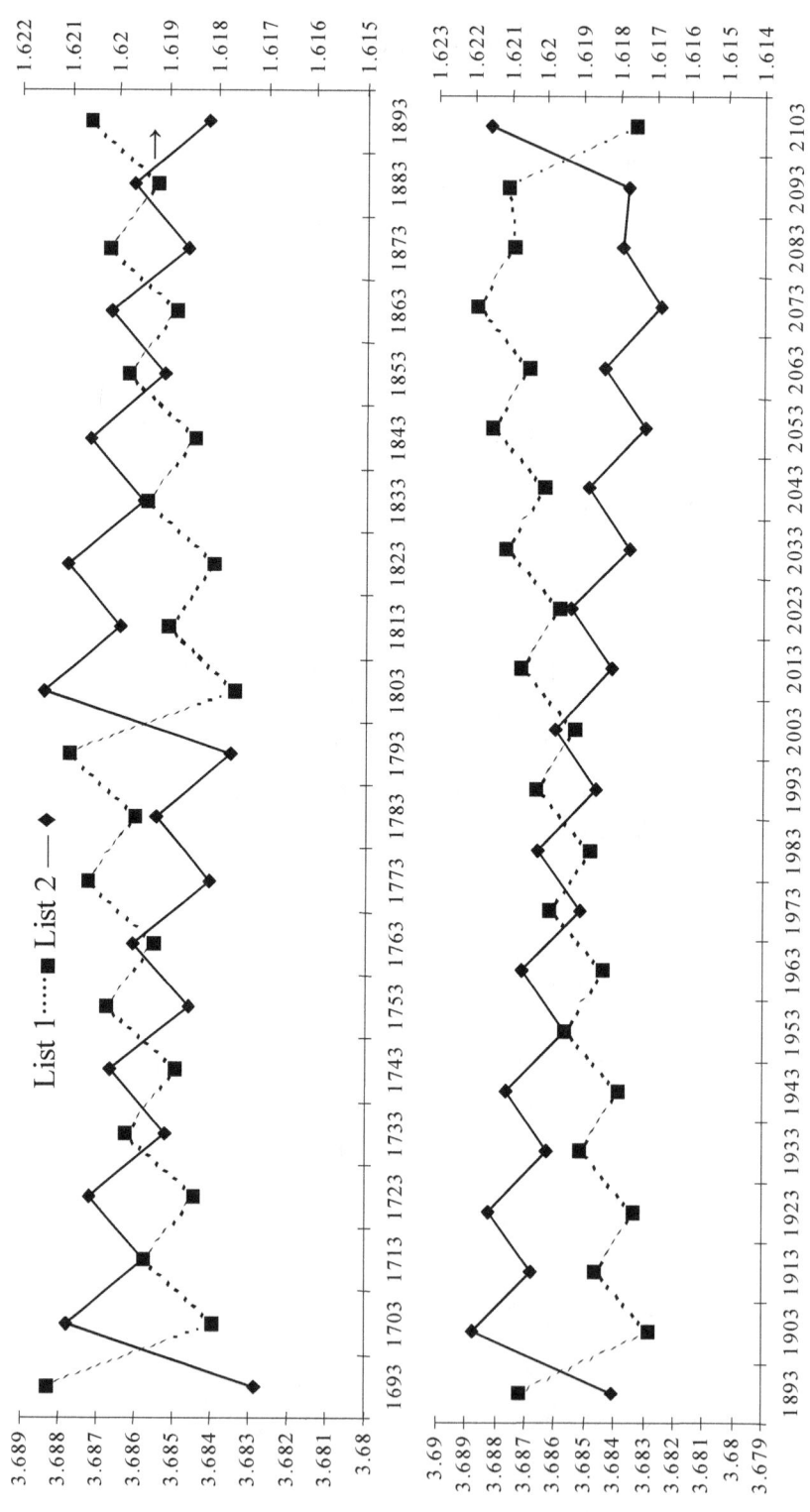

Mi mathematics Part 3: Notes:132

Special Section

Before we proceed any further there is one question that we need to address regarding ^{e}C and $^{\equiv}\partial$. We need to show that they combine to produce Time synchronicities and, additionally, are associated with Mi. We can begin with: -

S1

$$1536\,^{\equiv}\partial = 5632 = 22 \times 16^2 = 11 \times 8^3$$

Then continue with: -

S2

1. $\quad \sqrt[4]{\dfrac{\mp 5632}{^{\equiv}\partial}} - 2000 = 3.667918217 \approx\,^{\equiv}\partial$

2. $\quad \sqrt[8]{\dfrac{5632 \times 374 \times 182}{(222 + 78) \times 39}} = 3.667984331 \approx\,^{\equiv}\partial$

3. $\quad \dfrac{47 \times 5632}{42 \times 39 \times 22} = 7.345543346 \cong 2\,^{\equiv}\partial$

4. $\quad \dfrac{182 \times 5632}{374^2} = 7.328090595 \cong 2\,^{\equiv}\partial$

Or further still: -

5. $\quad \dfrac{\#3 + \#4}{4} = 3.668408485 \approx\,^{\equiv}\partial$

6. $\quad \sqrt[4]{\dfrac{222 \times 5632}{78^3}} = 1.274039676 \approx \dfrac{4}{\pi}$

7. $\quad \dfrac{66 \times 5632}{24^2 \times 22 \times 8} =\,^{\equiv}\partial$

8. $\quad \dfrac{5632}{24^2} =\,^{\equiv}\partial^2 -\,^{\equiv}\partial$

Even further: -

9. $\left[\sqrt{\dfrac{5632+2}{(374+182)}} - \pi\right]^{-1} = 24.00419642 \approx 24$

10. $\left[\log_n\left(\dfrac{5632}{374}\right)\right]^2 = 7.354749282 \cong 2\overset{\equiv}{\partial}$

11. $\sqrt[16]{\dfrac{+5632}{\overset{\equiv}{\partial}}} = 1.616836032$

12. $\sqrt{\log_n(5632 \times 124)} = 3.668310437 \rightarrow$

$\left(\log_n \sqrt{1536} = 3.668468457\right) \approx \overset{\equiv}{\partial}$

13. $\sqrt[16]{\dfrac{5632}{119}} \approx \overset{\equiv}{_2}\partial$

The year 2000, the year of the Mi entity experience plus Norman's and the author's full name count: the counts for 'Lawrencium', 'Lawrencium' +103 and 'Mira Ceti': the counts for 'Mi' and Mi's 'up to 24': counts for 'Enki', 'Odin', twin and 'time'. In item 9 the '2' might represent the two people with the name counts in the denominator or the result of the original °C. All these synchronicities were easy to find. Indeed, the number of synchronicities in the above list is almost embarrassing – and we haven't yet begun to look for any possibilities involving Time.
S3

$$\left[\log_n\left(\dfrac{5632 \times 365.256}{224.5^2}\right) - \left(\dfrac{5632 \times 365.256}{224.5^2}\right)^{-1}\right] = 3.684566589$$

In eq.S3 the denominator is the figure used in previous computations regarding the 12th of August, and the answer in days is synchronistic with computed seconds of List 1. If this answer is converted to seconds, 318346.5533, and then divided by the number of seconds of arc of the Sun's R.A. for the 12th of August 1943, the answer is also synchronistic with the Sun's R.A. for the same day. Of course, the dimensions there would be seconds and not hours.

S4

$$\log_n\left(\frac{5632}{141.3322292}\right) = 3.685106544$$

Equation S4 uses the number of degrees longitude for the Sun for the 12th of August 1943 in the denominator, and the answer is, once again, synchronistic with day 224.

The inference here then, is that the number 5632 has a connection to day 224. If this is the case then there should be other synchronicities with previous computations. The next equation set shows synchronicities with $^{\equiv}\partial$, τ and the Earth's sidereal year along with the author's analysis of names from Norman's research on the Philadelphia Experiment and the Montauk Laboratory.

S5

$$1. \quad \frac{5632}{^{\equiv}\partial\tau^4} = 224.0993797$$

$$2. \quad \sqrt[3]{\frac{1166 \times 5632}{365.256^2}} = 3.664844001,$$

$$3. \quad \sqrt[32]{916 \times 5632} = 1.620941873$$

Norman's contactee case study also shows synchronicities with 5632: -

S6

$$1. \quad \sqrt{\frac{110 \times 5632}{182}} = 58.34343188$$

$$2. \quad \frac{5632}{41} = 137.3658537, \sqrt{\frac{360}{137.3658537}} = 1.61889555$$

With the correction from the R.A. formula: -

S7

$$\frac{5632 + 8^{\equiv}\partial}{41} = 138.0813008$$

$$\left[\frac{\tan^{-1}\left(\tan\left(138.0813008\right)\cos 23.441884\right) + 180}{15}\right] = 9.363803693$$

In eq.S6 item 1, 182 might represent the number of the USS Eldridge or the author's full name count, while 110 is the count for Norman's contactee's name. The answer there is synchronistic with the distance of the Earth from the Sun, in days. In item 2, '41' might refer to the planets named in Norman's study or Mira, while the remaining items are synchronistic with the Golden Ratio and a circle. Equation S7 includes both 8's and $^{\equiv}\partial$ and the answer converts to a number synchronistic with previously mentioned details concerning day 224.

Finally S8, showing synchronicities concerning $^{\equiv}\partial$ and 3.68... using day 224, Norman's name count and Enki (introduced by Norman): using also the Sumerian counting system (60) and numbers from Montauk / Philadelphia Experiment study: -

S8

$$\sqrt{\frac{374 \times 224^{*,**}}{5632}} - \left(\left(\sqrt{1536}\right) - 39\right) = 3.664976271$$

$$*(224.5 = 3.669278349), **\frac{\{224.5 + 224\}}{2} = 3.66712731 \approx {}^{\equiv}\partial$$

$$\sqrt[3]{\frac{1166 \times 5632}{365.256^2}} = 3.664844001,$$

$$\sqrt{\frac{5632\pi}{\tau\left[\sqrt{\frac{374 \times 224}{5632}} - \left(\left(\sqrt{1536}\right) - 39\right)\right]^2 \times 60}} = 3.683542177$$

Note also that 5632 = 22 × 16.

So, our answer to the question – do ^{e}C and $^{\equiv}\partial$ effectively combine to produce Time synchronicities and be associated with Mi – must be in the affirmative.

Section 1

In the Mi book it was claimed that Mi seemed to be inclined to consider that the time categories were more concerned with magnetic properties, rather than electrical properties. However, who knows what the future will tell us – perhaps both electrical and magnetic properties will turn out to be similar, just 'viewed' from different 'points'. Perhaps Mi had no real preference and just cited magnetic properties as an example. Be that as it may, in Part 3 we did briefly examine both Gravitational and Electrostatic perspectives, so here we take a brief look at the Magnetic counterpart and search for any synchronicities.

4.1a

$$\mathbf{F}_{B} = (qv) \times \mathbf{B} = F_{B} = |q| vB \sin \phi$$

Equation 4.0 tells us that the force acting on the particle is perpendicular to the plane of the velocity of the particle and the magnetic field, that is to say, the force is in the same plane as the charge on the particle.

4.1b

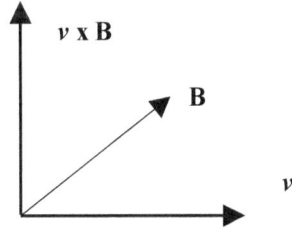

The differential equation of the motion for a particle in an electromagnetic field is classically: -

4.2

$$m\frac{dv}{dt} = q\mathbf{E} + (qv) \times \mathbf{B} =$$

$$(qv) = v_i = \mathbf{v} \times \mathbf{B} = \begin{vmatrix} i & j & k \\ v_1 & v_2 & v_3 \\ B_1 & B_2 & B_3 \end{vmatrix} =$$

$$(v_2 B_3 - v_3 B_2)\mathbf{i} - (v_1 B_3 - v_3 B_1)\mathbf{j} + (v_1 B_2 - v_2 B_1)\mathbf{k}$$

$$\mathbf{v} \times \mathbf{B} = \begin{pmatrix} 0 & B_3 & -B_2 \\ -B_3 & 0 & B_1 \\ B_2 & -B_1 & 0 \end{pmatrix}\begin{pmatrix} v_1 \\ v_2 \\ v_3 \end{pmatrix}$$

$$\begin{pmatrix} \dfrac{dv_1}{dt} \\ \dfrac{dv_2}{dt} \\ \dfrac{dv_3}{dt} \end{pmatrix} = \frac{q}{m}\begin{pmatrix} 0 & B_3 & -B_2 \\ -B_3 & 0 & B_1 \\ B_2 & -B_1 & 0 \end{pmatrix}\begin{pmatrix} v_1 \\ v_2 \\ v_3 \end{pmatrix} + \frac{q}{m}\begin{pmatrix} E_1 \\ E_2 \\ E_3 \end{pmatrix}$$

The third part of eq.4.2 is the usual anti-symmetric matrix. However, this is not an homogenous equation because of the second term on the right but the solution to the first part of the RHS will involve e^{At}. Firstly we set $q/m\, B_i = B_i$ and the 3×3 matrix = $\mathbf{A}$ and $\mathbf{B} = \mathbf{A}t$ so that we now have to compute $e^{\mathbf{B}}$. For this matrix, $n = 3$, so that for the expansion of $e^{\mathbf{B}}$ we have $n-1 = 2$.

4.3a

$$e^{\mathbf{B}} = a_2\mathbf{B}^2 + a_1\mathbf{B} + a_0 =$$

$$a_2\begin{pmatrix} 0 & B_3 & -B_2 \\ -B_3 & 0 & B_1 \\ B_2 & -B_1 & 0 \end{pmatrix}^2 + a_1\begin{pmatrix} 0 & B_3 & -B_2 \\ -B_3 & 0 & B_1 \\ B_2 & -B_1 & 0 \end{pmatrix} + \begin{pmatrix} a_0 & 0 & 0 \\ 0 & a_0 & 0 \\ 0 & 0 & a_0 \end{pmatrix} =$$

4.3a continued

$$a_2 \begin{pmatrix} -B_2^2 - B_3^2 & B_1 B_2 & B_1 B_3 \\ B_1 B_2 & -B_1^2 - B_3^2 & B_2 B_3 \\ B_1 B_3 & B_2 B_3 & -B_1^2 - B_2^2 \end{pmatrix} + \begin{pmatrix} a_1 a_0 & a_1 B_3 & -B_2 a_1 \\ -B_3 a_1 & a_1 a_0 & a_1 B_1 \\ a_1 B_2 & -B_1 a_1 & a_1 a_0 \end{pmatrix} =$$

$$\begin{pmatrix} a_2\left(-B_2^2 - B_3^2\right) + a_1 a_0 & a_1 B_3 + a_2 B_1 B_2 & a_2 B_1 B_3 + \left(-B_2 a_1\right) \\ a_2 B_1 B_2 + \left(-B_3 a_1\right) & a_2\left(-B_1^2 - B_3^2\right) + a_1 a_0 & a_2 B_2 B_3 + a_1 B_1 \\ a_2 B_1 B_3 + a_1 B_2 & a_2 B_2 B_3 + \left(-B_1 a_1\right) & a_2\left(-B_1^2 - B_2^2\right) + a_1 a_0 \end{pmatrix}$$

The next step is to find the eigenvalues and then find e^λ to find the values of a_1 and a_0.

4.3b

$$\begin{vmatrix} 0-\lambda & B_3 & -B_2 \\ -B_3 & 0-\lambda & B_1 \\ B_2 & -B_1 & 0-\lambda \end{vmatrix} =$$

$$-\lambda\left(\lambda^2 + B_1^2\right) + \left(-B_3^2 \lambda + B_1 B_2 B_3\right) - \left(B_1 B_2 B_3 + B_2^2 \lambda\right) =$$

$$-\lambda^3 - \lambda\left(B_1^2 + B_2^2 + B_3^2\right) =$$

$$-\lambda\left(\lambda - \left(B_1 + B_2 + B_3\right)\right)\left(\lambda + \left(B_1 + B_2 + B_3\right)\right) \therefore \lambda = \left(B_1 + B_2 + B_3\right)$$

or $\lambda = -\left(B_1 + B_2 + B_3\right)$

Choosing a unit magnitude for **B** there are three distinct values, no multiplicity, $\lambda = 1$, $\lambda = -1$, $\lambda = 0$, and $f(\lambda) = e^\lambda$. Therefore, since $r(\lambda) = a_{n-1}\lambda^{n-1}$...then $e^\lambda = a_2\lambda^2 + a_1\lambda^1 + a_0$.

4.3c

1. $e^1 = a_2\left(1\right)^2 + a_1\left(1\right) + a_0 = a_2 + a_1 + a_0$

2. $e^{-1} = a_2\left(-1\right)^2 + a_1\left(-1\right) + a_0 = a_2 - a_1 + a_0$

3. $e^0 = a_2\left(0\right)^2 + a_1\left(0\right) + a_0 = a_0$

4.3c continued

Solving for a_2, a_1 and a_0

$$1.+2.= e^1 + e^{-1} = 2(a_2 + a_0) = \frac{e^1 + e^{-1}}{2} - 1 = a_2 \text{ (since } e^0 = 1)$$

$$1.-2.= e^1 - e^{-1} = 2a_1 = \frac{e^1 - e^{-1}}{2} = a_1$$

Proof of 1. and 2.

$$1.\, e^1 = a_2 + a_1 + a_0 = \frac{e^1 + e^{-1}}{2} - 1 + \frac{e^1 - e^{-1}}{2} + 1 = \frac{2e^1}{2}$$

$$2.\, e^{-1} = a_2 - a_1 + a_0 = \frac{e^1 + e^{-1}}{2} - 1 - \frac{e^1 - e^{-1}}{2} + 1 = \frac{2e^{-1}}{2}$$

Inserting these into eq.3.59: -

4.3d

$$\begin{pmatrix} a_2\left(-B_2^2 - B_3^2\right) + a_1 a_0 & a_1 B_3 + a_2 B_1 B_2 & a_2 B_1 B_3 + \left(-B_2 a_1\right) \\ a_2 B_1 B_2 + \left(-B_3 a_1\right) & a_2\left(-B_1^2 - B_3^2\right) + a_1 a_0 & a_2 B_2 B_3 + a_1 B_1 \\ a_2 B_1 B_3 + a_1 B_2 & a_2 B_2 B_3 + \left(-B_1 a_1\right) & a_2\left(-B_1^2 - B_2^2\right) + a_1 a_0 \end{pmatrix}$$

$$a_2 = \left(\frac{3.6832694377}{2}\right)^{-1}, a_1 = 1.175201194, a_1 - a_2 = 0.632120558$$

$$a_2 + a_1 = 1.718281828, \frac{a_1}{a_2} = 2.163953414$$

$$a_2 a_1 a_0 = a_2 a_1 = \left(\frac{e^1 + e^{-1}}{2} - 1\right)\left(\frac{e^1 - e^{-1}}{2}\right) = 0.63822901$$

Our problem now is to search for any synchronicities, and we start with those associated with S_i, ^eC_s and $Ꮆ$. The forms $(a_2 a_1)$ and $(a_1 \div a_2)$ do not appear in the final matrix 4d so begin with these arrangements first.

1. Using 0.63822901 with the simultaneous equations and then using the author's name count we have: -

Mi Mathematics Part 4
G.A.T.E. (Ḡ)

$$0.63822901(3.2 - 1.8 - 0.8) = 0.382937406,$$

$$182^{0.382937406} = 7.336110676 = 2 \times 3.668055338 \approx 2^{\equiv}\partial$$

2. Next with Norman's name count, 'Enki' can be derived.

$$374 \times 0.382937406 = 143.219 \approx 39 \times {}^{\equiv}\partial$$

Using both name counts 182 and 374: -

$$2 \times (556^{(0.25 \times 0.382937406)}) = 3.66292436 \cong {}^{\equiv}\partial$$

$$68068/2.163953414^8 = 141.5662521 \left[R.A._{\odot} \, \text{day } 224 \right]$$

3. Using the constants, $kG = 0.599633$ from eq.3.33, $0.599633 \times 0.638229 = 0.38270317$, which is close to 0.382937406, and gives results in ${}^{\equiv}\partial$ fractionally lower than those just mentioned. Also: -

$$\sqrt[4]{\frac{1}{0.599633 \times 0.632822901}} \approx \frac{4}{\pi}$$

• The difference is less than 0.07 of 1%, and this result may be significant because we can form a geometrical arrangement representing gravitational, electrical and magnetic fields.

4. $360 \times 0.382937406 = 137.8574662$, which after conversion is synchronistic with the Sun's R.A. on day 224. Also: -

$$\frac{1}{3600} \left(\frac{\log_n 182}{0.382937406} \right)^4 \equiv 9.28'27''$$

5. Using ${}^{\equiv}\partial$ and Norman's word, 'twin', the result is 'time': -

$$66 \Big/ 0.382937406^{\equiv}\partial = 47.005$$

6. With 'Lawrencium' + 103 and 'Mira Ceti', 300, the result is: -

$$\frac{\left(\sqrt[4]{\dfrac{300^{\equiv\partial}}{0.382937406}} \right)}{2} = 3.6605 \cong {}^{\equiv}\partial$$

Synchronicities with the other forms are difficult to find so we can conclude that original differential equation might be applicable in some 'inverse' way.

Section 2

Just as we produced generating functions from the name counts we shall now use the digits in the counts as vector coordinates. Using the author's full name count and 'Lawrencium' + 103 first, for the obvious reason, we ask – what is the *vector projection* between the two vectors with coordinates of (1,8,2) and (2,2,2)?

4.4a

$$\frac{\mathbf{u \cdot t}}{\|t\|^2}\mathbf{t}, \quad \mathbf{u} = (1,8,2), \mathbf{t} = (2,2,2)$$

$$\frac{2+16+4}{2^2+2^2+2^2}(2,2,2) = \tfrac{22}{12}(2,2,2) = ({}^{\equiv}\partial, {}^{\equiv}\partial, {}^{\equiv}\partial)$$

Looking at this result we might feel that there must be some mistake, although with such an elementary equation there is not much to make a mistake with! What we seem to have here is a *vector definition* of ${}^{\equiv}\partial$. Is this an isolated case?

4.4b

$$1. \quad \frac{\mathbf{u \cdot t}}{\|t\|^2}\mathbf{t}, \mathbf{u} = (1,9,12), \mathbf{t} = (2,2,2)$$

4.4b continued

$$\frac{2+18+24}{2^2+2^2+2^2}(2,2,2) = \tfrac{44}{12}(2,2,2) =$$

$$2(\,^{\equiv}\partial,\,^{\equiv}\partial,\,^{\equiv}\partial)$$

2. $\mathbf{u} = (3,7,4), \mathbf{t} = (2,2,2)$

$$\frac{6+14+8}{2^2+2^2+2^2}(2,2,2) = \tfrac{28}{12}(2,2,2) =$$

$$(\,^{\equiv}\partial+1,\,^{\equiv}\partial+1,\,^{\equiv}\partial+1)$$

3. $\mathbf{u} = (1,5,2), \mathbf{t} = (2,2,2)$

$$\frac{2+10+4}{2^2+2^2+2^2}(2,2,2) = \tfrac{16}{12}(2,2,2) = (\,^{\equiv}\partial-1,\,^{\equiv}\partial-1,\,^{\equiv}\partial-1)$$

4. $\mathbf{u} = (1,9,3), \mathbf{t} = (2,2,2)$

$$\frac{2+18+6}{2^2+2^2+2^2}(2,2,2) = \tfrac{26}{12}(2,2,2) =$$

$$(\,^{\equiv}\partial+\,^{\equiv}\partial-3,\,^{\equiv}\partial+\,^{\equiv}\partial-3,\,^{\equiv}\partial+\,^{\equiv}\partial-3)$$

Mira Ceti has two counts so how do we decide which one to use. Use both at the same time, seems the logical choice (7,8) + (1,2,4) after all that is what the actual situation is. In eq.4.4b(1), the result is exactly double eq.4.4a which must rank as a incredible synchronicity. 4.4b(2) uses Norman's name count while 4.4b(3) is the count of the researcher and author (as mentioned in the Mi book) in affairs relevant to Norman's own researches. Add (2) and (3) together then divide by two and the answer is the same as eq.4.4a. Equations 4.4b(4) uses a random number 193 and not synchronistic with any material herein. However, all equations seem to indicate that the number 222, from a 3-D vector standpoint, is some kind of base from which $^{\equiv}\partial$ can be computed without direct use of the original methods. Very well then, let's try a 4 × 4 matrix with $^{\equiv}\partial$ in the last column.

4.5a

$$\mathbf{M_1} = \begin{pmatrix} 3 & 0 & 5 & ^{\equiv}\partial \\ 1 & 6 & 0 & ^{\equiv}\partial \\ 1 & 2 & 6 & ^{\equiv}\partial \\ 1 & 2 & 4 & ^{\equiv}\partial \end{pmatrix}, \mathbf{M_2} = \begin{pmatrix} 3 & 7 & 4 & ^{\equiv}\partial \\ 3 & 0 & 5 & ^{\equiv}\partial \\ 1 & 8 & 2 & ^{\equiv}\partial \\ 1 & 2 & 4 & ^{\equiv}\partial \end{pmatrix},$$

$$\left|\mathbf{M_1}\right| = \left|\mathbf{M_2}\right| = 16 ^{\equiv}\partial$$

$\mathbf{M_1}$ uses numbers that represent counts from the Philadelphia Experiment, 'USS Eldridge' + DE173 (182), 'Carl Meredith Allen', then both 'Duncan' and 'Edward Cameron', while $\mathbf{M_2}$ uses Norman's full name count, 'USS Eldridge' + DE173 (182), the author's full name count and 'Omicron Ceti' – the determinants are equal. On this occasion Omicron Ceti has been used because the count is the same as 'Edward Cameron'. If Omicron Ceti is replaced by the additive name counts as in eq.4.4b(1) the determinant is $142^{\equiv}\partial$ and 142° would be synchronistic with R.A. figures already mentioned. These synchronicities add support to the idea of these events being connected.

    We might be forgiven if we thought that all determinants with $^{\equiv}\partial$ in the fourth column would have a value of $(x.6666667)$, but might some determinants be simple integer multiples of $^{\equiv}\partial$? When $(1,1,0)$ replaces $(1,2,4)$ in both $\mathbf{M_1}$ & $\mathbf{M_2}$, the determinants are 220 and -154 respectively, and the synchronicity here is 220-154 = 66, the count for 'twin'.

    If 'Carl Meredith Allen' is replaced by the Mexican counterpart, the determinant is $24^{\equiv}\partial$, so the difference is $\underline{8}^{\equiv}\partial$. Now, Dividing the trace $\mathbf{M_1}$ by $\mathbf{M_2}$ the integer is $+182$: -

4.5b

$$\left(\frac{Tr.\mathbf{M_1}}{Tr.\mathbf{M_2}}\right)^8 = 463.14548... = 182 + 281 + \frac{1}{(1.61918...)^4}$$

The fractional part has a similarity to $^1/\tau$.

4.6

$$M_3 = \begin{pmatrix} 3 & 7 & 4 & \equiv\partial \\ 2 & 0 & 1 & \equiv\partial \\ 1 & 8 & 2 & \equiv\partial \\ 1 & 4 & 1 & \equiv\partial \end{pmatrix}, M_4 = \begin{pmatrix} 3 & 7 & 4 & \equiv\partial \\ 2 & 0 & 1 & \equiv\partial \\ 1 & 8 & 2 & \equiv\partial \\ -2 & -2 & -4 & \equiv\partial \end{pmatrix}$$

$$M_5 = \begin{pmatrix} 3 & 0 & 5 & \equiv\partial \\ 2 & 2 & 4 & \equiv\partial \\ 1 & 2 & 4 & \equiv\partial \\ 0 & 9 & 0 & \equiv\partial \end{pmatrix}, |M_3| = |M_4| = |M_5| = \equiv\partial,$$

$$M_6 = \begin{pmatrix} 2 & 6 & 3 & \equiv\partial \\ 1 & 1 & 0 & \equiv\partial \\ 1 & 8 & 2 & \equiv\partial \\ 2 & 3 & 2 & \equiv\partial \end{pmatrix}, |M_6| = -\equiv\partial$$

In M_3 we note Norman's full name count as r_1, the number of days to his birthday as r_2 (non-leap year), then the author's name count and 141 days to the author's birthday as r_3 and r_4. M_4 is a reversal inasmuch that r_4 counts backwards from Norman's birthday to the author's showing the surprise synchronicity of 224 days. $|M_3| = |M_4| = |M_5| = \equiv\partial$ (M_3 = -66, negative of 'twin' if 342 is used in r_4). M_5 is not really legitimate in the present context because r_4 is not a day number – r_3 and r_4 are the counts for Edward Cameron and Alfred Bielek respectively. $|M_5| = |M_4|$. In M_6 r_2 and r_4 are the anniversary of Jessup's (allegedly mysterious) death and the number of additional days to the author's birthday respectively.

Also $|\mathbf{M_6}|$ is the negative of $|\mathbf{M_4}|$ and $|\mathbf{M_5}|$. Substituting (264) for (263) and (183) for (182) as arbitrary numbers then $|\mathbf{M_6}| =$ -18.3333..., showing no similarity. However, the same is true using Norman's details with $|\mathbf{M_6}| = 10^{\equiv}\partial$. This situation is the reverse of what we should have expected because the suggestion might then be that the author was connected to Jessup and not to Norman – the apparent connection is 263-182 = 81. The number 81, however, is present in both Norman's and the author's name counts, so ideas become a little uncertain here. Nonetheless, this procedure does suggest that we investigate such vector quantities in more detail.

Below are some generated 3-D vectors, where eq.4.7a can be expressed as a linear combination, and that $d_1 + d_2 + d_3 = 0$, which is not the general case for linearity of 3-vectors.

4.7a

$$\mathbf{M_{1'}} = (3 \quad 0 \quad 5) = d_1(2 \quad 2 \quad 4) + d_2(1 \quad 2 \quad 6) + d_3(1 \quad 2 \quad 4)$$

$$\begin{array}{ll} & 2d_1 + \quad d_2 + \quad d_3 \\ = & 2d_1 + \quad 2d_2 + \quad 2d_3 \\ & 4d_1 + \quad 6d_2 + \quad 4d_3 \end{array} = \left(\begin{array}{ccc|c} 2 & 1 & 1 & 3 \\ 2 & 2 & 2 & 0 \\ 4 & 6 & 4 & 5 \end{array}\right)$$

$$= \left(\begin{array}{ccc|c} 2 & 1 & 1 & 3 \\ 0 & 1 & 1 & -3 \\ 4 & 6 & 4 & 5 \end{array}\right) = \left(\begin{array}{ccc|c} 2 & 1 & 1 & 3 \\ 0 & 1 & 1 & -3 \\ 0 & 4 & 2 & -1 \end{array}\right) = \left(\begin{array}{ccc|c} 2 & 1 & 1 & 3 \\ 0 & 1 & 1 & -3 \\ 0 & 0 & -2 & 11 \end{array}\right)$$

$$d_1 = 3, d_2 = 2.5, d_3 = -5.5$$

$$3(2 \quad 2 \quad 4) + 2.5(1 \quad 2 \quad 6) - 5.5(1 \quad 2 \quad 4) = (3 \quad 0 \quad 5)$$

4.7b

$$\mathbf{M_{2'}} = (3 \quad 7 \quad 4) = d_1(3 \quad 0 \quad 5) + d_2(1 \quad 8 \quad 2) + d_3(1 \quad 2 \quad 4)$$

$$= \left(\begin{array}{ccc|c} 3 & 1 & 1 & 3 \\ 0 & 8 & 2 & 7 \\ 5 & 2 & 4 & 4 \end{array}\right) = \left(\begin{array}{ccc|c} 15 & 5 & 5 & 15 \\ 0 & 4 & 1 & 3.5 \\ 15 & 6 & 12 & 12 \end{array}\right) = \left(\begin{array}{ccc|c} 15 & 5 & 5 & 15 \\ 0 & 4 & 1 & 3.5 \\ 0 & 1 & 7 & -3 \end{array}\right)$$

4.7b continued

$$= \begin{pmatrix} 3 & 1 & 1 & | & 3 \\ 0 & 1 & \frac{1}{4} & | & 0.875 \\ 0 & 1 & 7 & | & -3 \end{pmatrix} = \begin{pmatrix} 1 & \frac{1}{3} & \frac{1}{3} & | & 1 \\ 0 & 1 & \frac{1}{4} & | & 0.875 \\ 0 & 0 & 6.75 & | & -3.875 \end{pmatrix}$$

$$d_1 = 0.852, d_2 = 1.0185, d_3 = -0.574$$

Although technically (3,7,4) in $M_{2'}$ can be expressed as a linear combination of the others the argument is less certain because d_1 is an approximate figure.

4.7c

$$\mathbf{M}_{3'} = (3 \quad 7 \quad 4) = d_1(2 \quad 0 \quad 1) + d_2(1 \quad 8 \quad 2) + d_3(1 \quad 4 \quad 1)$$

$$= \begin{pmatrix} 2 & 1 & 1 & | & 3 \\ 0 & 8 & 4 & | & 7 \\ 1 & 2 & 1 & | & 4 \end{pmatrix} = \begin{pmatrix} 2 & 1 & 1 & | & 3 \\ 0 & 1 & 0.5 & | & \frac{7}{8} \\ 1 & 2 & 1 & | & 4 \end{pmatrix} = \begin{pmatrix} 1 & -1 & 0 & | & -1 \\ 0 & 1 & 0.5 & | & \frac{7}{8} \\ 1 & 2 & 1 & | & 4 \end{pmatrix}$$

$$= \begin{pmatrix} 1 & -1 & 0 & | & -1 \\ 0 & 1 & 0.5 & | & \frac{7}{8} \\ 0 & 3 & 1 & | & 5 \end{pmatrix} = \begin{pmatrix} 1 & -1 & 0 & | & -1 \\ 0 & 1 & 0.5 & | & \frac{7}{8} \\ 0 & 0 & -0.5 & | & 2\frac{3}{8} \end{pmatrix} = \begin{pmatrix} 1 & -1 & 0 & | & -1 \\ 0 & 1 & 0.5 & | & \frac{7}{8} \\ 0 & 0 & 1 & | & -4\frac{3}{4} \end{pmatrix}$$

$$d_1 = 2.25, d_2 = 3.25, d_3 = -4.75$$

$$(3 \quad 7 \quad 4) = 2.25(2 \quad 0 \quad 1) + 3.25(1 \quad 8 \quad 2) - 4.75(1 \quad 4 \quad 1)$$

4.7d

$$\mathbf{M}_{4'} = (3 \quad 7 \quad 4) = d_1(2 \quad 0 \quad 1) + d_2(1 \quad 8 \quad 2) + d_3(-2 \quad -2 \quad -4)$$

$$\begin{matrix} 2d_1 + & d_2 - & 2d_3 \\ 0d_1 + & 8d_2 - & 2d_3 \\ d_1 & 2d_2 - & 4d_3 \end{matrix} = \begin{pmatrix} 2 & 1 & -2 & | & 3 \\ 0 & 8 & -2 & | & 7 \\ 1 & 2 & -4 & | & 4 \end{pmatrix} = \begin{pmatrix} 1 & 0.5 & -1 & | & 1.5 \\ 0 & 8 & -2 & | & 7 \\ 1 & 2 & -4 & | & 4 \end{pmatrix}$$

$$\begin{pmatrix} 1 & 0.5 & -1 & | & 1.5 \\ 0 & 8 & -2 & | & 7 \\ 0 & 1.5 & -3 & | & 2.5 \end{pmatrix} = \begin{pmatrix} 1 & 0.5 & -1 & | & 1.5 \\ 0 & 1 & -\frac{1}{4} & | & \frac{7}{8} \\ 0 & 1.5 & -3 & | & 2.5 \end{pmatrix}$$

(equation 4.7d continued on next page)

147

$$= \begin{pmatrix} 1 & -1 & 2 & \vdots & -1 \\ 0 & 1 & -\frac{1}{4} & \vdots & \frac{7}{8} \\ 0 & 0 & -2.625 & \vdots & 1.1875 \end{pmatrix} = \begin{pmatrix} 1 & -1 & 2 & \vdots & -1 \\ 0 & 1 & 5 & \vdots & -7.5 \\ 0 & 0 & -1 & \vdots & \frac{1.1875}{-2.625}[-0.452....] \end{pmatrix}$$

Once again, while $\mathbf{M_{3'}}$ is a consistent set there is doubt about $\mathbf{M_{4'}}$ due to d_3 being approximate to three decimal places, which is why it was unnecessary to complete the computations. Why should there be doubt about counting backwards from Norman's birthday to the author's? We should not infer that it is because we cannot go back in time, but perhaps that Norman was born *before* the author and therefore it is legitimate to consider 141 days *after* Norman's birthday. Why then, did we not find $\mathbf{M_{4'}}$ to be totally inconsistent? Well, perhaps that would not have been correct either because in both the Mi book and this work, the elaborate network of synchronicities suggest that Norman and the author do have a connection in the Mi context. A similar explanation may be given to $\mathbf{M_{2'}}$. There is, however, an odd synchronicity with the d_i of $\mathbf{M_{1'}}$ – the ratios $^{5.5}\!/_3$ and $^{5.5}\!/_{2.5}$ are $\frac{1}{2}^{\equiv}\partial$ and 2.2 respectively and the ratio of 2.2 to $\frac{1}{2}^{\equiv}\partial$ is 1.2. The latter three are already familiar to us and they could indicate some underlying trend. Having said that, it may be important to realize that this procedure is no more than a linear mapping, and the conversion matrix is a transformation matrix, $T:\mathbb{R}^3 \rightarrow \mathbb{R}^3$. What is perhaps more important is that $(\mathbf{M_{1'}}d_i)(\mathbf{M_{3'}}d_j) = 41$ which brings us back to Mira, and the synchronicities involving Norman's contactee case.

We can proceed to evaluate $e^{\mathbf{Mi'}}$. This is a 3 ×3 matrix so we have $a_2 (\mathbf{M_{1'}})^2 + a_1 \mathbf{M_{1'}} + a_0$.

4.8a

$$a_2 \begin{pmatrix} 2 & 1 & 1 \\ 2 & 2 & 2 \\ 4 & 6 & 4 \end{pmatrix}^2 + a_1 \begin{pmatrix} 2 & 1 & 1 \\ 2 & 2 & 2 \\ 4 & 6 & 4 \end{pmatrix} + \begin{pmatrix} a_0 & 0 & 0 \\ 0 & a_0 & 0 \\ 0 & 0 & a_0 \end{pmatrix} =$$

(equation 4.8a continued on next page)

$$a_2 \begin{pmatrix} 10 & 10 & 8 \\ 16 & 18 & 14 \\ 36 & 40 & 32 \end{pmatrix} + a_1 \begin{pmatrix} 2 & 1 & 1 \\ 2 & 2 & 2 \\ 4 & 6 & 4 \end{pmatrix} + \begin{pmatrix} a_0 & 0 & 0 \\ 0 & a_0 & 0 \\ 0 & 0 & a_0 \end{pmatrix} =$$

$$\begin{pmatrix} 10a_2 + 2a_1 + a_0 & 10a_2 + a_1 & 8a_2 + a_1 \\ 16a_2 + 2a_1 & 18a_2 + 2a_1 + a_0 & 14a_2 + 2a_1 \\ 36a_2 + 4a_1 & 40a_2 + 6a_1 & 32a_2 + 4a_1 + a_0 \end{pmatrix}$$

$$\begin{vmatrix} 2-\lambda & 1 & 1 \\ 2 & 2-\lambda & 2 \\ 4 & 6 & 4-\lambda \end{vmatrix} =$$

$$2-\lambda \begin{vmatrix} 2-\lambda & 2 \\ 6 & 4-\lambda \end{vmatrix} = -8 + 8\lambda^2 - \lambda^3 - 8\lambda$$

$$-1 \begin{vmatrix} 2 & 2 \\ 4 & 4-\lambda \end{vmatrix} = -1(8 - 2\lambda - 8) = 2\lambda$$

$$1 \begin{vmatrix} 2 & 2-\lambda \\ 4 & 6 \end{vmatrix} = (4 + 4\lambda) = -\lambda^3 + 8\lambda^2 - 2\lambda - 4$$

$$(\lambda^3 - 8\lambda^2 + 2\lambda + 4)$$

$$\lambda_1 \cong -0.57622, \lambda_2 \cong 0.9049, \lambda_3 \cong 7.67132$$

4.8b

$$e^{-0.57622} = a_2(-0.57622)^2 + a_1(-0.57622) + a_0$$

$$e^{0.9049} = a_2(0.9049)^2 + a_1(0.9049) + a_0$$

$$e^{7.67132} = a_2(7.67132)^2 + a_1(7.67132) + a_0$$

$$0.56202 = a_2 0.33203 - a_1 0.57622 + a_0$$

$$2.4717 = a_2 0.818844 + a_1 0.9049 + a_0$$

$$2145.9122 = a_2 58.84915 + a_1 7.67132 + a_0$$

$$a_2 = 38.25222968,$$

$$a_1 = -11.28338078, a_0 = -18.64057749$$

Substituting these values into 4.8a: -
4.8c

$$\begin{pmatrix} 10a_2 + 2a_1 + a_0 & 10a_2 + a_1 & 8a_2 + a_1 \\ 16a_2 + 2a_1 & 18a_2 + 2a_1 + a_0 & 14a_2 + 2a_1 \\ 36a_2 + 4a_1 & 40a_2 + 6a_1 & 32a_2 + 4a_1 + a_0 \end{pmatrix} = e^{M_1}$$

$$= \begin{pmatrix} 341.3149578 & 371.238916 & 294.7344567 \\ 589.4689133 & 647.3327952 & 512.964454 \\ 1331.946745 & 1462.388903 & 1160.297249 \end{pmatrix}$$

Any synchronicity here is well hidden, if present at all, but: -
4.9a

$$|M| = 2981.0661761, tr. = 2148.945002$$

$$a_{ij} = 6711.68739,$$

The determinant of e^{M_1} contains the most obvious synchronicity because $e^8 = 2980.958$, but using the nearest integer for the determinant and the trace is perhaps more interesting. Equation 4.9b might be an introduction to something not yet mentioned.
4.9b

$$\sqrt{\left(\log_n (2981.0661761 - 2148.945002)^2\right)} = 3.667145504 \approx \,^{\equiv}\partial$$

$$\frac{2981 - 2149}{8} = 104, \quad \sqrt[4]{\dfrac{\left(\dfrac{2981 - 2149}{8}\right) \times 39}{22}} = 3.684841539$$

The first and third results show obvious synchronicities but we might ask what the number 104 represents. Just by coincidence 104 is the word count for 'Roswell'. (The town of Roswell, New Mexico, U.S.A. was the area where something crashed in July 1947 – see pages 233-234.)

We use the same procedure on e^{M_3}: -

4.10

$$a_2 \begin{pmatrix} 2 & 1 & 1 \\ 0 & 8 & 4 \\ 1 & 2 & 1 \end{pmatrix}^2 + a_1 \begin{pmatrix} 2 & 1 & 1 \\ 0 & 8 & 4 \\ 1 & 2 & 1 \end{pmatrix} + \begin{pmatrix} a_0 & 0 & 0 \\ 0 & a_0 & 0 \\ 0 & 0 & a_0 \end{pmatrix} =$$

$$a_2 \begin{pmatrix} 5 & 12 & 7 \\ 4 & 72 & 36 \\ 3 & 19 & 10 \end{pmatrix} + a_1 \begin{pmatrix} 2 & 1 & 1 \\ 0 & 8 & 4 \\ 1 & 2 & 1 \end{pmatrix} + \begin{pmatrix} a_0 & 0 & 0 \\ 0 & a_0 & 0 \\ 0 & 0 & a_0 \end{pmatrix} =$$

$$\begin{pmatrix} 5a_2 + 2a_1 + a_0 & 12a_2 + a_1 & 7a_2 + a_1 \\ 4a_2 & 72a_2 + 8a_1 + a_0 & 36a_2 + 4a_1 \\ 3a_2 + a_1 & 19a_2 + 2a_1 & 10a_2 + a_1 + a_0 \end{pmatrix}$$

$$\begin{vmatrix} 2-\lambda & 1 & 1 \\ 0 & 8-\lambda & 4 \\ 1 & 2 & 1-\lambda \end{vmatrix} = x^3 - 11x^2 + 17x + 4$$

$$\lambda_1 \approx -0.20704, \lambda_2 \approx 2.12801, \lambda_3 \approx 9.07903$$

Evaluating a_2, a_1 and a_0 : -

4.11

$$e^{-0.20704} = a_2 (-0.20704)^2 + a_1 (-0.20704) + a_0$$

$$e^{2.12801} = a_2 (2.12801)^2 + a_1 (2.12801) + a_0$$

$$e^{9.07903} = a_2 (9.07903)^2 + a_1 (9.07903) + a_0$$

$$0.81299 = a_2 0.04286556 - a_1 0.20704 + a_0$$

$$8.39814 = a_2 4.52842656 + a_1 2.12801 + a_0$$

$$8769.45553 = a_2 82.42878574 + a_1 9.07903 + a_0$$

$$a_2 = 135.3802447, a_1 = -256.8130001$$

$$a_0 = -58.16072355$$

Substituting these values: -
4.12

$$\begin{pmatrix} 105.1144998 & 1096.989447 & 690.8487128 \\ 541.5209788 & 7634.712894 & 3846.436809 \\ 149.327734 & 2058.598649 & 1038.828723 \end{pmatrix}$$

$$|M| = -3143881.955, tr. = 8778.656117$$

The synchronicity concerns the trace: -
4.13

$$\sqrt{tr.M_1 + tr.M_3} = \frac{\sqrt{2148.945002 + 8778.656117}}{e^{2.405}} = 9.435918649,$$

$$\frac{tr.M_1 + tr.M_3 + 9.435918649^2}{8 \times 374} = 3.68203131, \frac{2(tr.M_1 + tr.M_3)}{77^2}$$

$$= 3.686153186, \left(\sqrt[3]{tr.M_1 + tr.M_3} - 22 + 39\right)^2 = 1535.926756$$

Three of the items of eq.4.13 are synchronistic with day 224 while the last suggests a connection to ^eC: the first item is coincidental with topics to be discussed in Section 4. Other synchronicities not given here also involve day 224 and this suggests that the evaluation of e^{Mx} is a good indicator that we should continue with, and focus on exponential values. This is the approach that we shall concentrate on in the next section.

Section 3

Our inference has been be that some combination of e^i and $^{\equiv}\partial$ ($i = 3.2, -1.8, -0.8, -0.6$) does have a connection with Mi's ideas about Time but what we need is a direct 'test', in our context, to check the validity of e^i and hence, that inference. The 'test' should contain time values that are consistent with the material herein, and the result should be immediately obvious to us.

Mi Mathematics Part 4
G.A.T.E. (G_4)

Since calculations for the Sun's R.A. use the tropical year, 365.2422 days, we shall use this and Moon's sidereal period of revolution, 27.3217 days: -
4.14

$$\sqrt{\frac{365.2422}{27.3217}} = 3.656256166, \frac{1}{3.656256166} = 0.273503812$$

$$2\left(\frac{1}{3.656256166} + 1\right)^2 = 1.62181196 \times 2 = 3.24362392,$$

$$e^i - (3.24362392)^{-3} - {}^{\equiv}\partial = 22.00000026$$

The square root of the Sun / Moon ratio is approximately 99.72% of ${}^{\equiv}\partial$ and the inverse allows us to use the form of ${}^{\equiv}_2\partial$ by adding 1 then squaring. The result is synchronistic with $(^4\!/\pi)^2$, but using ^{e}C we multiply by 2. Finally, subtracting the cubed inverse and ${}^{\equiv}\partial$ from e^i the result is so close to 22 ('Mi'?) that it could hardly be a more obvious synchronicity (a result of 21.99999955 is obtained if 365.256 is used). So we can conclude that G_4 is consistent with Mi's ideas, but we have to include ${}^{\equiv}\partial$, that is: -
4.15

$$f\left({}^{\equiv}\partial \propto e^i\right), \left(x = \left({}^e C_S\right)_i, i = a, b, c, d\right)$$

We refer back to eq.3.46 and notice that 3.46(1) & 3.46(4) have some resemblance to what we are looking for in eq.4.15, ignoring items 3.46(2), 3.46(3) and 3.46(4) as they contain additional numbers and roots. Equation 4.16 displays several synchronicities but if eq.4.15 is equal to the Sun's R.A. then clearly there must be –
4.16 (includes eq.3.46

$$\sqrt{\left(2e^{3.2}\right)^2 + \left(-2e^{-1.8}\right)^2 + \left(-4e^{-0.8}\right)^2 + \left(4e^{-0.6}\right)^2} = 49.14813219$$

$$= (3.66298949)^3$$

4.16 continued

$$\sqrt{\left(2e^{3.2}\right)^2 +\left(-2e^{-1.8}\right)^2 +\left(-4e^{-0.8}\right)^2 +\left(4e^{-0.6}\right)^2} = 49.14813219$$

$$= (3.66298949)^3 \approx \; {}^{\equiv}\partial^3$$

$$\sqrt{\left(2e^{3.2}\right)^2 +\left(-4e^{-1.8}\right)^2 +\left(-12e^{-0.8}\right)^2 +\left(16e^{-0.6}\right)^2} =$$

$$50.13976613 = (3.68740991)^3 \equiv \text{day } 224$$

$\alpha \qquad \sqrt[4]{50.13976613^{\equiv}\partial} = 3.68225138$

$\beta \qquad \dfrac{\left(50.13976613^{\equiv}\partial\right)^2}{3600} = 9.388689318$

– another variable, Δ, contained in eq.4.15 so that the magnitude can be calculated at any moment, and this is shown in eq.4.17: -

4.17

$$\sqrt{\left(2e^{3.2}\right)^2 +\left(-4e^{-1.8}\right)^2 +\left(-12e^{-0.8}\right)^2 +\left(16e^{-0.6}\right)^2} = \mathbf{V}$$

$$\therefore f\left({}^{\equiv}\partial \propto e^x\right) = \Delta \mathbf{V}^{\equiv}\partial^k = \text{R.A.}_{\odot}, k \geq 1$$

$$\text{but } \dfrac{\left(50.13976613^{\equiv}\partial\right)^2}{3600} = 9.388689318 \therefore$$

$$\mathbf{V}^{2\equiv}\partial^2 = 33799.28154 \therefore \Delta = 120.45346$$

$$\therefore 47 \times \left(9.4 - \dfrac{1}{342}\right) {}^{\equiv}\partial^{-1} + \mathbf{V}^{2\equiv}\partial^2$$

$$= \mathbf{V}^{2\equiv}\partial^2{}_{224} = 33919.735 \therefore k = 2$$

The penultimate line of eq.4.17 uses 9.4 & 342 as two time-based synchronicities and the count for 'time' to show one possible way to obtain Δ. However, the basic expression is the expanded form of ^{e}C and we already know that $\left|{}^e\text{C}\right| = 24\times64 = 3\times8^3$: we have the synchronicity of '8' & '3'. Because the Sun's R.A. on day $224 \approx (^=\partial+0.017)^8 = (^=\partial+0.017)^{2\times4}$ then we might use ^{e}C as a Quartic equation with a constant of 64: -

4.18

$$2x^4 - 4x^3 - 12x^2 + 16x - 64 =$$

$$2x^4 - 4x^3 - 12x^2 + 16x - 24(^=\partial-1) = 0, x_1 = 3.681096,$$

$$(x_1)^8 = 3.681096^8 = 33714.53306 = \text{V}^2 \; {}^=\partial^2{}_{224} - 205.2$$

Solving Quartic equations is quite a long job so the details are not given here, but the other three solutions are two Complex and one negative Real. Therefore x_1 is the only solution of interest at this time. Although using the solution $(x_1)^8$ gives a result less than day 224 it remains an obvious synchronicity. The range of Δ in $(64+\Delta_x)$ for day 224 (year 1943) from the first second to one second before midnight is $0.20533615(=\Delta_1)$ to $0.7124167(=\Delta_2)$. Note also that $\text{V}(\Delta_1+ \Delta_2) = 46.01...: 46$ is 64.

These synchronicities seem to suggest that Mi should be associated with day 224, but Why? Looking at eq.4.17 & 4.18 perhaps an answer is provided by Norman's birthday, 23 days prior to day 224, and the author's, 23 days prior to the end year: -

4.19a

$$\sqrt{\left(2e^{3.2}\right)^2 + \left(-4e^{-1.8}\right)^2 + \left(-12e^{-0.8}\right)^2 + \left(16e^{-0.6}\right)^2} = \text{V},$$

$$\left(2x^4 - 4x^3 - 12x^2 + 16x - 64\right)_{224} = {}^e\text{C}_q \therefore {}^e\text{C}_q\text{V} =$$

$$0.45915543 \times 50.13976613 \approx 23.022, (64 \times 0.45915543 \approx 8^=\partial)\,*$$

$$3\left(^=\partial+4\right)\times8 = 23\times8 = 24\left(^=\partial+4\right) = 184$$

A $$\left(\frac{184}{224-\text{int.}\left(\frac{184\tau}{^=\partial}\right)-4}\right)^8 = \left(\frac{184}{\left(39^=\partial\right)-4}\right)^8 = 9.428100039,$$

4.19a continued

$$\frac{184^2}{3600} = 9.404444444$$

$$\mathrm{B} \quad \frac{\tan^{-1}\left(\tan\left(224 - \text{int.}\left(\frac{184\tau}{\overset{\equiv}{\partial}}\right) - 4\right) \times \cos\left(23.441884\right)\right) + 180}{15} =$$

$$9.428417449 \approx \mathrm{A}$$

Note the additional synchronicity (*).

    We can now associate the work of Part 3, eq.3.53 and Graph 3 where we used the slope value of the graph, 2.7000235, with the Earth's sidereal period, day 224.5 and $\overset{\equiv}{\partial}$: -
4.19b

$$\mathrm{C} \quad \frac{\left(\dfrac{365.256}{2.7000235} \times 224.5\right) + \left(365.256 \times \left(\overset{\equiv}{\partial}^2 - \overset{\equiv}{\partial}\right)\right)}{3600} =$$

$$9.428191019 \approx \mathrm{B} \approx \mathrm{A}$$

Actually there is a difference of 0.00009098, which would be just over 0.3 of an arc second. Indeed, if we use the constant (a), (say 0.305) of graph 3 and divide it by 3600, then add it to 9.428100039 the difference becomes even less. For our purposes here, surely we could regard the two equations as being identities and that the number 23 is important and we shall revisit the number 23 later.

    Returning to our previous objective, in the last section we demonstrated how $\overset{\equiv}{\partial}$ was also connected to a possible vector, **V,** which might be associated with our time. So how might **V** and $\mathrm{G}_\partial 4$ be connected? If the vector **V** represents a point from the four time categories to our time then it should also represent $\mathrm{G}_\partial 4$.
4.20

$$\prod_{x=a}^{x=d} e^i = v\,\mathbf{V}$$

We shall approach this problem from a Set Theoretic position and review a common type of textbook example, though the final step is about Sets and not about their content.

In the table below are four categories, top = t, left side = l, right side = r, bottom = b.

T.1

Group
t & l
t & r
b & l
b & r
t & l & r
b & l & r
b & l & t & r

Next, draw a Venn diagram

V.1

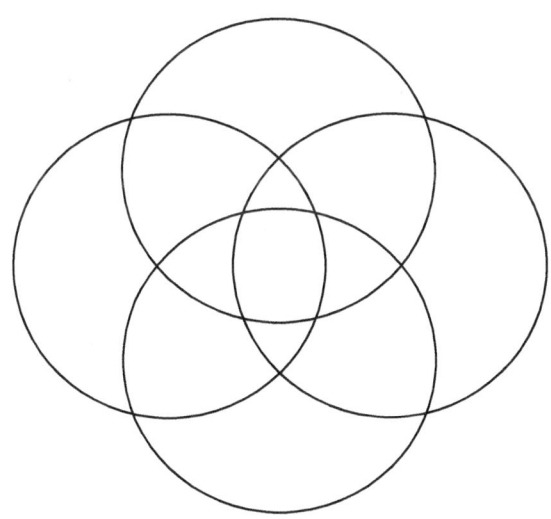

V.2

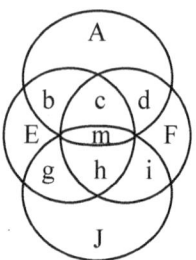

Analytically: -
4.21

$$n(A) = X_1 - n(t \cap r) - n(t \cap l) - n(l \cap r \cap t) - n(l \cap r \cap t \cap b)$$
$$= X_1 - d - b - c - m = A$$
$$n(J) = X_2 - n(b \cap r) - n(b \cap l) - n(l \cap r \cap b) - n(l \cap r \cap t \cap b)$$
$$= X_2 - i - g - h - m = J$$
$$n(E) = X_3 - n(t \cap l) - n(l \cap r \cap t) - n(b \cap l) - n(l \cap r \cap b)$$
$$-n(l \cap r \cap t \cap b)) = X_3 - b - c - g - h - m = E$$
$$n(F) = X_4 - n(t \cap r) - n(l \cap r \cap t) - n(b \cap r) - n(l \cap r \cap b)$$
$$-n(l \cap r \cap t \cap b) = X_4 - d - c - i - h - m = F$$

In eq.4.21 X_1 to X_4 is some maximum value allowed for each set. If the total of the subsets fulfils this maximum but is less than ΣX_i then the excluded figure can be found by applying the inclusion / exclusion theorem as shown in eq.4.22: -
4.22

$$n(t \cup b \cup l \cup r) = n(t) + n(b) + n(l) + n(r) - n(t \cap b) - n(t \cap l)$$
$$-n(t \cap r) - n(b \cap r) - n(b \cap l) - n(l \cap r) + n(t \cap b \cap l \cap r)$$

However, if such elementary procedures are applicable in the Mi context then we should find synchronicities reflecting this idea. For example, we only have a limited number of inputs to the four sets, which should, according to our 'synchronicity rule', produce synchronicities. Indeed, if four sets with the same construction as V.1 are to be considered *at all*, then they should produce a synchronicity <u>without</u> any given content. Finding the total number of subsets: -

4.23

$$n(t), n(t \cap r), n(t \cap l), n(l \cap r \cap t), n(l \cap r \cap t \cap b)$$

$$n(b), n(b \cap r), n(b \cap l), n(l \cap r \cap b), n(l \cap r \cap t \cap b)$$

$$n(l), n(t \cap l), n(l \cap r \cap t), n(b \cap l), n(l \cap r \cap b), n(l \cap r \cap t \cap b)$$

$$n(r), n(t \cap r), n(l \cap r \cap t), n(b \cap r), n(l \cap r \cap b), n(l \cap r \cap t \cap b)$$

$$S_4 = A\left[\sum n(t)\right] + A\left[\sum n(b)\right] + A\left[\sum n(l)\right] + A\left[\sum n(r)\right] =$$

$$5 + 5 + 6 + 6 = 22$$

The total number of sets in class S_4 (S = the four sets) is equal to the name count of 'Mi' and it would difficult to think of a more appropriate synchronicity than that. The diagram, V.2, also obeys a V.3

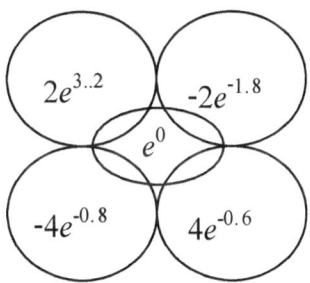

theorem in geometry concerning circles intersecting at *eight* points.

Although in the diagram V.3 the central portion is shown as a separate shape, this has only been done for convenience and we have to remember that it is part of the four sets. This diagram suggests that there is some function, or functions, from each set that will give a mapping into the central section. We could find numerical relationships in the above example but we have a serious contradiction here. In fact the contradiction exists in previous work but it was left unmentioned – ^eC. Mi seemed to have made it quite clear that as far as Mi was concerned negative numbers don't exist, and, of course, in reality they don't. In ^eC we can answer the contradiction by saying that $(-2b)$ and $(-4c)$ are *subtractions* of nonnegative quantities but in a multiplication using just one of these, *subtraction* is obviously unsatisfactory. This means that V.3 above cannot represent that which would satisfy Mi's constraint. However, this constraint arithmetically vanishes because these two negative quantities would, when multiplied together, give the same answer as if the two terms were positive. This might have been one reason why Mi described the 'number' situation in the nonnegative sense, because it makes ^eC positive under multiplication: perhaps that is why ^eC has the symmetry of containing two negatives and two positives.

Be that as it may, such a representation does conflict with our own everyday experience because: -
4.24a

$$2e^{3.2} \times (-2e^{-1.8}) \times (-4e^{-0.8}) \times 4e^{-0.6} = 64e^0 = 8^2 e^0$$

– but it does equal the Quartic equation 4.18 and dividing one by the other the answer *is* one. (Just a reminder, 'Eldridge' = 64. As a very short digression, and a bit of a 'long shot' at that, one wonders about the alleged displacement and forty-year 'journey' of the USS
4.24b (40× 365.256) -141=14469.24

$$\frac{\sqrt{\log_n \left(14469.24 \times (64 + \overset{=}{\partial}) \right)}}{\overset{=}{\partial}} \times 24900 = 25222m \, (\approx 40582.2km)$$

If 24900 miles is one complete Earth rotation then the resulting difference is not that far out from the alleged displacement.)

We shall complete this section by combining eq.4.18 and eq.4.24a (× & ÷) noting that although they are identities and have the same ^eC coefficients, the variables are different. However, we might have the same 'local' system but viewed from different perspectives.

4.25a

$$\frac{2e^{3.2} \times (-2e^{-1.8}) \times (-4e^{-0.8}) \times 4e^{-0.6}}{2x^4 - 4x^3 - 12x^2 + 16x} = \frac{64e^0}{64}$$

$$(2e^{3.2} \times 2x^4) + (-2e^{-1.8} \times -4x^3) + (-4e^{-0.8} \times -12x^2) + (4e^{-0.6}16x)$$

$$= 18505.68934$$

We have multiplied two 'four dimensional' equations that are both equal to 64 and we have eight components so divide by eight. But if $^{\equiv}\partial$ *is actually part* of this time component system then multiply each component by $^{\equiv}\partial$, which is, of course, the same as just multiplying the result by $^{\equiv}\partial$: -

4.25b

$$^{\equiv}\partial 18505.68934 = 67854.19425 = {}^eC33927.09712$$

$$33927.09712 = 8(\tfrac{1}{2} {}^{\equiv}\partial) \times 18505.68934$$

The figure of 33927.09712 is exactly (2×3.68106) more than the figure for day 224.5, 1943. Even this difference is synchronistic with the x_1 solution of the Quartic equation.

These equations provide us with clear (synchronistic) proof that Norman's Chimes experience, from whatever source, connects the author's Mi entity experience, Mi's four Time categories and Norman's own studies.

Section 3

Having finished the last Section with comments on the importance of Norman's Chimes experience, we now examine some of the synchronistic dates, 23, 201, 224.5, 342 and 365.256, in some basic sound-frequency models.

4.26

$$\sum_{i=1}^{4} \frac{x_i}{23} = \frac{201 + 224.5 + 342 + 365.256}{23} = 49.25026087$$

$$\sqrt[3]{49.25026087} = 3.665524937 = 0.999689 \stackrel{\equiv}{=} \partial$$

Again, we have an incredible synchronicity. If we add 0.5 to both 201 and 342 signifying that the births occurred sometime during the day and not in the first hour, the answer is even closer to $\stackrel{\equiv}{\partial}$, 3.666603265. Insert each of these into the 'first harmonic': -

4.27

$$\sum_{i=1}^{4} \frac{343}{x_i} = 343 \times \left(\frac{23}{201} + \frac{23}{224.5} + \frac{23}{342} + \frac{23}{365.256} \right) = 119.0548695$$

119 is synchronistic with the count for 'Lawrencium', but it was also part of replacement in eq.3.38. We now rearrange the items and combine them with ^eC directly as four 'first harmonics': -

4.28

$$\log_n H_1 = \log_n \left(\left(2 \times \frac{343}{23} \right) - \left(2 \times \frac{343}{201} \right) - \left(4 \times \frac{343}{224.5} \right) + \left(4 \times \frac{343}{342} \right) \right)$$

$$= 3.191031298$$

This answer is close to (3.2) of S_1, so let us now replace the dates with name counts 374 and 182, 78 and 119 (+103): -

4.29

$$\log_n H_2 = \log_n \left(\left(2 \times \frac{343}{78} \right) - \left(2 \times \frac{343}{222} \right) - \left(4 \times \frac{343}{182} \right) + \left(4 \times \frac{343}{374} \right) \right)$$

$$= 0.603918786, \left[2H_2 = 3.669538728 \approx \frac{4 \times 343}{374} \cong \stackrel{\equiv}{\partial} \right]$$

4.30

$$\log_n \left(\left(2 \times \frac{343}{22} \right) - \left(2 \times \frac{343}{300} \right) - \left(4 \times \frac{343}{182} \right) + \left(4 \times \frac{343}{374} \right) \right)$$

$$= 3.219880887$$

The result of eq.4.29 is not synchronistic but two items are $\approx \overset{=}{\partial}$. In eq.4.30, the counts for 'Mira Ceti' and 'Lawrencium' have been combined and 22 substituted for 78.

Subtracting eq.4.29 from eq.4.30 gives a result reminiscent of τ^2 while eq.4.28 and 4.30 $\cong$ 3.2. These two equations might suggest that the constant of 3.2 in the simultaneous equations could be important as far as Norman's Chimes are concerned but we would need a corrective calculation. The denominators of eq.4.28 are days of the year and we have the astronomical calculation correction formula for the Earth's inclination. Therefore, it would be legitimate for us to use here, so let's try it: -

4.31(Days in ascending order)

$$\left(2 \times \frac{343}{23}\right) - \left(2 \times \frac{343}{201}\right) - \left(4 \times \frac{343}{224.5}\right) + \left(4 \times \frac{343}{342}\right) = {}^eC_\lambda$$

$$\tan^{-1}\left(\frac{\sin\left({}^eC_\lambda\right) \times \cos\left(23.441884\right)}{\cos\left({}^eC_\lambda\right)}\right) - {}^eC_\lambda =$$

$$\tan^{-1}\left(\tan\left(24.31348897\right) \times \cos\left(23.441884\right)\right) - 24.31348897$$

$$= 22.51454296 - 24.31348897 = -1.798946012$$

This result is just over 99.94% of (-1.8) and is much closer to the second constant of the simultaneous equations. What is required now is a reverse procedure that will give a result that is synchronistic with the original ^eC.

Norman made two other major contributions Enki and twin, with counts 39 and 66 , so we might start with one of these. Since 66 is 3 × 22, and 'twin' means 'two of ', let 66 substitute $^eC_\lambda$, and also let 66 = 66° because 90° - 66° = 24° (and $^{66}/_{90} = 0.2\overset{=}{\partial}$). Also use -66 because of the negative result of eq.4.31.

4.32

$$\left(\tan^{-1}\left(\tan\left(-66\right) \times \cos\left(23.441884\right)\right)\right) + 90$$

$$= 25.88645883, 25.88645883 + 39 = 64.888645883,$$

$$\left(64.888645883 - 64\right)^4 = 0.617496188$$

Equation 4.32 continued

$$25.88645883 - (e^{3.2} + e^{-1.8} + e^{-0.8} + e^{-0.6}) =$$

$$0.190489144, (0.190489144 + 39)^2 = 1535.894439 =$$

$$0.999931275 \times \left|{}^{e}C\right| \approx 1536$$

Using the second number, 39, we find the result is synchronistic with the Quartic equation where the decimal part is coincidental with τ^{-1}. Alternatively, by subtracting the exponential figures and then adding 39 we find an answer synchronistic with ${}^{e}C$.

We can conclude that it is legitimate to employ the astronomical correction formula although where the constant 3.2 was originally indicated as the main component, this is not the case now. Let us try anther combination, this time in descending order: -
4.33

$$\left(2 \times \frac{343}{342}\right) - \left(2 \times \frac{343}{224.5}\right) - \left(4 \times \frac{343}{201}\right) + \left(4 \times \frac{343}{23}\right) = {}^{e}C_{\lambda r}$$

$$\tan^{-1}\left(\tan\left({}^{e}C_{\lambda r}\right) \times \cos(23.441884)\right) = \kappa^{e}C_{\lambda r}$$

$$\sqrt[3]{\frac{\kappa^{e}C_{\lambda r} + \dfrac{201}{23} + \dfrac{224.5}{23} + \dfrac{342}{23} + \dfrac{365.256}{23}}{2}} =$$

$$\sqrt[3]{\frac{49.35589975 + 49.25026087}{2}} = 3.666834858 \approx {}^{\equiv}\partial$$

While the above equations are synchronistic they do not present any single conclusive result but they do suggest that degrees of arc continue to be important. They also present us with another question – why does the number 343 give synchronicities? After all, it is not synchronistic with anything in the Mi Book and its closest neighbor herein is day 342, December 8th. According to family the author was born sometime after 8pm of the 8th which is day 342.8333. Perhaps under other circumstances this might be considered synchronistic with 343, but here it would seem to be an 'artificial' move. Perhaps pursuing equations in degrees $(x°)$ might reveal something. We saw in eq.3.53 that the slope of 2.7 produced synchronicities with the correction formula, if we now reversed the procedure and inserted 343 in to the linear expression, along with $\overline{\overline{\equiv}}\partial$, then a periodic function would be the result: -

4.34

$$a = 0.30490084, b = 2.7000235$$

$$\left(\sin(x)b + a\right) \overset{\equiv}{=} \partial, \left(\sin(343)b + a\right) \overset{\equiv}{=} \partial = \left(\sin(-17)b + a\right) \overset{\equiv}{=} \partial$$

$$= -1.776535323 \approx \frac{3.2}{-1.8} \therefore \sin^{-1}\left(\left(\frac{-1.8}{\overset{\equiv}{\equiv}\partial} - a\right)\Big/b\right) = b_f$$

$$= -17.14205843, (360 - 17.14205843 = 342.8579416)$$

The result of (x_f) has the dimension of degrees and therefore is not a true synchronicity with the birthday 342, though it is strange that the numbers should bear any resemblance at all. At this point, it would seem that 3.2 and -1.8 are paired together. Moreover: -

4.35a

$$\overset{\equiv}{=}\partial b = C, \frac{dy}{dx} = \frac{d\left(\sin(b_f)b + a\right)\overset{\equiv}{=}\partial}{dx} = C\frac{d\left(\sin(b_f) + \overset{\equiv}{=}\partial a\right)}{dx} =$$

$$C\cos(b_f) = 9.460293795$$

Although the result has the dimension of degrees, the figure is synchronistic the R.A. of the Sun on day 224. Using eq.4.34 with 3.2, -0.8 and -0.6: -

4.35b

$$a_f = 12.140183, b_f = -17.14205843, c_f = -11.17069697$$

$$d_f = -9.993170339, \exp\left(^e C_{Sf}\right) =$$

$$\exp\left(\left(2 \times 3.2 a_f\right) - \left(2 \times -1.8 b_f\right) - \left(4 \times -0.8 c_f\right) + \left(4 \times -0.6 d_f\right)\right)$$

$$= 68.247401604$$

Mi Mathematics Part 4
G.A.T.E. (G̯)

Remember that 68 is the count for 'Cetus' so repeat eq.4.35a using the result of 4.35b: -
4.35c

$$\frac{dy}{dx} = \frac{d\left(\sin(68.247401604)b + a\right) \overset{\equiv}{=} \partial}{dx} =$$

$$C\cos(68.247401604) = 3.668967569$$

This result is obviously synchronistic with $\overset{\equiv}{=}\partial$ but it is also synchronistic with other items herein, the second half of eq.3.56 being an example. The cube root of $^{e}C_{\lambda r}$ (eq.4.33) is 3.668143843 provides another example. Perhaps an interesting synchronicity is that although $182 \div \overset{\equiv}{=}\partial^3$ gives a result just outside of day 224, dividing 182 by (eq.4.35c)^3 gives 3.685019321 which is consistent with the figures of List 1 of Part 3. (The function of eq.4.34 is named the Tridel Slope function and eq.4.35a-c will be known as the Chimes Derivative – $\overset{\equiv}{=}\partial$ & D^{e}C respectively. The graph for the Tridel Slope function (sinusoidal) is shown in Notes.).

Section 4

Because of the relationships between 3.2, -0.8, -1.8 & -0.6, we have: -
4.36a

$$\text{Let } c = -\frac{1}{4}a, d = \frac{1}{3}b$$

$$\therefore 2e^a - 2e^b - 4e^{-\frac{1}{4}a} + 4e^{\frac{1}{3}b} = 49.13239331 \cong \overset{\equiv}{=}\partial^3$$

Equation 4.36a indicates that we have two variables, which brings us back to Mi's original idea of two main categories, 'active' and 'passive' Time. With reference to e^i we have: -
4.36b

$$(e^a e^b e^{-\frac{1}{4}a} e^{\frac{1}{3}b}) = e^{\frac{3a}{4}} e^{\frac{4b}{3}} = e^{2.4} e^{-2.4} = e^0$$

166

By using PDE methods eq.4.36b can be reduced to zero because the results cancel: -

4.37

$$\frac{\partial e^i}{\partial e^a}e^{-2.4} + \frac{\partial e^i}{\partial e^b}e^{2.4} = \left(e^{2.4}e^{-2.4}\right) - \left(e^{-2.4}e^{2.4}\right) = 1 - 1 = 0$$

These equations suggest that the two constants, 3.2 and -1.8, need special consideration – but is there a connection to $^{\equiv}\partial$?

4.38

$$\frac{|3.2|}{|-1.8|} = {}^{\equiv}\partial^2 - {}^{\equiv}\partial - 8$$

The Oliver Ratio can now be used to define other properties and synchronicities: -

4.39

$$O_\tau = 1.61805063159354$$

$$\frac{{}^{\equiv}\partial\left(O_\tau\right)^4}{\pi} - \frac{3.2}{-1.8} = {}^{\equiv}\partial^2 - {}^{\equiv}\partial, \frac{{}^{\equiv}\partial\left(O_\tau\right)^4}{\pi} + \frac{3.2}{-1.8} = 6.2\dot{2}$$

$$\sqrt[4]{\frac{360\pi}{6.2\dot{2}}} = 3.671780525 \therefore \sqrt[4]{\frac{365.256\pi}{6.2\dot{2}}} = 3.685109766$$

$$\frac{\left(\tan^{-1}\left(\tan\left(*e^{\frac{1}{O_=}+\frac{3.2}{-1.8}} - 365.256\right) \times \cos\left(23.441884\right)\right)\right) + 180}{15} = \frac{\xi}{15}$$

$$9.399886842 \approx 9.4, \left(*e^{\frac{3.2}{O_=}-1.8}\text{ in }\xi = \xi_2\right), \sqrt[4]{\xi_2} = 3.669583778 \approx {}^{\equiv}\partial$$

It is also coincidental that a number equal to $\frac{1}{10}$ of 24 should be produced in both positive and negative forms, so does this have a meaning? The number 2.4 presents us with yet another challenge – whether or not it connects to the Earth's orbital period.

If we use the integers of the Earth's orbital period and diameter along with day 224, converting these into vector

coefficients and then we compute equation of the plane that such vectors would produce. First we need to compute the normal: -
4.40

$$P = (3,6,5), Q = (1,1,6), R = (2,2,4)$$

$$\overrightarrow{PQ} = (1,1,6) - (3,6,5) = (-2,-5,1), \overrightarrow{PR} =$$

$$(2,2,4) - (3,6,5) = (-1,-4,-1)$$

$$\det. \begin{bmatrix} i & j & k \\ -2 & -5 & 1 \\ -1 & -4 & -1 \end{bmatrix} = \begin{vmatrix} i & j & k \\ -2 & -5 & 1 \\ -1 & -4 & -1 \end{vmatrix} = (9i - 3j + 3k) = n$$

We then convert n, into the equation of the plane: -
4.41

$$9(x-3) - 3(y-6) + 3(z-5) =$$

$$9x - 27 - 3y + 18 + 3z - 15 = 9x - 3y + 3z = 24$$

The equation $9x - 3y + 3z$ needs to be normalized to find the perpendicular distance from the plane to the origin: -
4.42

$$\frac{9}{\sqrt{(9^2 - 3^2 + 3^2)}} + \frac{-3}{\sqrt{(9^2 - 3^2 + 3^2)}} + \frac{3}{\sqrt{(9^2 - 3^2 + 3^2)}} =$$

$$= \frac{24}{\sqrt{(9^2 - 3^2 + 3^2)}} = \frac{24}{\sqrt{3^3 = \partial}} = \frac{24}{\sqrt{+81}} = \frac{24}{\sqrt{81 + 18}} = 2.412090757$$

In eq.4.42 the intermediate figures are all multiples of three and the equation of the plane equals 24 while the denominator of can be expressed as the integer of the period of revolution for the Moon × $\equiv\partial$. The denominator can also be expressed in terms of the name count for 'Oliver' or 'Lawrence', plus the mirror image. Finally, the answer is close to the figure of 2.4. Now convert (9, -3, 3) back into days we have 900 - 30 + 3 = 873 which is 2 years 143 days, or May 23 (2.391780822 non-leap years), 2 = twin or the constant of ^eC? $143 = 39^{=}\partial$ and 23 are also synchronistic. Does 873 days provide any synchronicities with the original number of days of the generated vectors: -

4.43

a. $\quad v = \dfrac{\sqrt{\left(\dfrac{873}{365}\right)^{2*} + \left(\dfrac{873}{116}\right)^{2} + \left(\dfrac{873}{224}\right)^{2}}}{^{=}\partial} = 2.401678076,$

b. $\quad (2.412090757 + (2.391780822)*, \bar{X} = 2.4019355789)$

c. $\quad \sqrt[3]{\dfrac{873}{365} + \dfrac{873}{116} + \dfrac{873}{224}} = 2.39995, 365 + 116 + 224 = 705$

d. $\quad \left.\begin{array}{l} \left(\dfrac{873-705}{873} + 39\right)^{2} = 1536.047342 \\ (\sin(e^{v}) + 39)^{2} = 1535.975491 \end{array}\right\} \approx |^{e}C| = 1536$

f. $\quad \dfrac{873-705}{873} - \sin(e^{v}) = 0.00091666476$

The results of eq.4.43 confirm that $e^{2.4}$, and as its reciprocal $e^{-2.4}$, are probably the nearest we have come to a possible meaning to Mi's 'active' and 'passive' Time categories, with possibly -1.8 and -0.6 in the former, 3.2 and -0.8 in the latter.

The figure of 2.4 seems to have a profound effect on several numbers synchronistic herein: -

4.44a (All numbers are in degrees)

$$\sin(374 \times 2.4) = \sin(224 \times 2.4) = \sin(2.4)$$
$$\sin(374 \times 224 \times 2.4) = \sin(-2.4)$$

Equation 4.44 must be a candidate for the title of being the most incredible synchronicity so far. Using Norman's full name count, with day 224 and 2.4, we are able to achieve precisely what was achieved with the constants *a*, *b*, *c* and *d*, on page 167. This then raises the question as to why separately they are the same as a

positive angle while combined they produce a negative. What might be a synchronistic 'runner up' is: -
4.44b

$$\sin(365 \times 2.4) = \sin(365 \times 224 \times 2.4) =$$
$$\sin(365 \times 374 \times 2.4) = \sin(305 \times 182 \times 2.4) = \sin(24)$$

Furthermore: -
4.44c

$$\frac{\sin^{-1}(\sin(182 \times 2.4))}{24} = 3.2, \frac{\sin^{-1}(\sin(182 \times 2.4))}{-(39 + \,^{\equiv}\partial)} = -1.8$$

$$\frac{\dfrac{\sin^{-1}(\sin(182 \times 2.4))}{182 - 374}}{2} = -0.8, \frac{\sin^{-1}(\sin(182 \times 2.4))}{246 - 374} = -0.6$$

$$(143 + 103) = (222 + 24) = 246, \sin(182 \times 2.4) = \sin(343 \times 2.4)$$

Equation 4.44c provides us with trigonometric definitions of the four constants of $^e C_S$. There are several other sums that are interesting, such as $(305 \times 2.4) = 12$ and $(305 \times 556 \times 2.4) = -12$, but what this study shows is that numbers synchronistic herein can be paired so that trigonometrically they are equivalent. If 2.3 or 2.5 are used instead of 2.4, there are no identities. Again, this is an indication that a geometrical analysis is required.

Since the figure of 2.4 was derived from the four constants, it might be instructive to see how it affects them.
4.45

$$\left(\frac{3.2}{-2.4}\right) + \left(\frac{-0.8}{-2.4}\right) = \left(\frac{-1.8}{2.4}\right) + \left(\frac{-0.6}{2.4}\right) = -1$$

If the idea that the two main (Mi) Time categories can be represented by 2.4 and -2.4 then one interpretation might be that the 'reversal' mentioned in $\mathcal{G}_4$ is possible from either 'active' or 'passive' Time. However, using division and multiplication: -

4.46a

$$\frac{\left(\dfrac{3.2}{-2.4}\right)+\left(\dfrac{-0.8}{-2.4}\right)+\left(\dfrac{-1.8}{2.4}\right)+\left(\dfrac{-0.6}{2.4}\right)}{\left(\dfrac{3.2}{-2.4}\right)\times\left(\dfrac{-0.8}{-2.4}\right)\times\left(\dfrac{-1.8}{2.4}\right)\times\left(\dfrac{-0.6}{2.4}\right)}=24$$

Equation 4.46a plus eq.4.45$_R$ (rearranged = -2) equals 22 and as far as the name 'Mi' is concerned these equations could not be more synchronistic. If we now invert eq.4.46a and apply ^{e}C the answer is 2^eC: -

4.46b

$$\frac{\left(2\dfrac{3.2}{-2.4}\right)\times\left(-2\dfrac{-0.8}{-2.4}\right)\times\left(-4\dfrac{-1.8}{2.4}\right)\times\left(4\dfrac{-0.6}{2.4}\right)}{2\left(\dfrac{3.2}{-2.4}\right)-2\left(\dfrac{-0.8}{-2.4}\right)-4\left(\dfrac{-1.8}{2.4}\right)+4\left(\dfrac{-0.6}{2.4}\right)}=4$$

Therefore: -
4.46c

$$\text{Eqs.}\frac{\left[(4.46a)+(4.45_R)\right]\times 4.46b}{4.46a}=\;^{\equiv}\partial$$

As far as we are concerned here the figure of 2.4 has a special significance and as such is worth some further study. We continue with e^i.

4.47

$$e^{\left(\frac{3.2}{-2.4}\right)}+e^{\left(\frac{-0.8}{-2.4}\right)}+e^{\left(\frac{-1.8}{2.4}\right)}+e^{\left(\frac{-0.6}{2.4}\right)}=2.910376899$$

$$\frac{33920}{2.910376899^2}=4004.583693,\frac{33920}{2.910376899^2\times 22}=182.0265315$$

$$\frac{33920^{\;\equiv\partial^{-1}}}{2.910376899^2}=1092.159189$$

The numbers 1092 and 4004 can be found on pages 35 & 36 in reference to the clock page diagrams. The numbers 182 & 22 need no introduction and 33920 is the R.A of the Sun on day 224.5, 1943, to the nearest arc second. The clock diagrams were concerned with justification of 'moving' the position of M77, so: -

4.48a

$$77 \times 2.910376899 = 224.0990212$$

$$M77 = 13 \times 77 = 1001, \log_n \left(\frac{1001}{\equiv \partial (2.910376899)^3} \right) = 2.404624021$$

$$\left(\frac{\frac{1001}{224.5} + 2.910376899}{2} \right) = 3.684587113,$$

$$\frac{13 \times 77 \times 41}{\equiv \partial^4} - 2.910376899 = 224.1452204$$

It would seem that no matter which way we turn we find that day 224 is involved, including where 'Mira' is used and therefore the places involved in Norman's recent contactee case.

Having mentioned Mira without the other identifying name, Ceti (37), can Lawrencium (119), without the identifying number, 103, be derived? It would seem so: -

4.48b

$$41 \times 2.910376899 = 119.3254529$$

$$\left(\frac{222 + 78}{2.910376899} \right) = 103.0794328$$

$$\frac{(3.684587113 + 1) + 103}{2.910376899} = 37.00022054$$

The figure of 3.684587113+1 is the counterpart of the $\equiv \partial + 1$ mentioned in the earlier 4×4 matrices. Now that the Mi book 'central components' can be derived, what about Time?

4.49

$$47 \times 2.910376899 = 136.7877143$$

$$136.7877143 + 2.404624021^{\uparrow} = 139.1923383$$

There are two ways in which we can view the second result of eq.4.49 Firstly, Mira-culously, it is almost Mira Ceti's R.A. of 2hr. 19min.20secs.,139.3333333 arc minutes (current estimates – but strangely enough the first part is very close to estimates of the 1980's). Secondly, after applying the correction formula, the result is consistent with the Sun's R.A. on day 224 ('↑' see eq.4.48a).

We now turn to the e^i applying ^eC as before: -

4.50

$$\frac{e^{(2\times3.2)} + e^{((-2\times-1.8))} + e^{(-4\times-0..8)} + e^{(4\times-0.6)}}{\equiv \partial^4} = 3.668355178 \approx {}^{\equiv}\partial$$

$$\sqrt{e^{(2\times3.2)} \times e^{(-2\times-1.8)} \times e^{(-4\times-0..8)} \times e^{(4\times-0.6)}} \times \frac{365.256}{360} = 224.638949881$$

The equations of Part 3 and Part 4 have further increased the number of synchronicities from those of Part 1 and Part 2 and we have shown that numbers important to certain branches of scientific topics also exhibit synchronicities. The nature in which the Earth orbits the Sun is fundamental to all life on Earth, yet the equations that rely partly on that nature also provide synchronistic figures. The Lists and graphs of Part 3 seem to indicate that day 224 has some specific periodic anomaly that might be connected to any number of important ideas, the Golden Ratio for example. In Part 4, the idea that day 224 is important has continued to the point where it seems 'all roads' lead to it.

With regard to Mi's four Time categories, Ǥ4 presented a 'first step', suggesting that at least an exponential function might be involved, an hypothesis supported by various synchronistic rearrangements. The derivation of the numbers -2.4 and 2.4 would be, in the present context, suitable candidates for Mi's 'active and 'passive' time zones. However, ($e^{-2.4}e^{2.4} = 1$) would suggest the 'active and 'passive' time zones balance one another but unfortunately, Mi did not seem to have clarified whether or not the 'active and 'passive' time zones balance one another. Perhaps the author's own background about oriental philosophies might have had an influence in that regard. Nevertheless, the two numbers produced synchronicities that are, most definitely, uncanny and serve to deepen the mystery. We shall revisit -2.4 and 2.4 later.

Several more synchronicities could have been included but there comes a point where we start to expect synchronicities, as for example in the case of e^x. On one hand, [exp.($\sqrt{e^{3.2}}$) =141.6037161] which is synchronistic with the Sun's R.A. on day 224, and on the other hand [exp.$\sqrt{(e^{(-1.8 \times -0.8 \times -0.6)}})]^2 \approx 3.6635$, close to the value of $^{\equiv}\partial$. Each synchronicity might have a specific role to play under certain conditions but at this point they only (re) confirm what we already know. In other words, we might 'not see the woods for the trees'. What we need to do now is ask broader questions and this we do in the Part 5.

Notes

Some more synchronicities that use the constants 3.2, -1.8, -0.8, -0.6 are: -

$$\sqrt[4]{e^{22+(-2.8\times6)}} = 3.669296668 \approx {}^{\equiv}\partial, \log_n 182e^{-2.8} = 2.40407$$

$$\sqrt[4]{\frac{556}{e^{-2.8}}} = 9.778558432 \approx {}^{\equiv}\partial^2 - {}^{\equiv}\partial$$

$$\sqrt[4]{e^{22+(-2.8\times6)}} = \sqrt[4]{\exp\left(\left(\frac{234^{\equiv}\partial}{39}\right)+(-2.8\times6)\right)} =$$

$$\sqrt[4]{\exp\left(\left(\frac{182}{8+{}^{\equiv}\partial^{-1}}\right)+(-2.8\times6)\right)} = \sqrt[4]{\exp\left(\left(6^{\equiv}\partial\right)+(-2.8\times6)\right)}$$

$$*\log_n \sqrt[8]{e^{22} \times \left(e^{-0.8}e^{-0.6}\left(e^{-1.8}\right)^{-1}\left(e^{3.2}\right)^{-1}\right)} = 2.4$$

These examples are taken from Part 1 eq.1.4 and 1.10 and lastly from the most important source, the original derivation of $\overset{\equiv}{\partial}$. Equation (*) clearly shows the expansion and the connection between the count of 'Mi' and the constants. Examples from Part 2 include replacing (22) with other numbers from the study: -

$$\sqrt[4]{e^{22+(-2.8\times6)}} = 3.669296668 =$$

$$\sqrt[4]{e^{182-119-41+(-2.8\times6)}} = \sqrt[4]{e^{1+6+9+6+(-2.8\times6)}} =$$

$$\sqrt[4]{e^{\left(2\times3.2-(2\times-1.8)-(4\times-0.8)+(4\times2.2)\right)+(-2.8\times6)}} = \sqrt[4]{e^{\sqrt{374+110}+(-2.8\times6)}}$$

The first is from eq.2.18 involving the author's name count, 'Lawrencium' and 'Mira', while the second is from page 47 concerning the sequential addition. The third is eq.2.32, the Chimes expression equal to 22. The fourth uses Norman's full name-count along with the name count for his recent contactee case.

$((\sin(x)\times2.7)+0.305)\times3.66667$

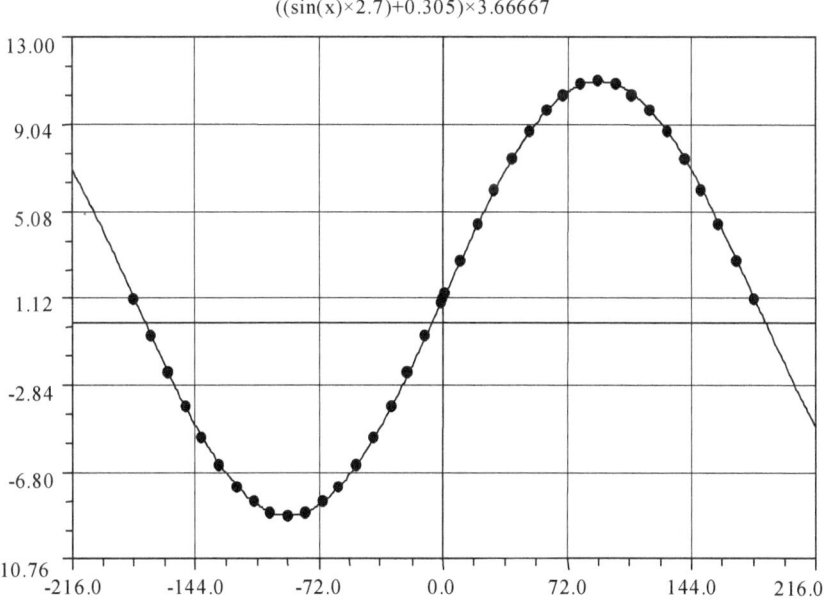

G.A.T.E. ($\overset{\circ}{\mathbb{G}}$)

Section 1

Mi's apparent preference for a flat dimension (mentioned in the Mi book, Chapter 10) raises the question about whether Mi's perception of the four Time categories is also preferentially flat. There are several alternatives as to why Mi might perceive our time as flat, among them the possibility that (Mi's idea of) the four time categories might actually be flat.

It might be instructive to compute the metric of a flat space using Polar coordinates, with e^i representing a Mi Time field, that is $x = r \cos \theta, y = r \sin \theta, \theta = e^i$

5.0

1. $x = r\cos\theta = \overline{x}^1 = x^1 \cos x^2, y = r\sin\theta = \overline{x}^2 = x^1 \sin x^2$

2. $x = -r\cos\theta = \overline{x}^1 = -x^1 \cos x^2, y = -r\sin\theta = \overline{x}^2 = -x^1 \sin x^2$

1. $J = \begin{bmatrix} \dfrac{\partial(x^1 \cos x^2)}{\partial x^1} & \dfrac{\partial(x^1 \cos x^2)}{\partial x^2} \\ \dfrac{\partial(x^1 \sin x^2)}{\partial x^1} & \dfrac{\partial(x^1 \sin x^2)}{\partial x^2} \end{bmatrix} = \begin{bmatrix} \cos x^2 & -x^1 \sin x^2 \\ \sin x^2 & x^1 \cos x^2 \end{bmatrix}$

$J^T J = \begin{bmatrix} \cos x^2 & \sin x^2 \\ -x^1 \sin x^2 & x^1 \cos x^2 \end{bmatrix}\begin{bmatrix} \cos x^2 & -x^1 \sin x^2 \\ \sin x^2 & x^1 \cos x^2 \end{bmatrix} =$

$\begin{bmatrix} (\cos x^2)^2 + (\sin x^2)^2 & 0 \\ 0 & (x^1)^2 \sin^2 x^2 + (x^1)^2 \cos^2 x^2 \end{bmatrix} = \begin{bmatrix} 1 & 0 \\ 0 & (x^1)^2 \end{bmatrix}$

2. $J = \begin{bmatrix} \dfrac{\partial(-x^1 \cos x^2)}{\partial x^1} & \dfrac{\partial(-x^1 \cos x^2)}{\partial x^2} \\ \dfrac{\partial(-x^1 \sin x^2)}{\partial x^1} & \dfrac{\partial(-x^1 \sin x^2)}{\partial x^2} \end{bmatrix} = \begin{bmatrix} -\cos x^2 & x^1 \sin x^2 \\ -\sin x^2 & -x^1 \cos x^2 \end{bmatrix}$

$J^T J = \begin{bmatrix} -\cos x^2 & -\sin x^2 \\ x^1 \sin x^2 & -x^1 \cos x^2 \end{bmatrix}\begin{bmatrix} -\cos x^2 & x^1 \sin x^2 \\ -\sin x^2 & -x^1 \cos x^2 \end{bmatrix} = \begin{bmatrix} 1 & 0 \\ 0 & (x^1)^2 \end{bmatrix}$

Case 2 uses negative r which seems a little strange, but has been included because ^cC has both positive and negative coefficients which are used in the recalculation below: -

5.1

3. $x = -2r\cos\theta = \bar{x}^1 = -2x^1\cos x^2, y = -2r\sin\theta = \bar{x}^2 = -2x^1\sin x^2$

4. $x = 2r\cos\theta = \bar{x}^1 = 2x^1\cos x^2, y = 2r\sin\theta = \bar{x}^2 = x^1\sin x^2$

3. $J = \begin{bmatrix} \dfrac{\partial(-2x^1\cos x^2)}{\partial x^1} & \dfrac{\partial(-2x^1\cos x^2)}{\partial x^2} \\ \dfrac{\partial(-2x^1\sin x^2)}{\partial x^1} & \dfrac{\partial(-2x^1\sin x^2)}{\partial x^2} \end{bmatrix} =$

$\begin{bmatrix} -2\cos x^2 & 2x^1\sin x^2 \\ -2\sin x^2 & -2x^1\cos x^2 \end{bmatrix}$

$J^T J = \begin{bmatrix} -2\cos x^2 & -2\sin x^2 \\ 2x^1\sin x^2 & -2x^1\cos x^2 \end{bmatrix}\begin{bmatrix} -2\cos x^2 & 2x^1\sin x^2 \\ -2\sin x^2 & -2x^1\cos x^2 \end{bmatrix} =$

$\begin{bmatrix} (4\cos x^2)^2 + (4\sin x^2)^2 & 0 \\ 0 & 4(x^1)^2\sin x^2 + 4(x^1)^2\cos x^2 \end{bmatrix} =$

$\begin{bmatrix} 4 & 0 \\ 0 & 4(x^1)^2 \end{bmatrix}$

4. $J = \begin{bmatrix} \dfrac{\partial(2x^1\cos x^2)}{\partial x^1} & \dfrac{\partial(2x^1\cos x^2)}{\partial x^2} \\ \dfrac{\partial(2x^1\sin x^2)}{\partial x^1} & \dfrac{\partial(2x^1\sin x^2)}{\partial x^2} \end{bmatrix} = \begin{bmatrix} 2\cos x^2 & -2x^1\sin x^2 \\ 2\sin x^2 & 2x^1\cos x^2 \end{bmatrix}$

$J^T J = \begin{bmatrix} 2\cos x^2 & 2\sin x^2 \\ -2x^1\sin x^2 & 2x^1\cos x^2 \end{bmatrix}\begin{bmatrix} 2\cos x^2 & -2x^1\sin x^2 \\ 2\sin x^2 & 2x^1\cos x^2 \end{bmatrix} =$

$\begin{bmatrix} 4 & 0 \\ 0 & 4(x^1)^2 \end{bmatrix}$

The equivalent in cylindrical coordinates is: -

$$\overline{x}^1 = r\cos\theta, \overline{x}^2 = r\sin\theta, \overline{x}^3 = x^3, \begin{bmatrix} 1 & 0 & 0 \\ 0 & (x^1)^2 & 0 \\ 0 & 0 & 1 \end{bmatrix} \begin{bmatrix} 4 & 0 & 0 \\ 0 & 4(x^1)^2 & 0 \\ 0 & 0 & 1 \end{bmatrix}$$

Because of the negative sign in eq.5.1b, the coordinates are not the usual Polar coordinates given in textbooks, although the results are the same.

It is possible to have another interpretation of ^eC, because 4 can be represented as 2^2, so the radius, r, becomes $r^2 = (x^1)^2$. In this case, the next equation, eq.5.2 below, shows that both g_{11} and g_{22} contain x^1.

5.2

$$x = -r^2\cos\theta = \overline{x}^1 = -(x^1)^2\cos x^2$$

$$y = -r^2\sin\theta = \overline{x}^2 = -(x^1)^2\sin x^2$$

$$J = \begin{bmatrix} \dfrac{\partial\left(-(x^1)^2\cos x^2\right)}{\partial x^1} & \dfrac{\partial\left(-(x^1)^2\cos x^2\right)}{\partial x^2} \\ \dfrac{\partial\left((-x^1)^2\sin x^2\right)}{\partial x^1} & \dfrac{\partial\left((-x^1)^2\sin x^2\right)}{\partial x^2} \end{bmatrix} =$$

$$\begin{bmatrix} -2x^1\cos x^2 & (x^1)^2\sin x^2 \\ -2x^1\sin x^2 & -(x^1)^2\cos x^2 \end{bmatrix}, J^T J =$$

$$\begin{bmatrix} -2x^1\cos x^2 & -2x^1\sin x^2 \\ (x^1)^2\sin x^2 & -(x^1)^2\cos x^2 \end{bmatrix}\begin{bmatrix} -2x^1\cos x^2 & (x^1)^2\sin x^2 \\ -2x^1\sin x^2 & -(x^1)^2\cos x^2 \end{bmatrix}, =$$

(Eq.5.2 continued on next page)

$$\left[\begin{array}{cc} \left(4(x^1)^2\cos^2 x^2\right)+\left(4(x^1)^2\sin^2 x^2\right) & 0 \\ 0 & (x^1)^4\sin^2 x^2+(x^1)^4\cos^2 x^2 \end{array}\right]$$

$$=\left[\begin{array}{cc} 4(x^1)^2 & 0 \\ 0 & (x^1)^4 \end{array}\right]$$

$$x=r^2\cos\theta=\bar{x}^1=(x^1)^2\cos x^2, y=r^2\sin\theta=\bar{x}^2=(x^1)^2\sin x^2$$

$$=\left[\begin{array}{cc} 4(x^1)^2 & 0 \\ 0 & (x^1)^4 \end{array}\right]$$

$$\left[\begin{array}{cc} 4(x^1)^2 & 0 \\ 0 & (x^1)^4 \end{array}\right],\left[\begin{array}{cc} 4(x^1)^2 & 0 \\ 0 & (x^1)^4 \end{array}\right]$$

From the short excursion to the Complex numbers we found that the coefficients were the radii and we have a = 2 = r, b = -4 = -r^2 or 2r,c = -12 = -($r^3 + r^2$) or 6r and d = 16 = r^4 or 8r. That is, all are multiples of r = 2, which gives us another two possibilities in the expanded form of ^{e}C.

5.3

3. $x=-6r\cos\theta=\bar{x}^1=-6x^1\cos x^2, y=-6r\sin\theta=\bar{x}^2=-6x^1\sin x^2$

$$3.\ J=\left[\begin{array}{cc} \dfrac{\partial(-6x^1\cos x^2)}{\partial x^1} & \dfrac{\partial(-6x^1\cos x^2)}{\partial x^2} \\ \dfrac{\partial(-6x^1\sin x^2)}{\partial x^1} & \dfrac{\partial(-6x^1\sin x^2)}{\partial x^2} \end{array}\right]=\left[\begin{array}{cc} -6\cos x^2 & 6x^1\sin x^2 \\ -6\sin x^2 & -6x^1\cos x^2 \end{array}\right]$$

$$J^T J=\left[\begin{array}{cc} -6\cos x^2 & -6\sin x^2 \\ 6x^1\sin x^2 & -6x^1\cos x^2 \end{array}\right]\left[\begin{array}{cc} -6\cos x^2 & 6x^1\sin x^2 \\ -6\sin x^2 & -6x^1\cos x^2 \end{array}\right]=$$

$$\left[\begin{array}{cc} (36\cos x^2)^2+(36\sin x^2)^2 & 0 \\ 0 & 36(x^1)^2\sin^2 x^2+36(x^1)^2\cos^2 x^2 \end{array}\right]$$

5.3 continued

4. $x = 8r \cos\theta = \bar{x}^1 = 8x^1 \cos x^2$, $y = 8r \sin\theta = \bar{x}^2 = 8x^1 \sin x^2$

$$4.\ J = \begin{bmatrix} \dfrac{\partial(8x^1 \cos x^2)}{\partial x^1} & \dfrac{\partial(8x^1 \cos x^2)}{\partial x^2} \\ \dfrac{\partial(8x^1 \sin x^2)}{\partial x^1} & \dfrac{\partial(8x^1 \sin x^2)}{\partial x^2} \end{bmatrix} = \begin{bmatrix} 8\cos x^2 & -8x^1 \sin x^2 \\ 8\sin x^2 & 8x^1 \cos x^2 \end{bmatrix}$$

$$J^T J = \begin{bmatrix} 8\cos x^2 & 8\sin x^2 \\ -8x^1 \sin x^2 & 8x^1 \cos x^2 \end{bmatrix} \begin{bmatrix} 8\cos x^2 & -8x^1 \sin x^2 \\ 8\sin x^2 & 8x^1 \cos x^2 \end{bmatrix} =$$

$$\begin{bmatrix} (64\cos^2 x^2) + (64\sin^2 x^2) & 0 \\ 0 & 64(x^1)^2 \sin^2 x^2 + 64(x^1)^2 \cos^2 x^2 \end{bmatrix}$$

$$\therefore 3. = \begin{bmatrix} 36 & 0 \\ 0 & 36(x^1)^2 \end{bmatrix}, 4. = \begin{bmatrix} 64 & 0 \\ 0 & 64(x^1)^2 \end{bmatrix}$$

Next we shall calculate the tensor derivatives for: -

$$\begin{bmatrix} 1 & 0 \\ 0 & (x^1)^2 \end{bmatrix}, \begin{bmatrix} 4 & 0 \\ 0 & 4(x^1)^2 \end{bmatrix}$$

5.4

$$[ij,k] = \Gamma_{ijk} = \frac{1}{2}\left(\frac{\partial g_{kj}}{\partial x^i} + \frac{\partial g_{ki}}{\partial x^j} - \frac{\partial g_{ij}}{\partial x^k} \right), \Gamma^i_{jk} = g^{ir}\Gamma_{ijr}, g^{ir} = \frac{1}{g_{ir}}$$

$$[11,1] = \Gamma_{111} = \frac{1}{2}\left(\frac{\partial g_{11}}{\partial x^1} + \frac{\partial g_{11}}{\partial x^1} - \frac{\partial g_{11}}{\partial x^1} \right) = \frac{1}{2}\frac{\partial g_{11}}{\partial x^1} = 0$$

$$[22,2] = \Gamma_{222} = \frac{1}{2}\left(\frac{\partial g_{22}}{\partial x^2} + \frac{\partial g_{22}}{\partial x^2} - \frac{\partial g_{22}}{\partial x^2} \right) = \frac{1}{2}\frac{\partial g_{22}}{\partial x^2} = 0$$

$$[12,1] = \Gamma_{121} = \frac{1}{2}\left(\frac{\partial g_{11}}{\partial x^2} + \frac{\partial g_{21}}{\partial x^1} - \frac{\partial g_{12}}{\partial x^1} \right) = \frac{1}{2}\frac{\partial g_{11}}{\partial x^1} = 0$$

(Equation 5.4 continued)

$$[21,1] = \Gamma_{211} = \frac{1}{2}\left(\frac{\partial g_{21}}{\partial x^1} + \frac{\partial g_{11}}{\partial x^2} - \frac{\partial g_{21}}{\partial x^1}\right) = \frac{1}{2}\frac{\partial g_{11}}{\partial x^1} = 0$$

$$[11,2] = \Gamma_{112} = \frac{1}{2}\left(\frac{\partial g_{12}}{\partial x^1} + \frac{\partial g_{12}}{\partial x^1} - \frac{\partial g_{11}}{\partial x^2}\right) = \frac{1}{2}\frac{\partial g_{11}}{\partial x^1} = 0$$

$$[22,1] = \Gamma_{221} = \frac{1}{2}\left(\frac{\partial g_{21}}{\partial x^2} + \frac{\partial g_{21}}{\partial x^2} - \frac{\partial g_{22}}{\partial x^1}\right) = -\frac{1}{2}\frac{\partial g_{22}}{\partial x^1} = -x^1, -4x^1$$

$$[12,2] = \Gamma_{122} = \frac{1}{2}\left(\frac{\partial g_{12}}{\partial x^2} + \frac{\partial g_{22}}{\partial x^1} - \frac{\partial g_{12}}{\partial x^2}\right) = \frac{1}{2}\frac{\partial g_{22}}{\partial x^1} = x^1, 4x^1$$

$$[21,2] = \Gamma_{212} = \frac{1}{2}\left(\frac{\partial g_{22}}{\partial x^1} + \frac{\partial g_{12}}{\partial x^2} - \frac{\partial g_{21}}{\partial x^2}\right) = \frac{1}{2}\frac{\partial g_{22}}{\partial x^1} = x^1, 4x^1$$

$$\Gamma^1_{22} = -\frac{1}{2g_{11}}\frac{\partial g_{22}}{\partial x^1} = -x^1, -4x^1, \Gamma^2_{12} = \Gamma^2_{21} = \frac{1}{2g_{22}}\frac{\partial g_{22}}{\partial x^1} = \frac{1}{x^1} =, \frac{1}{x^1}$$

It is obvious that in the case of $r = 1$, the tensor derivative is zero. The angles sin e^i and cos e^i vanish, so it would seem that we have reached some type of limit, which is a problem.

The problem is this. The exponential values of e^i have been introduced as a matter of synchronicity so their absence would not be consistent with material herein. Sine and cosine angles can be inferred from the radius, r, but given only the metric of eq.5.1b etc., e^i of ^eC_S would remain elusive. If we introduced e^i just because it was convenient then we would not be pursuing the study in an objective manner. If we want to consider flat dimensions in Polar Coordinates, along with e^i, then we have to add e^i as another differential function (or some other differential equation with ce^i as a solution). This might then suggest that Cylindrical Coordinates are more appropriate since they would represent a flat sheet in 3-D, a tube (though this might present another problem in the topology of such a field – a non-convex set). Equation 5.5 is the calculation of this metric, but with z at the origin, equal to zero, $e^i = x^3$.

5.5a

$$x = e^i r \cos\theta = \overline{x}^1 = e^i x^1 \cos x^2, y = e^i r \sin\theta = \overline{x}^2 = e^i x^1 \sin x^2,$$

$$z = x^3 = \overline{x}^3, x^i = x^1, x^2, e^i$$

$$\frac{\partial \overline{x}^1}{\partial x^i} = e^i \cos x^2 - e^i x^1 \sin x^2 + e^i x^1 \cos x^2$$

$$\frac{\partial \overline{x}^2}{\partial x^i} = e^i \sin x^2 + e^i x^1 \cos x^2 + e^i x^1 \sin x^2$$

$$\frac{\partial \overline{x}^3}{\partial x^3} = 0 + 0 + 1$$

$$J^T J =$$

$$\begin{bmatrix} e^i \cos x^2 & e^i \sin x^2 & 0 \\ -e^i x^1 \sin x^2 & e^i x^1 \cos x^2 & 0 \\ e^i x^1 \cos x^2 & e^i x^1 \sin x^2 & 1 \end{bmatrix} \begin{bmatrix} e^i \cos x^2 & -e^i x^1 \sin x^2 & e^i x^1 \cos x^2 \\ e^i \sin x^2 & e^i x^1 \cos x^2 & e^i x^1 \sin x^2 \\ 0 & 0 & 1 \end{bmatrix}$$

$$= \begin{bmatrix} \left(e^i\right)^2 & 0 & \left(e^i\right)^2 x^1 \\ 0 & \left(e^i\right)^2 \left(x^1\right)^2 & 0 \\ \left(e^i\right)^2 x^1 & 0 & \left(e^i\right)^2 \left(x^1\right)^2 + 1 \end{bmatrix}$$

5.5b (for a negative index)

$$x = e^{-i} r \cos\theta = \overline{x}^1 = e^{-i} x^1 \cos x^2, y = e^{-i} r \sin\theta = \overline{x}^2 = e^{-i} x^1 \sin x^2,$$

$$z = x^3 = \overline{x}^3, x^i = x^1, x^2, e^{-i}$$

$$\frac{\partial \overline{x}^1}{\partial x^i} = e^{-i} \cos x^2 - e^{-i} x^1 \sin x^2 - e^{-i} x^1 \cos x^2$$

$$\frac{\partial \overline{x}^2}{\partial x^i} = e^{-i} \sin x^2 + e^{-i} x^1 \cos x^2 - e^{-i} x^1 \sin x^2$$

$$\frac{\partial \overline{x}^3}{\partial x^i} = 0 + 0 + 1,$$

(Equation 5.5b continued)

$$J^T J = \begin{bmatrix} e^{-i}\cos x^2 & e^{-i}\sin x^2 & 0 \\ -e^{-i}x^1\sin x^2 & e^{-i}x^1\cos x^2 & 0 \\ -e^{-i}x^1\cos x^2 & -e^{-i}x^1\sin x^2 & 1 \end{bmatrix}$$

$$\times \begin{bmatrix} e^{-i}\cos x^2 & -e^{-i}x^1\sin x^2 & -e^{-i}x^1\cos x^2 \\ e^{-i}\sin x^2 & e^{-i}x^1\cos x^2 & -e^{-i}x^1\sin x^2 \\ 0 & 0 & 1 \end{bmatrix} =$$

$$\begin{bmatrix} \left(e^{-i}\right)^2 & 0 & -\left(e^{-i}\right)^2 x^1 \\ 0 & \left(e^{-i}\right)^2 \left(x^1\right)^2 & 0 \\ -\left(e^{-i}\right)^2 x^1 & 0 & \left(e^{-i}\right)^2 \left(x^1\right)^2 + 1 \end{bmatrix}$$

Substituting with the constants: -

5.6

$$\begin{vmatrix} \left(e^{3.2}\right)^2 & 0 & \left(e^{3.2}\right)^2 \\ 0 & \left(e^{3.2}\right)^2 & 0 \\ \left(e^{3.2}\right)^2 & 0 & \left(e^{3.2}\right)^2 + 1 \end{vmatrix}, \begin{vmatrix} \left(e^{-i}\right)^2 & 0 & -\left(e^{-i}\right)^2 \\ 0 & \left(e^{-i}\right)^2 & 0 \\ -\left(e^{-i}\right)^2 & 0 & \left(e^{-i}\right)^2 + 1 \end{vmatrix} = \mathcal{G}5$$

$$r = 1, \left|\mathcal{G}5\right|_{3.2} \times \left|\mathcal{G}5\right|_{-1.8} \times \left|\mathcal{G}5\right|_{-0.8} \times \left|\mathcal{G}5\right|_{-0.6} = 1$$

5.7

$$\log_n \frac{1}{\left|\mathcal{G}5\right|_{3.2}} = -12.8, \log_n \frac{1}{\left|\mathcal{G}5\right|_{-1.8}} = 7.2, \log_n \frac{1}{\left|\mathcal{G}5\right|_{-0.8}} = 3.2$$

$$\log_n \frac{1}{\left|\mathcal{G}5\right|_{-0.6}} = 2.4, e^{-12.8+7.2+3.2+2.4} = e^{3.2-1.8-0.8-0.6} = e^0 = 1$$

Equation 5.6, $r = 1$ is important result because it coincides with $\mathcal{G}4$ and also complies with the set theoretic hypothesis that when all four Time categories come together they produce a situation consistent with our reality. Equation 5.7 exposes some

synchronicities by taking the inverse of the determinant for each metric computation and then using the constants from (^eC_S). Synchronicities for inverses 3 & 4 are obvious while inverse 2 is three times inverse 4. Inverse 1 is 'uncanny' because when using the author's name count, 182:
5.7b

$$\log_n \frac{1}{\left|G_5 5\right|_{3.2}} = (1)a + 8b + 2c = 3.2 - 14.4 - 1.6 = -12.8$$

The figure of -12.8 was found in eq.3.29 that also contained Norman's name count, and if the figure there, -6.2, is taken away from -12.8 the result is precisely that found in eq.2.35, -6.6, also involving Norman's name count.

Having said that we must confront the issue of what happens when $r = 2$, because this was the original value of ^eC: -
5.8

$$t(a,b,c,d) = \left(re^{3.2}\right)\left(-re^{-1.8}\right)\left(-r^2 e^{-0.8}\right)\left(r^2 e^{-0.6}\right) = G_5 6$$
$$r = 1, \left|G_5 6\right| = 1, r = 2, \left|G_5 6\right| = 64$$

The name 'Eldridge' has a count of 64 (as well as being 8^2) and this might be an indication that we should explore this idea further.

Proceeding as before, from the general to the particular, we compute the gradient and substituting $r = 2 = {}^eC$
5.9

$$t(a,b,c,d) = \left(re^{3.2}\right)\left(-re^{-1.8}\right)\left(-r^2 e^{-0.8}\right)\left(r^2 e^{-0.6}\right)$$

$$\frac{\partial t(a,b,c,d)}{\partial x^1} + \frac{\partial t(a,b,c,d)}{\partial x^2}, r = x^1, e^i = x^2$$

$$= \left(e^{3.2} + re^{3.2}\right) + \left(-e^{-1.8} + re^{-1.8}\right) + \left(-2re^{-0.8} + r^2 e^{-0.8}\right) +$$
$$\left(2re^{-0.6} - r^2 e^{-0.6}\right)$$

$$= e^{3.2}(r+1) + \left(e^{-1.8}(r-1)\right) + \left(e^{-0.8}\left(-2r + r^2\right)\right) + e^{-0.6}\left(2r - r^2\right)$$

$$\therefore \left(r = {}^eC\right) \Rightarrow r = 2, 3e^{3.2} + e^{-1.8} + 0 + 0 = G_5 7$$

This result in matrix form has the determinant of 12.1655999. This number seems a very unlikely one to provide synchronicities, but let's try a few sums anyway. Since the general pattern of the equations originated from ^eC, which in turn, the author claims, was 'designed' by Mi, therefore: -

5.10a

$$\frac{374\left(3e^{3.2}\right)\left(e^{-1.8}\right)}{22^2} = 9.400690832, \frac{182\left(3e^{3.2}\right)\left(e^{-1.8}\right)}{47} = 47.1093443$$

$$\frac{141\left(3e^{3.2}\right)\left(e^{-1.8}\right)}{182} = 9.424997725, \frac{374\left(3e^{3.2}\right)\left(e^{-1.8}\right)}{39} = 116.6649837$$

$$\frac{\pi^{\equiv}\partial\left(3e^{3.2}\right)\left(e^{-1.8}\right) + {}^{\equiv}_{2}\partial}{15} = 9.42735853,$$

$$\frac{15 \times 182}{\left(3e^{3.2}\right)\left(e^{-1.8}\right)} = 224.4032372,$$

Equation 5.10 provides numerous synchronicities. Using Norman's and Mi's name count, resulting in a figure similar to the Sun's R.A. on day 224: the author's name count used along with 'time' results in a figure similar to that of 'time'. The author's name count along with the degrees of the Sun / Earth longitude gives a figure that would be just 19 arc seconds different from the Sun's R.A. on the 12th of August 1943. Norman's name count with the count for 'Enki', gives a result very close to diameter of the Earth's orbit around the Sun, in days. Using π, $^{\equiv}\partial$ and $^{\equiv}_{2}\partial$ divided by the number of degrees in one hour R.A. gives a figure synchronistic with Sun's R.A. on the 12th of August 1943. Lastly, The author's name count with the number of degrees in one hour R.A. results in a figure synchronistic with day 224.

Further synchronicities arise from using powers of 12.1655999, given in eq.5.10b below. In eq.5.10b(1) Norman's birthday and the author's, result in a figure close to $^{\equiv}\partial$ while in (2) the name count of Norman's recent contactee case and the count for the names synchronistic with 'Mira', along with 'twin', gives a

result synchronistic with day 224. Item (3) shows the area of a circle divided by our year and squared, also gives a synchronistic –
5.10b

1. $$\frac{201+342}{\left[\left(3e^{3.2}\right)\left(e^{-1.8}\right)\right]^2} = 3.668873778$$

2. $$\sqrt{\frac{110 \times 41 \times 66}{\left[\left(3e^{3.2}\right)\left(e^{-1.8}\right)\right]^4}} = 3.686321251$$

3. $$\left(\frac{\left[\left(3e^{3.2}\right)\left(e^{-1.8}\right)\right]^2 \pi}{365.256}\right)^2 = 1.620463098$$

$$\frac{22^4}{3600\left(1.620463098\right)^4} = 9.436949713$$

4. $$\left(\frac{182 - \left[\left(3e^{3.2}\right)\left(e^{-1.8}\right)\right]^2}{\equiv\partial} - 8\right)^2 = 1.618570834 \approx \tau$$

– result. Item (4) uses the author's name count, $\overset{\equiv}{\partial}$ and eight to give a result very close to the Golden Ratio.

That $G_97 \neq 1$ is acceptable because we are considering the properties of the system and not its affect on ours. However, should such a requirement be necessary then G_97 immediately suggests the solution. All the constants are so aptly given in terms of each other, that by using the inverse of g_{11} and g_{22} for g_{33} and g_{44}, when multiplied by the elements achieves a determinant of one. The synchronicity here is that the d value in eq.2.33, -2.8, is the figure that satisfies this condition: -
5.11

$$e^{-0.8}e^{-0.6}\log_n\left(e^{-1.8}\right)^{-1}\log_n\left(e^{3.2}\right)^{-1} = e^{-0.8}e^{-0.6}\left(e^{1.8}\right)\left(e^{-3.2}\right) = e^{-2.8}$$

$$G_98 = 3e^{3.2}e^{-1.8}\sqrt{\frac{e^{-2.8}}{\left(3e^{-0.8}\right)^2}}\sqrt{\frac{e^{-2.8}}{\left(e^{-0.6}\right)^2}} = 1\left[= e^{3.2}e^{-1.8}\sqrt{e^{-2.8}}\right]$$

Mi Mathematics Part 5
G.A.T.E. (G_{g})

Equation 5.11 was computed for $r = 2$, the Chimes Expression having four terms, but further 'adjustments' are necessary in g_{33} and g_{44} for $r = 1$. This means that $G_{g}8$ could be incorporated into any equation that involves Time, such as the Wave equation: -

$$x + y + z = ct = x + y + z = ct(G_{g}8)$$

$G_{g}8$ is almost certainly a matrix field and as such would be effective throughout its domain. If this is so, then we should expect some synchronicities to be derived when applying the suspected vector from eq.3.63, viz. (* & **)

$$\sqrt{\left(2e^{3.2}\right)^2 + \left(-2e^{-1.8}\right)^2 + \left(-4e^{-0.8}\right)^2 + \left(4e^{-0.6}\right)^2} = 49.14813219$$

5.12 (using $(G_{g}7)^2$)

$$*49.14813219 \times 148.0018209 = 7274.013058$$

$$\frac{7274.013058}{\equiv \partial} = 1983.821743$$

$$**50.13976613 \times 148.0018209 = 7420.776688$$

$$\frac{7420.776688}{\equiv \partial} = 2023.848188$$

The interesting point about eq.5.12 is that both suspected vector forms of ^{e}C from eq.3.63 give answers that are synchronistic with the 'biorhythmic' years for the Earth. The day number is somewhat later than day 224 – 300 and 310 respectively. This is unexpected because previously we have been deriving figures that were more related to the Sun's R.A. on day 224. (The synchronicity concerning the day numbers is that there is a total difference of (300-224)+(310-224) = 162 and when this is divided by 'Mi', 22, the answer is twice 3.681818182. Note the obvious synchronicity – that 162 = 2 × 81, the count for 'Lawrence' and 'Oliver'.) The inference here might be the number of orbits rather than a point on the orbit, and perhaps a geometric approach might reveal more.

We might decide to do the reverse: -

5.13a

$$\log_n \left(\frac{365.256}{7274} \times 224 \right) = 2.420183, \log_n \left(\frac{365.256}{7420} \times 224 \right) = 2.40031$$

$$\frac{2.420183 + 2.40031}{2} = 2.4102465$$

The average of 2.4102465 $\cong$ eq.4.42, which was derived from 365, 224 and 116, as coordinates. This might mean that with 224 as a reference point, Mi was able to establish contact within a certain range of 2.4 units. If this is so then year number 2000 should reveal a synchronicity.

5.13b

a. $\log_n \left(\frac{365.256}{\equiv \partial 2000} \times 224 \right) = 2.412059086$

b. $\log_n \left(\frac{365.256}{\equiv \partial 2000.232240437} \times 224 \right) = 2.411942972$

c. $\log_n \left(\frac{365.256}{\equiv \partial 1978.6} \times 224 \right) = 2.422816742$

d. $\log_n \left(\frac{365.256}{\equiv \partial 2002.169863} \times 224 \right) = 2.410974742$

There is very little difference between eq.4.42(a) and 5.13a, while eq.5.13b(b) represents the day of the Mi experience. Equation 5.13b(c) represents the approximate date of the 'first crying' while 5.13(d) represents the date when Norman's Chimes experience began.

The results of eq.5.13b are similar in the first decimal place, so it might be that they represent the limit of Mi's contact.

Mi Mathematics Part 5
G.A.T.E. (Ģ)

For example, when considering Mi's 'up to twenty four' what years would 2.4 and 2.424 represent?

5.14a

$$1 \quad \frac{224 \times 365.256}{\equiv \partial e^{2.4}} = 2024.264179$$

$$2 \quad \frac{224 \times 365.256}{\equiv \partial e^{2.424}} = 1976.260191$$

These two periods are just 1.5 days short of a 48 year span and represent the 5th and 4th of April respectively. So to all intents and purposes represent the year 2000 ± 24, and is too coincidental with Mi's '... twenty four' not to be relevant. What about 3.2 and -1.8?

5.14b

$$1 \quad \frac{224 \times 365.256}{\equiv \partial e^{3.2}} = 909.5605268$$

$$2 \quad \frac{224 \times 365.256}{\equiv \partial e^{-1.8}} = 134990.7512, \frac{134990.7512}{909.5605268} = 148.4131591$$

$$3 \quad \frac{224 \times 365.256}{\equiv \partial e^{-0.8}} = 49660.32211$$

$$4 \quad \frac{224 \times 365.256}{\equiv \partial e^{-0.6}} = 40658.43292$$

The ratio of items 1 and 2 is close enough to 148.0018209, $(Ģ7)^2$, to be a synchronicity. In addition, note the similarity of 134990 to 13.4444, $\equiv\partial^2$, and that: -

5.15

$$\left(\frac{134990.7512}{374 \times 182}\right)^2 = {\equiv}\partial + \left({\equiv}\partial + \frac{1}{e^{2.427365147}}\right)^{-1}$$

Using both Norman's and the author's name counts $\equiv\partial$ can be derived where even the index of 2.427365147 is synchronistic with the computations involving 2.4. Equation 5.14b(3), has another interesting slant to it and could be interpreted as confirmation for using the exponential function: -

5.16

$$\frac{e^{-0.8}}{e^{-1.8}} = \frac{134990.7512}{49660.32211} = 1 + \frac{1}{2!} + \frac{1}{3!} + \frac{1}{4!} + \frac{1}{5!} + ...\infty = e^1$$

As we all know, there is not a branch of mathematics that does not use the exponential series at some ponit or other, and strange that we should find an exact identity amongst the synchronicities.

It would seem therefore, that there is some type of intricate web between the set of figures concerning the 'biorhythmic' years and Mi's 'up to twenty four'.

At this point, it would seem to be appropriate to ask what values (sine $e^{3.2}$) etc. might have.

5.17

$$\sin \theta° = \sin e^{3.2} = 0.415209814, \phi = e^{-1.8}, e^{-0.8}, e^{-0.6}$$

$$\sec \theta° = \frac{1}{\sin \theta} = 2.40840912$$

$$= \frac{\cos \phi°}{\sin \theta°} = 2.408410889, 2.408346852, 2.408310427$$

$$\theta° = e^{3.1}, e^{3.3}, \frac{1}{\sin \theta°} = 2.646849315, 2.194227445$$

The constant of 3.2 is just the right figure to give a synchronicity with 2.4, while figures of 3.1 and 3.3 would be outside acceptable limits. The other constants do not give genuine synchronicities because any figure below, or approaching zero, will give similar results. Having said that, they are synchronistic in that they conveniently lie within the range of figures that give these results.

We already know that: -

$$(2 e^{3.2}) (-4 e^{-1.8}) (-12 e^{-0.8}) (16 e^{-0.6}) = 1536$$

and

$$(2\ e^{3.2})\ (-2\ e^{-1.8})\ (-4\ e^{-0.8})\ (4\ e^{-0.6})\ =\ 64$$

therefore: -

5.18

$$\frac{(2\ e^{3.2})\ (-4\ e^{-1.8})\ (-12\ e^{-0.8})\ (16\ e^{-0.6})}{(2\ e^{3.2})\ (-2\ e^{-1.8})\ (-4\ e^{-0.8})\ (4\ e^{-0.6})}\ =\ 24$$

$$\frac{\left((2\ e^{3.2})\ (-4\ e^{-1.8})\ (-12\ e^{-0.8})\ (16\ e^{-0.6})\right)\times 22 + 64}{3600}\ =\ 9.404\dot{4}$$

$$\frac{(2\ e^{3.2})\ (-4\ e^{-1.8})\ (-12\ e^{-0.8})\ (16\ e^{-0.6})}{\tau^{4}}\ =\ 224.0993797$$

$$\left(22\times 24\times 64\right)+124 = 33916, \left(22\times 24\times 64\right)+222 = 34014$$

Finally, eq.5.18 shows the relation between the two forms of the Chimes expression, with day 224, 9.4, 22 and 24. With the additions of 'Omicron Ceti' and 'Lawrencium' + 103 we arrive at the Sun's R.A. in seconds of arc for day 224, 1943 and 1983 respectively. This is probably as close as we shall come to a 'confirmation' that Mi was involved with Norman's Chimes experience.

However, does G̨7 *actually* work on a 2-D coordinate system and for us, produce synchronicities? The answer is yes, but the author's analysis will appear in his next book. Perhaps you could try a computation of your own. (Technically, you should also check that the original line length is preserved, but that requires knowledge of Linear Algebra.) Try using Norman's and the author's name counts and birthdays (182,342) and (374,201): -

$$\sqrt{(374-182)^{2}+(201-342)^{2}}\ =\ \sqrt{192^{2}+(-141)^{2}}\ =\ 238.2121$$

By calculating $(3e^{3.2}x+y)$ and $(x+e^{-1.8}y)$ a series of synchronicities can be established especially those that relate to day 224. (If you are interested in some brief details, you can e-mail the author)

Mi Mathematics Part 6
G.A.T.E. ($\frac{G}{g}$)

In this final part of Mi Mathematics I want to discuss, on a more personal level, some of the ideas used in this work and some extensions. There are three categories: criticisms, extrapolations of Parts 1 to 5, and, a 'glimpse beyond'. In the latter third category there are some deep mathematical issues, but as I mentioned in the Prologue, this is not a book on mathematics and therefore I shall give just one or two examples.

Perhaps you, the reader, have agreed in principle with the inferences and deductions made on the basis of the synchronicities, ignoring any personal doubt just for the sake of being able to proceed from one section to the next. I have encouraged this by using such phrases as '...we shall....', '...we would...' and so on. Here I will discuss some criticisms in the hope that I can address some doubts you may have.

Probably by far the most important criticism would be that of using name counts. Although the synchronicities were perhaps convincing, the basis on which they were produced is questionable. How can **I** say this, and yet write two books such that the trend depends very much on these quantities? The truth is that before my Mi entity experience I most certainly would have had doubts about name count validity.

The main problem here is that we are now so far removed from the earliest spoken word, that we cannot appreciate what problems early parents had in naming their children. A thousand years ago a child might have been named according the place of birth, or to some mystical or religious belief. Ten thousand, maybe twenty thousand years ago, children were probably called the equivalent of 1st, 2nd and so on. My point is, at that time a 'name' probably had a greater significance than a 'name' has today. In all probability, in very ancient times one's name would actually carve out one's destiny, that is to say, that one would try to live up to the position to which the name referred.

I was named according to my father's first name and another member of the family, and many other people have been named in the same way. However, how many children are named by using other devices such as movie stars, books etc. It becomes difficult understand how present day names can be related to physical events but there could be reasons for such developments. Firstly, in the Mi book I suggested that perhaps external agents have deliberately engineered languages: secondly, that there is a subconscious drive to pursue a certain course related to names. Thirdly, that it is not true of all people but only of some, that destinies might be related to a name. The latter might be more acceptable because it might cover a 'pure coincidence'.

A fourth category is to claim that all of the numbers that we can think of are already in existence in one form or another, such as flower patterns and other natural designs. These were here long before the Fibanacci sequence and the Golden Ratio were discovered. Having said that, why and how does nature follow such designs? What part of DNA is designed to follow something *resembling* a diagram of a Fibonacci spiral?

In eq.1.5 the second sequence is generated by the seed number 11 and therefore every number there is devisable by $^{\equiv}\partial$, but two name counts stands out, that of Norman, 374 and Mi, 22. Following 374 is 605, which just happens to be equal to that of 'USS Eldridge' 'D' + 'E' + 173, plus ' Lawrencium' + 103, plus 'Mira Ceti'. Is it therefore possible, that in some other 'dimension' Norman's name takes on a different form and the other members of the sequence are linked together? The Fibonacci sequence is not the only 'natural' set that connects Norman's name count to Lawrencium. Using the one and only π: -

$$374/\pi = 119.0478974$$

Indeed, one begins to wonder why Mi contacted me and not Norman.

Be that as it may, one problem is that both Lawrencium and the USS Eldridge were not around (here on Earth) when Norman was born, but Mira Ceti was. So is this star Norman's connection to later events? Below are six Fibonacci sequences: -

Mi Mathematics Part 6
G.A.T.E. ($\overset{?}{G_{j}}$)

6.1

$0,1,1,2,3,5,8,13,21,34,55,89,\boxed{144},233,377$

$0,3,3,6,9,15,\boxed{24},\boxed{39},63,102,165,267,432,699,1131$

$0,5,5,10,15,25,40,65,105,170,275,445,720,1165,1885$

$0,6,6,12,18,30,48,\boxed{78},126,204,330,534,864,1398,2262$

$0,11,11,\boxed{22},33,55,88,\boxed{143},231,\boxed{374},\boxed{605},979,1584,2563,4147$

$0,14,14,28,42,70,112,\boxed{182},294,476,770,1246,2016,3262,5278$

$(0,8,8,16,24,40,64,104,168,272,440,712,1152,1864,3016,4880)$

Perhaps the most important point to notice is that the 11th position in each sequence (using zero as position one) is a multiple of $\overset{\equiv}{\partial}$ – $15\overset{\equiv}{\partial}$, $45\overset{\equiv}{\partial}$, $90\overset{\equiv}{\partial}$, $102\overset{\equiv}{\partial}$ and $210\overset{\equiv}{\partial}$. The proof that all sequences of the natural counting numbers, $\mathbb{N}$, will contain $\overset{\equiv}{\partial}X$ is that they are simply multiples of the first original sequence. If such patterns exist in the natural world this would be conclusive proof that $\overset{\equiv}{\partial}$ *is* all around us, contained in the point that corresponds to the 11th position in the natural design representing the Fibonacci sequence. More generally, whatever happens in the original sequence will happen in the others.

However, with regard to Norman and Mira Ceti, the count for 'Mira Ceti' is in the group that has the ratio of $\frac{1}{2}\overset{\equiv}{\partial}$ to the sequence containing Norman's name count. At the same position as Mira Ceti in Norman's group is 143 which is of course, 'Enki' multiplied by $\overset{\equiv}{\partial}$, so: -

6.2

$$\frac{1}{2}\overset{\equiv}{\partial}78 - \frac{1}{2}\overset{\equiv}{\partial} - \frac{374}{143} = 138.5512821$$

After using the correction for Earth's inclination eq.6.2 equates to 9hrs.23min.56secs (to the nearest arc second) for the early morning of August 12th 1943. Interesting may be but without the number 224, eq.6.2 alone might not be enough for you – it certainly isn't for me. In eq.6.1, 374 is divided by τ^2 because 143 is the second number going back in sequence and 78 is added from the previous sequence. The result of eq.6.2 was interpreted as degrees R.A. so in eq.6.3 the result is: -

6.3

$$\left(\frac{374}{\tau^2} + 78\right)^0 \times \frac{365.256}{360} = 224.0797754$$

Equation 6.3 has the dimension of days. Using the ephemeris program at 224.0797754 days, the Sun's R.A. would have been 9hrs.23min.44secs (to the nearest arc second). The difference between the R.A of eq.6.2 and eq.6.3 is only 12 arc seconds. Therefore, there might be a possible connection between Norman and Mira Ceti, and day 224, in the Fibonacci sequences of eq.6.1.

An unexpected synchronicity in eq.6.1 is that the ratio of the sequence that contains my name count to that containing Norman's, is exactly Tridel 2, $\overline{\overline{2}}\partial = 1 +(1 \div \overline{\overline{}}\partial) = 1.2727....$ This has an important consequence because 'Enki' is $143 \div \overline{\overline{}}\partial$ so that my name count becomes: -

6.4

$$39\overline{\overline{}}\partial\,\overline{\overline{2}}\partial = 182$$

This clearly connects Norman's name count with mine, through "Enki' and the Tridel factors. 'Lawrencium' with or without 103, does not form a sequence according to the rules of eq.6.1. So as far as the name counts are concerned the Fibonacci sequence illustrates that at least Norman's name and mine, along with Mira Ceti and Enki, very likely exist in the form of some natural pattern.

A brief digression here. Mirror image numbers seem to display a pattern with Norman's name count and mine.

6.5

$$\sum(182,821,218),(281,812,128) = 2442$$

$$\sum(374,743,437),(473,734,347) = 3108$$

6.5 continued

$$\frac{3108}{2442} = 1 + \frac{1}{\overset{\equiv}{\partial}} = \overset{\equiv}{2}\partial$$

$$\sum (119,191,911),(911,119,191) = 2442$$

In eq.6.5 I have used a rotation similar to that of the so-called Epsilon Tensor and the numbers produced by the rotation of digits of both the original and mirror image, are then summed. In this case the ratio of Norman's count to mine is the same as in the Fibonacci sequences, $\overset{\equiv}{2}\partial$. The count for 'Lawrencium' is the same as the count for my name. However, we needn't stop there: -

6.6

$$\text{⅄}\varepsilon_{224} = \text{⅄}\varepsilon_{305} = \text{⅄}\varepsilon_{152} = 1776, \text{⅄}\varepsilon_{124} = 1554$$

$$\frac{(3108 + 1776)}{\overset{\equiv}{\partial}} = \frac{(2(2442))}{\overset{\equiv}{\partial}} =$$

$$3108 - 1776 = 6(222) = 1332$$

$$1776 - 1554 = 222$$

Equation 6.6 shows further relationships between the counts involving the Philadelphia Experiment where in the last but one line the result is exactly that for a rotation of 'Lawrencium' + 103, with the last line also resulting in 'Lawrencium' + 103. A word of caution here – if we take an arbitrary number, say 229, the summed rotation is 2886, which when taken away from Norman's count, 3108-2886 = 222, and 2886-1554 = 1332. The synchronicities involving $\overset{\equiv}{\partial}$ and $\overset{\equiv}{2}\partial$, however, remain valid. As part of the third category another issue concerning $\text{⅄}(x)$ will be mentioned later.

Returning to the Fibonacci sequences, is there a connection to day 224? The only number in eq.6.1 that is a multiple of 224 is in the 5th sequence containing my name count, 2016. The synchronicity here is that there are nine 224's in 2016, precisely the number of hours in the Sun's R.A. on day 224. However, 224 is the result of 9×(sequence seed number) ×…: -

6.7

$$\left(\equiv\partial^2 - \equiv\partial - 8\right) \times 9 \times 14 = 224$$

The (Tridel, eight) items on the LHS are those from eq.4.38. Because the number 224 was 'hidden' in the sequence could any connection between 22 and 224 be 'hidden' – actually it is there in all the sequences, synchronistic with the seconds of arc for the Sun's R.A. on day 224 (F_n, $n<14$ give figures > 34210): -

6.8

$$\left(\frac{22 \times F_{14}}{F_{15}}\right)^4 = 341.., \left(\frac{22 \times 1165}{1885}\right)^4 = 34178.18582$$

Why Lawrencium is not represented by a sequence (in the present context) is a reasonable question but we need to remember that it was formed from two processes and not one. The formula for the synthesis of Lawrencium is: -

6.9

$$^{252}_{98}\text{Cf} + ^{11}_{5}\text{B} \rightarrow ^{257}_{103}\text{Lw} + 6^1_0 n, \quad ^{252}_{98}\text{Cf} + ^{10}_{5}\text{B} \rightarrow ^{257}_{103}\text{Lw} + 5^1_0 n$$

The sequential count of 222 is 6, which matches the number of neutrons emitted using Boron 11. However, the second part of the Boron mixture uses Boron 10 and if 222 is converted to be the coefficients of a, b and c of the equations given to Mi, the result is 1.2 and 'Mi' divided by 1.2 is exactly $5^{\equiv}\partial$,. Also: -

6.10

$$\sqrt{\frac{222 \times 5^{\equiv}\partial}{(222 + 78)}} = 3.683295626$$

We are back in the realm of day 224.

I have to conclude that using name counts is valid, within the Mi context, even though it does have a strange and bizarre connotation – but I am getting used to it.

Mi Mathematics Part 6
G.A.T.E. ($\frac{G}{g}$)

It is time to move on and discuss some extrapolations.

The classical gravitational force expression used in eq.3.33 made me wonder whether there were any parallels using the synchronicities. Because I have continually suggested that Norman is the connection between my Mi experience and Norman's own studies, why not put it to the 'gravitational' test. Let the two Fibonacci sequences containing Norman's name count and mine substitute mass m_1 and mass m_2. Substitute the connection between the two series, $\overset{\equiv}{_2}\partial$, for the Gravitational constant G, then substitute 182 and 605 for m_1 and m_2. 605 is equivalent to the counts of Mira Ceti, Lawrencium + 103 and USS Eldridge D + E + 173, and let the force be equal to one. What is the value of r?

6.11

$$\frac{\overset{\equiv}{_2}\partial(182 \times 605)}{r^2} = 1 \therefore r = \sqrt{140140} = 374.3527748$$

Again, this clearly demonstrates that Norman is the important connection between the relevant events. In eq.6.12 is an expression taken from Black Hole theory: so let's try again.

6.12

$$\frac{2GM}{r} = G_{nc} = \frac{2\,\overset{\equiv}{_2}\partial 605}{224} = 6.875$$

$$\left(r = 374 + 22 + 24 \Rightarrow G_{nc} = \overset{\equiv}{}\partial \right)$$

6.875 is synchronistic with details from day 224. However, take it a stage further and use $(S_i + {}^e C_{=d})$ that we know is equal to zero: -

6.13

$$\left(3.2 \times \frac{2\,\overset{\equiv}{_2}\partial 605}{224} \right) + \left(-1.8 \times \frac{2\,\overset{\equiv}{_2}\partial 605}{224} \right) + \left(-0.8 \times \frac{2\,\overset{\equiv}{_2}\partial 605}{224} \right)$$

$$+ \left(-0.6 \times \frac{2\,\overset{\equiv}{_2}\partial 605}{224} \right) = [a] - [b + c + d] = 22 - 22 = 0$$

Mi Mathematics Part 6
G.A.T.E. (^C_G)

Technically speaking we cannot combine the 'gravitational' expressions of eq.6.11 and eq.6.12, because r has different values hence I have not done so. Nevertheless, these substitutions do result in synchronicities that cannot be simply explained away as coincidence, especially where eq.6.13 could be interpreted as the appearance of the Mi entity and its 'program', then the removal of the 'program' (Curious –'program' minus 'Mi' = 'twin'). Equation 6.13 does really bring us back to very beginning of 'Mi then No Mi'. Because of the origin of eq.6.11 and eq.6.12 one might be inclined to theorize that Mi's contact has something to do with gravity.

One might now criticize the methods just used, but such ideas of substitution into an existing formula with new material is not unusual in science. For example, researchers in Superstring Theory apparently tried many mathematical functions to find one that would fit a certain problem.

Based on actual data, today, many theories spring up as possibilities to explain certain exotic effects. One of these theories is based on the Heisenberg's Uncertainty Principle, that to view certain properties of particles one has to apply energy to do so. However, the applied energy affects the system under analysis and so results have to be take this into account. Some people think that when an object has a velocity, or acceleration, this changes the immediate environment accordingly and therefore may change the metric. Now, there is no intention here to debate this point of view, but suppose the 2-D metric derivative of eq.5.1b initiated a new metric in its own image: -

6.14

$$\Gamma^1_{22} = -\frac{1}{2g_{11}}\frac{\partial g_{22}}{\partial x^1} = -x^1, \Gamma^2_{12} = \Gamma^2_{21} = \frac{1}{2g_{22}}\frac{\partial g_{22}}{\partial x^1} = \frac{1}{x^1}$$

$$\left(-x^1\right)^2 + \left(\frac{1}{x^1}\right)^2 = \begin{bmatrix} \left(x^1\right)^2 & 0 \\ 0 & \left(\frac{1}{x^1}\right)^2 \end{bmatrix}$$

In eq.6.14 I have ignored the repetition of $(x^1)^{-1}$, Γ^2_{12}, Γ^2_{21}, because they apply to the same condition, x^1. Therefore, let $x^1=1$, as in earlier equations, and that $^1\!/x^1$ is some other parameter, say time, $^1\!/t$. Now it is possible to have a curve with parameters $[1,t]$ and the metric of: -

6.15

$$\mathcal{C} = \begin{cases} x^1 = 1 \\ x^2 = t_1 \end{cases}, \begin{bmatrix} (1)^2 & 0 \\ 0 & \left(\dfrac{1}{t_1}\right)^2 \end{bmatrix}$$

The arc length distance is then determined by: -

6.16

$$\mathcal{C} = \begin{cases} x^1 = 1 \\ x^2 = t_1 \end{cases} \therefore dx^i = [0,1]$$

$$(ds)^2 = [0 \ 1] \begin{bmatrix} (1)^2 & 0 \\ 0 & \left(\dfrac{1}{t_1}\right)^2 \end{bmatrix} \begin{bmatrix} 0 \\ 1 \end{bmatrix} = \begin{bmatrix} 0 \\ \left(\dfrac{1}{t}\right)^2 \end{bmatrix} \therefore ds = \int_a^b \sqrt{\left(\dfrac{1}{t_1}\right)^2}$$

Next, substitute the upper limit with the Earth's sidereal year and the lower limit with the Earth's distance from the Sun in days, and multiply the integral by $^\circ C = 2$: -

6.17

$$C_1 = 365.256, r = 58.1323, \therefore 2\int_r^{C_1} \left(\frac{1}{t_1}\right) = \log_n C_1 - \log_n r =$$

$$2(5.900598478 - 4.062721447) = 3.67575406$$

Taking the Sun's R.A. on day 224.5 to the nearest arc second, 33920 to the eighth root, 3.683892771, the figure of 3.67575406 is very close to the average of $^{\equiv}\partial$ and 3.683892771, and eq.3.10. The question now becomes – is there a relationship between two curves with the same metric, using day 224.5?

6.18

$$C_2 = 365.256 - 224.5 = 140.756, r = 58.1323,$$

$$\left(\frac{2\int_r^{C_2}\left(\frac{1}{t_2}\right)}{2\int_r^{C_1}\left(\frac{1}{t_1}\right)}\right) = \left(\frac{\int_r^{C_2}\left(\frac{1}{t_2}\right)}{\int_r^{C_1}\left(\frac{1}{t_1}\right)}\right) = \frac{0.884306447}{1.83787703} =$$

0.481156482

Since we have been using exponential sums: -
6.19

$$\exp\left(\frac{\int_r^{C_2}\left(\frac{1}{t_2}\right)}{\int_r^{C_1}\left(\frac{1}{t_1}\right)}\right) = \exp(0.481156482) = 1.617944445$$

Now compute the lower limit of day 224, namely 224: -
6.20

$$C_3 = 365.256 - 224 = 141.256, r = 58.1323,$$

$$\exp\left(\frac{\int_r^{C_3}\left(\frac{1}{t_2}\right)}{\int_r^{C_1}\left(\frac{1}{t_1}\right)}\right) = \exp(0.483085856) = 1.621069079$$

Therefore the Golden Ratio will lie in the interval: -
6.21

$$[(365.256 - 224.5) \leq \tau \leq (365.256 - 224)]$$

There is more to add, because the figure of 2.4 that was used in Part 4 is also intricately involved.
6.22

$$\frac{365.256}{2.4} - e^{2.4} = 141.1668236$$

(I agree that $r = 58.1323$ days is an unusual unit for a radius.)

However, because the figure of 2.4 was originally derived from e^i it follows that e^i must be involved also. Reversing the method, the radius of 58.1323 days gives a similar result: -
6.23

$$58.1323 \times 2.4 + 2\log_n 2.4 =$$

$$139.51752 + 1.750938475 = 141.2684575$$

The final figure has the dimension of days and converts to 139.236175°, which in turn coverts to 141.6581534°, equivalent to 9.443876894 hours R.A.

In a further possible extension of ideas I make some very rough calculations based on the material so far. Let day 224 be equal to day one, or the starting point in the Mi environment (see also page 127), perhaps more specifically, a point where the four time categories are conducive to Mi's ideas. If this is the case then it is reasonable to suppose that there should be synchronicity with the day of contact with me. If Mi, either by calculation or mistake, decides to contact me on day 224 by Mi's reckoning, what day would that be as far I am concerned? $224+141=365=(Mi)0+141$, therefore $141+83=224$. Day 83 is March 23rd (leap year). Now considering that the figure of 2.4 has been widely seen earlier add this to the result and the answer is 10 a.m. on March 25th. This is very close to the actual time (noon) when I saw the Entity. March 23rd is also synchronistic in terms being the 23rd day and also remembering that Norman's birthday is 141 days prior to mine. Additionally my name count divided by 83 just happens to be the 4th root of 23.12, so that if this figure was used the addition of 2.4 is about three-quarters of an hour after noon – not bad for a 'rough' calculation.

In the third and final extrapolation I will theorize about Time travel, in the Mi context, based on the above and the rotating square plus the rotating tetrad element of 6 and the $\mathbb{C}$, or Gauss, plane. Because Mi seemed to prefer a 'flat' system, and since some previous computations have been considered from that standpoint, then that will be the approach taken here. Einstein's theory of

Mi Mathematics Part 6
G.A.T.E. (C_g)

Special Relativity is concerned with this type of space so below is a brief revision of some of the equations in S.R.

A beam of light traversing a tube, length L, that has a velocity v travelling perpendicular to its orientation, and with a reflecting mirror at the end, will have a triangular displacement and light travel time of: -

6.24a

$$c^2 (\Delta t)^2 = 4L^2 + v^2 (\Delta t)^2 \therefore (\Delta t)^2 = \frac{4L^2}{c^2} + \frac{v^2 (\Delta t)^2}{c^2}$$

Rearranging: -

6.24b

$$\therefore (\Delta t)^2 - \frac{v^2 (\Delta t)^2}{c^2} = \frac{4L^2}{c^2} = 1 - \frac{v^2}{c^2} =$$

$$\frac{4L^2}{(\Delta t)^2 c^2} = (\Delta t)^2 \left(1 - \frac{v^2}{c^2}\right) = \frac{4L^2}{c^2}$$

$$\therefore \Delta t = \frac{2L}{c \sqrt{\left(1 - \frac{v^2}{c^2}\right)}} = \frac{\Delta t_0}{\sqrt{\left(1 - \frac{v^2}{c^2}\right)}}$$

That is to say, a person in the proper frame (travelling with the experiment), will see the beam of light simply travel up to the mirror and be reflected straight down. The calculation for the time of travel for the beam of light will be ($\Delta t_0 = \frac{2L}{c}$). However, a person in a *different* frame will observe the experiment as travelling from one point to another point in a 'triangular' motion and taking time (Δt). For example, consider a person performing the experiment on a moving train, they will observe the former, while another person on a platform, say, will observe the latter. Therefore there will be a disagreement in the value of the light travel time in the order of $\sqrt{(1-\beta^2)}^{-1/2}$, where $\beta^2 = \frac{v^2}{c^2}$. For example say $\Delta t_0 = 1$(day, year etc), $\frac{v^2}{c^2} = 0.999$, we have: -

6.25

$$\therefore \Delta t = \frac{1}{\sqrt{\left(1 - 0.999^2\right)}} = 22.36627204$$

Someone travelling at 0.999 of the speed of light on a round tip of 1 year will find that almost 22.4 years have elapsed at the starting point. If we put the RHS of eq.6.25 equals γ, then $\Delta t = \gamma \Delta t_o$. A similar result holds for length and mass.

If two frames of reference use a different origin and are moving relative to each other, the position of an object considered stationary by both would be calculated as being different. If the object's position differed only in the x coordinate then the position was given by the (Galilean) transformation equations: -
6.26

$$\overline{x} = x - vt, \overline{y} = y,$$
$$\overline{z} = z, \overline{t} = t$$

This does not agree with the work done by Maxwell and the wave front equation.
6.27

$$x^2 + y^2 + z^2 = c^2 t^2,$$
$$(x - vt)^2 + y^2 + z^2 =$$
$$x^2 - 2xvt + (vt)^2 + y^2 + z^2 = c^2 t^2$$

The work of Lorentz suggested that the transformation equations should be: -
6.28

$$x \rightarrow \overline{x} = f(x) - g(vt)$$
$$y \rightarrow \overline{y} = y$$
$$z \rightarrow \overline{z} = z$$
$$t \rightarrow \overline{t} = j(t) + h\left(\frac{x}{v}\right)$$

6.28 continued

$$\therefore \left[f(x) - g(vt) \right]^2 + y^2 + z^2 = c^2 \left[j(t) + h\left(\tfrac{x}{v}\right) \right]^2$$

$$= f^2(x) + g^2(vt) - 2f(x)g(vt) + y^2 + z^2 =$$

$$c^2 j^2(t) + c^2 h^2 \left(\tfrac{x}{v}\right) + 2c^2 j(t)h\left(\tfrac{x}{v}\right)$$

Since the result of eq.6.28 must agree with the first of eq.6.27 suitable units must be chosen for $f(x)$, $g(vt)$ and $j(t)$. These are $f(x) = x$, $g(vt) = vt$ and $j(t) = t$. Substituting we have: -

6.29

$$x^2 + v^2 t^2 - 2xvt + y^2 + z^2 = c^2 t^2 + c^2 h^2 \left(\tfrac{x}{v}\right) + 2c^2 th\left(\tfrac{x}{v}\right)$$

$$\left[-xvt = c^2 th\left(\tfrac{x}{v}\right) \Rightarrow h\left(\tfrac{x}{v}\right) = -\frac{xv}{c^2} \right]$$

$$\therefore c^2 t^2 + c^2 h^2 \left(\tfrac{x}{v}\right) + 2c^2 th\left(\tfrac{x}{v}\right) = c^2 t^2 + 2c^2 t\left(\frac{-xv}{c^2}\right) + c^2\left(\frac{x^2 v^2}{c^4}\right)$$

$$x^2 + v^2 t^2 - 2xvt + y^2 + z^2 = c^2 t^2 - 2c^2 xvt + \left(\frac{x^2 v^2}{c^2}\right)$$

$$x^2 - \left(\frac{x^2 v^2}{c^2}\right) + y^2 + z^2 = c^2 t^2 - v^2 t^2$$

$$\therefore = x^2 \left(1 - \frac{v^2}{c^2}\right) + y^2 + z^2 = c^2 t^2 \left(1 - \frac{v^2}{c^2}\right)$$

The result of eq.6.29 reduces to common experience as $c \to 0$, but it must be reduced to the mappings of eq.6.28: -

6.30

$$x^2 \left(1 - \frac{v^2}{c^2}\right) = (x - v)^2 \therefore \bar{x} = \frac{(x - v)}{\sqrt{\left(1 - \frac{v^2}{c^2}\right)}}$$

6.30 continued

$$t^2\left(1-\frac{v^2}{c^2}\right)=\left(t-\frac{vx}{c^2}\right)^2 \quad \therefore \overline{t}=\frac{\left(t-\dfrac{vx}{c^2}\right)}{\sqrt{\left(1-\dfrac{v^2}{c^2}\right)}}$$

There is no need to go into further detail of S.R. because the expressions so far will suffice.

Many of the synchronicities have been close to τ or $^4\!/\pi$ and because τ is inversely symmetric the question arises whether or not τ retains this symmetry in the relativistic equation. By inserting $^1\!/\tau$ as the fraction of light speed the answer is indeed proportional to τ.

6.31

$$\Delta t = \frac{1}{\sqrt{\left(1-\left(1/\tau\right)^2\right)}}=\sqrt{\tau}, \frac{1}{\sqrt{\left(1-\left(1/\sqrt{\tau}\right)^2\right)}}=\tau$$

The next question is – because $\overset{\equiv}{_2}\partial^2$ approximates τ, can the 5th and 6th Fibonacci sequences of eq.6.1 be used? We leave that question for some other occasion.

The figure U$\subset$ **M** on page 128 is repeated on the following page with two additions, a larger inscribed circle and its outer square. If the innermost square has a perimeter of 4 units the circle, created by revolving the square, will then have a perimeter of $\pi\sqrt{2}$: the middle square a perimeter of $^4\!/\pi$ $(\pi\sqrt{2})$: the larger inscribed circle will be 2π and finally the outer square, $(^4\!/\pi)2\pi = 8$ units. (See diagram G)

Diagram G is an example showing a possible single-state connection for travelling from one time category to the other. The larger square has a $^4\!/\pi$ relation to an inscribed circle, so that a velocity of 0.618034c on the circle would produce an observed time dilation of $\sqrt{1.618034}$. A particle moving on the circle with a velocity of 0.6189901c would produce an observed time dilation of

$^4/\pi$ – that is, the particle would have the increased lifetime equivalent to the perimeter of the inscribing square. However the particle would maintain its direction unless affected by a suitable electromagnetic / gravitational potential. The synchronicity here is that such a possible field has already indicated previously in equations 4.2 and 4.3, and from the list of synchronicities there, where item 3 is repeated on the next page: -

Diagram G

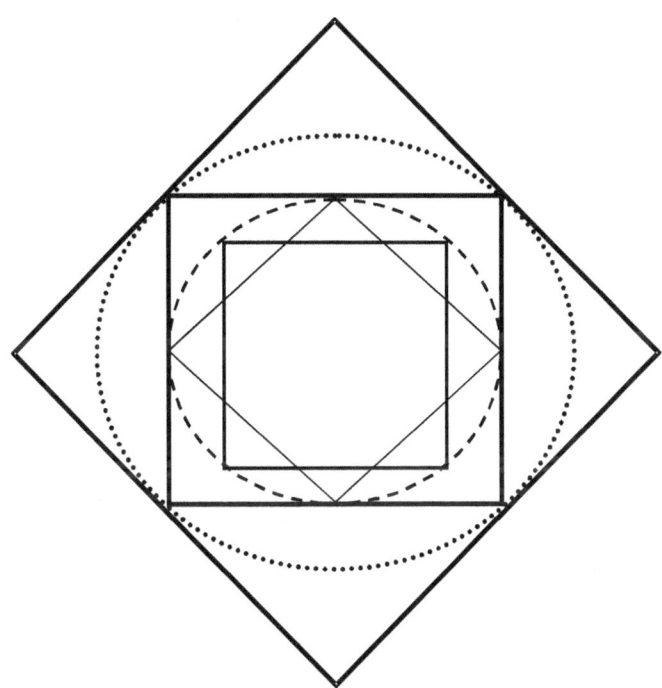

6.32

$$\sqrt[4]{\frac{1}{0.599633 \times 0.632822901}} = 1.000686298\frac{4}{\pi}$$

I doubt the accuracy here for an exact match for energy-velocity-area / perimeter 'jump', but several methods might be available such as the 'error function', $^2/\sqrt{\pi} \int_b^a e^{-u^2}$, because of the constant, which is $\sqrt[4]{}/\pi$, and the inverse exponential function.

Before such ideas can be explored there would be a need to know what our three dimensions, (x, y, z), requirement would be. Again, appealing to the synchronicities herein, use day 224.5, 1943, as the standard, and using the eq.3.20: -

6.33

$$(xyz)\sqrt{\frac{22^4}{(x+y+z)\times 33919.735}} = \sqrt[3]{\frac{22^4}{3 \times 33919.735}} =$$

$$\sqrt[3]{12.19975345}, 12.19975345 = |\mathcal{G}_\partial 7| + \frac{1}{8 \times 3.66}$$

For the year 1983 the figure is $\mathcal{G}_\partial 7$- $(22+[0.001\times(12.19591653)^2])^{-1}$. The synchronicities here, using 1943, the (x, y, z) coordinates are equal to the metric $\mathcal{G}_\partial 7$ plus almost the inverse of $8^{\equiv}\partial$. 1983 on the other hand, is $\mathcal{G}_\partial 7$ minus the inverse of the count for 'Mi' plus one thousandth of a squared figure almost the same as the total for 1943. Next, use the velocity of $0.6189901c$ (which would produce an observed time dilation of $^4/\pi$) from the previous page and the three (x, y, z) values for 1943: -

6.34

$$\left(\sqrt[3]{12.19975345} \times 3\right) = vt = 0.6189901t \therefore t = 11.15718334$$

$$\log_n t = 2.412083698 \approx 2.412090757$$

The value of $\log_n t$ is almost exactly that calculated for the perpendicular distance in eq.4.42. To establish the connection between the 4-D time-field, eq.6.34 and $^{\equiv}\partial$ (since by previous synchronicities I have concluded that Time is connected to $^{\equiv}\partial$): -

6.35

$$4\left(^{\equiv}\partial - \left(\frac{4}{\pi}\right)^{-2}\right) = 4\left(^{\equiv}\partial - 0.616850275\right) = 12.19926557$$

Even the difference between 12.19975345 and 12.19926557 is synchronistic, $(0.000487883)^{-1} \div 556 = 3.68645544$. Similarly, there is not much effort involved in connecting eq.6.35 with day 224: -

6.36

$$2\sqrt{\left(^{\equiv}\partial - 0.616850275\right)} + \sqrt{1536} - 39 = 3.684580588$$

Equation 6.36 uses the value of the original $^{\circ}C = 2$, and the determinant of the expanded form of $^{\circ}C$ and the count for 'Enki'.

So, in total these synchronicities suggest that by using an electromagnetic/gravitational potential and a fraction of the speed of light, a 'jump' to the four Time categories might be possible. However, it would seem that the 'jump' should have a perpendicular distance in the region of 2.412 units.

One or two glimpses beyond begin with an idea of where to start on a geometrical interpretation, and the obvious place to start is where this study began, with me and Mi.

6.37

$$\frac{182}{22} = 8 + {}^{\equiv}\partial^{-1}, \frac{1942}{22} = 88 + {}^{\equiv}\partial^{-1}$$

Important here is that if $^{\equiv}\partial^{-1}$ is cancelled then $88 = 11 \times 8$ and if 88 is considered to be the area of a square then: -

6.38

$$88 = \frac{4}{\pi}(r^2\pi), \therefore r^2 = 22, d = 9.38083152, c = 8 \times 3.683843923$$

That is to say that the inscribed circle would have a squared radius value equal to that of the count for 'Mi', and a diameter of a little over 9.38. The circumference would them be eight times a figure synchronistic with day 224.5 1943 (just under 3⅓ arc seconds). The figure of 9.38 is also synchronistic with day 224.

The obvious question is what does $22 \times (888 + {}^{\equiv}\partial^{-1})$ represent? Well firstly, $19542 = (305 \times 8^2) + 22$, which involves the total count for the 'Eldridge', but perhaps more important is that: -
6.39

$$\frac{19542}{88} = 222.0681818$$

This result is almost exactly the count for 'Lawrencium' +103, and has the obvious connection to yours truly. The count for 'Mira', 41, and hence Norman's contactee case study, appear in the next stage in the series along with Earth's orbit around the Sun.

The next extrapolation is taken from Superstring theory but I emphasize that here I am not expressing an opinion about Superstring theory. My opinion, such as it is from an unqualified laypersons point of view, is left until later but *my* Martial Art stance leans toward String Theory, while from a physical point of view I tend to towards Particle Theory. You will find examples in the literature that report the 'SuperString Revolution', and The Theory of Everything, while others reflect the ideas of the famous Physicist Wolfgang Pauli who apparently replied that SuperString theory was '…not even wrong'. (See book references)
6.40

$$v = \sqrt{\frac{T}{\mu}}, \mu = m/l, \sqrt{\left[\left(\frac{1963}{556}\right)^4 - (^{\circ}C = 2)\left(\sqrt[8]{3600\sqrt{\frac{1963}{22}}}\right)\right]} \approx |\mathfrak{G}_g^{\circ}7|$$

The first part of eq.6.40 is the equation for a vibrating string under tension *T*. In the second part I have said that the average 'tension' for the years 1943 to 1983 is the mid point year, 1963, and that $\mu =$ 'Mi'. Coincidentally, the square root of this is 9.446018882. This

Mi Mathematics Part 6
G.A.T.E. ($\mathcal{G}$)

is synchronistic with The Sun's R.A. on day 224, so I have simply multiplied by 3600 and the taken the eighth root as in previous computations, 3.685054488. Using the same year, but divided by Norman's name count plus mine, taken to the fourth power. The square root of the result is almost exactly the determinant of the metric $\mathcal{G}7$ (1.000011448 × $|\mathcal{G}7|$ to be more precise).

Now, in ordinary strings and wires the formula in eq.6.40 is sufficient, but in Superstring theory additional items are considered. The expression below shows one of the early considerations where items (σ) and ($\partial\eta$) are other multiple elements. The underlined elements h^{ab} and $\sqrt{h}$ represent a 2-D metric and the square root of the determinant for that metric, respectively, a so-called flat world sheet: -

$$S = -\frac{T}{2}\int(\sigma)\underline{h^{ab}\sqrt{h}}(\partial\eta)$$

Substituting σ with eq.1.17 and h with $\mathcal{G}7$ the resulting equation is $\int(\sigma)\mathcal{G}7\sqrt{\det.\mathcal{G}7}$ and is equal to: -
6.41

$$\left\|\left(\int_0^3 \left(2x^4 + 2x^2 - 180\right)dx\right)\right\| \times \mathcal{G}7 \times |\mathcal{G}7| = 424.8\mathcal{G}7|\mathcal{G}7|$$

$$\begin{pmatrix} 380348.4356 \\ 854.2559 \end{pmatrix} = \begin{pmatrix} 47^3 \times 3.6634 \\ \sqrt{e^{3.6743^2}} \end{pmatrix}$$

47 ='time': 3.6634 & 3.6743 $\cong$ $\overset{\equiv}{\partial}$, and again we have some incredible synchronicities. I am not suggesting that Superstring theory and the ideas herein support each other, I have just used similar constructions to show how far the synchronicities may go.

The next topic concerns Spinor theory, or perhaps more correctly here, 'Spinorial Object' theory. Basically a 'Spinorial Object' is an object that is capable of rotation while being attached to something that can be twisted. When the object is rotated through 720°, 4π radians, the attachment twists but the twists can be removed without rotating the object. Appendix 3 illustrates how this can be done using a belt (a Tae Kwon Do belt actually) and a book (the replacement book on mentioned on page 104). Any flat length of material, such as a piece of ribbon, can be used as long as it is firmly held in place by a weight on the table. One must be able to twist the belt without it becoming dislodged at the 'fixed' end.

Attach the 'free' end to an object that can be freely rotated, perhaps a two-inch square (5cm square) piece of cardboard. Put a mark on the cardboard so that you can identify your starting point. Hold the piece of cardboard at full belt length as shown and rotate the piece of cardboard a full 360° <u>anti-clockwise</u>, so that your mark is in the original position. Now repeat the full 360° turn. The belt is now twisted twice over. Keeping hold of the piece of cardboard in the rotated position, move it the inward towards the fixed end until it and the fixed end are side by side, with the cardboard slightly to your right. Keeping the cardboard *precisely* in the same rotated position move it away from you going beyond and under the fixed end. Now move the cardboard in an anti-clockwise direction behind the belt and take it in your left hand keeping it *precisely* in the same rotated position. Move outward from the table and pull the belt out to full length so that the cardboard is now at the original starting point. You will find that the belt is also in the original, untwisted position.

In the above example the piece of cardboard is the spinorial object. However, other spinorial objects display deeper ideas, such as the rotations of the corners of a cube. One corner can remain in the same position but the faces of the cube will be in a different orientation.

In the above exercise both object and connection were physical items, but there have been various formulations that use a 'non-physical' or 'imaginary' connection so it is not surprising that Time has been considered in this way. However, as in the above exercise, the connection must be firmly fixed at both ends. Though it is not hard to visualize Time perhaps being fixed on an object, or all objects, the question then arises about the fixture of Time at the 'other end' – what and where is it?

Though the content of the previous paragraph is important is not my main point here. The spinorial object can be tracked in various ways, one of which is with Quaternion Algebra, but here, I just want to consider the process of Quaternion multiplication.

6.42a

$$r = qp = (a + ib + jc + kd)(x + iy + jz + kw) =$$
$$a(x + iy + jz + kw) + ib(x + iy + jz + kw) +$$
$$jc(x + iy + jz + kw) + kd(x + iy + jz + kw) =$$
$$ax + aiy + ajz + akw + ibx - by + kbz - jbw$$
$$jcx - kcy - cz + icw + kdx + jdy - idy - dw$$
$$[ij = k, jk = i, ki = j, ik = -j, kj = -i, ji = -k]$$

Rearranging we have: -
6.42b

$$r_1 = (ax - by - cz - dw)$$
$$r_2 = (ay + bx + cw - dz)$$
$$r_3 = (az - bw + cx + dy)$$
$$r_4 = (aw + bz - cy + dx)$$

Now, if $q = a,b,c,d$ and $p = x,y,z,w$ we find that when $q = 22,5,5,6$ and $p = 24,2,2,4$ then $r_1 = 484 = 22^2$! Given the apparent complexity of quaternion multiplication this result involving 'Mi' and $182 + 374$, '...up to twenty four...' and day 224, must rank very high on the scale of synchronicities. Substituting 22,1,8,2 in to a,b,c,d and 'time' with my birthday 47,3,4,2 in to x,y,z,w, the total r_1 to r_4 is 1702, which is very close to the synchronicities 1702.1961 (see page 54). Stranger still is that when the same process is used for 'USS Eldridge DE173' = 3,0,5 = b,c,d, 2,2,4 = y,z,w the result of the total r_1 to r_4 is $1702 - 148$, the difference is very close to $|℟7|^2$. There are other synchronicities (such as one that might connect to the Chimes expression and the simultaneous equations) and even though I might be criticized for using quaternion algebra in this way, it may have a role to play herein.

The idea of spinorial objects is all very well but what about the ideas presented in this work – where is the connection? Good question. The answer is perhaps not as simple as I might hope as it uses mixture of ideas. Return to the piece of cardboard that was our spinorial object and write on the upper surface the number 182, my name count. On the underside write the +number, 281. Now repeat the spinorial experiment, only this time write down the number of occurrences of both numbers appearing on the upper side: -
Sp.1

$$a.0° = 182, \quad b.180° = 281, \quad c.360° = 182,$$
$$d.540° = 281, \quad e.720° = 182$$

We have three occurrences of 182 and two occurrences of 281. Adding together equals 1108. Do exactly the same with Norman's name and the answer is 2068.
Sp.2

$$\frac{\dfrac{1108}{182} \times 281}{180} = 9.503907204, \quad \frac{\dfrac{2068}{374} \times 473}{360} = 7.26503268$$

The idea here is that we divide by the source number then multiply by the image number and then divide the result by the nearest multiple of 180°.
Sp.3

$$(9.503907204 + 7.26503268)^2 = 281.1973448$$
$$9.503907204 \times 7.26503268 = 69.04619642$$
$$\frac{2068 - 1108}{360} = \stackrel{\equiv}{\partial} - 1$$

There are two (very) approximate synchronicities in the first equation, Sp.2, and three reasonable synchronicities in the second, Sp.3. The figure of 9.5 is reminiscent of the Sun's R.A. on day 224 and 7.265 is reminiscent of $2^{\equiv}\partial$. The figure approximating 281.2 has the integer value of the mirror image of 182: 69 is synchronistic with the count for Thailand, while the last result is the same as that found in previous matrix work. However, there are 'deeper' synchronicities here and they relate to day 224. Firstly, the second line of eq.Sp.3 suggests multiplying the Sun's R.A. on day 224.5, 1943, by $2^{\equiv}\partial$, which of course would give a result similar to the one given in eq.Sp.3. Secondly, multiply the first line of eq.Sp.3 by the second and take the square root and apply the Earth's inclination correction formula and the result consistent with the Sun's R.A. on day 224. Thirdly, multiply the second line of eq.Sp.3 by the third line then take the 4th root and the answer again is consistent with day 224 figures in the Lists of Part 3. These ideas are not so simple but they seem to be relevant here.

There has been considerable reference to the Golden Ratio (Golden Mean) and to numbers that are close to 1.618033989. Can the Silver Mean, $(\sqrt{2})-1$ (sometimes denoted as Ag_σ), be used at all? Three results of eq.6.43 are all synchronistic.

6.43

$$\frac{\tau}{Ag_\sigma} - Ag_\sigma + \left(\sqrt{1536} - 39\right) = 3.683901922$$

$$\frac{^{\equiv}\partial^3}{Ag_\sigma} = 119.0117871, \frac{1}{Ag_\sigma} = 2.414213562$$

Finally, we enter the topic of Number theory. If we concern ourselves with $(\mp N)+1$ and finding the prime under 2^n we have: -

6.44

$$(\mp 374 + 1) + (\mp 182 + 1) = (847 + 1) + (463 + 1) =$$

$$(2^4 \times 53) + (2^4 \times 29) = 1312 = 41 \times 2^5, 2160 - 1312 = (\mp 374 + 1),$$

$$(53 \times 29) - 1 = 1536$$

The number 1312 is synchronistic with several items including the

count for 'Mira' and Norman's contactee case. Perhaps important is that there is a direct connection to the determinant of the expanded form of ^eC and day 224: -
6.45

$$1536 - 1312 = 224, \frac{1312}{2.4^2} \times \frac{360}{365.256} = 224.5000767$$

The number 23 combined with the other prime 73 produced the SETI number, eq.1.25, 1679, and there are further Number theory synchronicities evident here.

In conclusion there are one or two numbers that I would stress as being important throughout.
6.46

$$\frac{374}{22} = 17, \sqrt{119 + 188 + 160 + 17} = \sqrt{182 + 78 + 224} =$$

$$\sqrt{182 + 110 + 124 + 68} = \sqrt{111 + 123 + 250} = \sqrt{374 + 110} =$$

$$\sqrt{66 \times 2 ^{\equiv} \partial} = \sqrt{224 + \left| \mathbf{M}_c^s \right|} = \sqrt{124 + 224 + tr.\left(\mathbf{M}_c^s \right) + 123} =$$

$$\sqrt{188 + 160 + 123 + tr.\left(\mathbf{M}_c^s \right)} = \sqrt{+\left(39 ^{\equiv} \partial \right)} = \sqrt{+47 \times 4} = 22$$

- CMA both American and Mexican 188,160: 'Edward Cameron' and 'Duncan Cameron', 124 & 126: 'Enki', 39. 'Andrew Hero', 111: Lawrencium, 119: my name count (or DE173), 182: 'Mira Ceti',78: Norman's name, 374: Norman's contactee study name, 110: 'Omicron Ceti' 124: 'Time', 47: 'Twin', 66 & 'USS Eldridge', 123: $^{\equiv}\partial$: Day 224 and Matrix **M** from page 88.

<u>Interpretation of eq.6.46</u>

It might be argued that the fourteen numbers were bound to produce some numerical synchronicities, and I am sympathetic to that point of view. However, we are dealing with numbers that represent events that would otherwise be unrelated and it may have been Mi's intention that we *should* connect them.

Mi Mathematics Part 6
G.A.T.E. (G_{∂}°)

- I find it very strange that Norman's name count plus the count for the name of his contactee study should equal the square of 'Mi', and a little disconcerting. Whether what the contactee believed happened, did *actually happen or not* is irrelevant, the numbers 'add up', deepening the mystery even further. Indeed, the way in which Norman's study and investigation unfolded did so with coincidences – but that is for Norman to tell and not I. However, the question is that if Mi wanted Norman and I to know that Mi was involved in this witness's experience, what would be the reason? If we infer that this is connected to the USS Eldridge, and the Montauk Laboratory, what are we to deduce from that? The plot thickens, so to speak when: -
6.47

$$110 + [188 + 160] + [124 + 126] + 263 + 305 + 111 + 152 = 1539$$

$\sqrt{1539}$ is very close to the result of item 1a of eq.3.15, 39.2, which was computed using the simultaneous equations and Chimes expression. One criticism of eq.6.47 is that there must have been more people involved with the events from USS Eldridge, and the Montauk Laboratory, than I will ever be aware of, but for sure, the USS Eldridge *was* involved in some mysterious affair, so: -
6.48

$$22^2 - (110 + 305) = 69$$

Thailand has a count of 69, which of course, then involves Norman, Mi, and me. However, is the '69' in eq.6.48 only a name count, or could it also refer to something else?
6.49

$$\left(\frac{1}{110} + \frac{1}{305} + \frac{1}{484} \right) = \varepsilon, \left[\varepsilon^{-1} - 68 \right]^2 = 1.619617538,$$

$$\varepsilon^{-1} = 69 + \frac{1}{3.6678}, \sqrt{\log_n (110 + 305 + 484 - 68)^2} = 3.666778$$

The number 68 represents the count for 'Cetus'.

• When 'twin', 66 = 3 ×22, is multiplied by $\overset{=}{\partial}$, the result is 11 × 22. What might be the message here? I am not suggesting biological twins, but previously we had C.M.A., American and Mexican 188 & 160, 'Duncan Cameron' and 'Edward Cameron' = 250: -

6.50

$$([188+160]+[124+126])-374=224$$

$$\frac{(188+160+124+126+66)}{\overset{=}{\partial}^4}=3.673519568\cong\,\overset{=}{\partial}$$

The message seems clear. Norman was meant to suggest 'twin' so that we might connect to day 224.

• The items involving the matrix **M** (item 8 of eq.3.15) might be important, and if we consider the number 124 as 'Edward Cameron', then the other numbers associated matrix **M** are all from the same events mentioned herein. Furthermore: -

6.51

$$\sqrt{\log_n\left(tr.\underset{C}{\overset{S}{\mathbf{M}}}\times\left|\underset{C}{\overset{S}{\mathbf{M}}}\right|\times224\right)}=3.67930388$$

This figure is close to the midpoint of $\overset{=}{\partial}$ plus the figure for day 224.5, 1943. This raises the question – what does the matrix **M** of eq.3.15, with the simultaneous equations and the Chimes expression, really represent? A clue may be provided in a_{ij} of **M**: -

6.52

1. $\sqrt{\sum\left(a_{ij}\right)^2}=\sqrt{29+38+41+40}=\sqrt{148}=12.16552506$

$2+9+3+8+4+1+4=31,7\times31=217,365-217=\sum\left(a_{ij}\right)^2$

2. $r_L=qp=(22+i1+j8+k2)(47+i3+j4+k2)$

$r_E=qp=(22+i3+j0+k5)(47+i2+j2+k4)$

$\therefore\sum_r\left(r_L-r_E\right)=\sum\left(a_{ij}\right)^2$

Mi Mathematics Part 6
G.A.T.E. (Ɠ)

The first result is $0.999993848 \times |Ɠ7|$ and therefore is also very close the to the string analogy but the next result is obtained by taking the sequential addition of the four parts under the radical. Since there are seven months in our current year that have 31 days, this leaves 148 days for the other months. The second equation involves the quaternion equations previously mentioned which indicates a connection to the matrix **M**. These considerations are part of ongoing study.

• The remaining two items of eq.6.46 involve mirror image numbers of 'Enki' and 'time' along with $\overset{\equiv}{\partial}$. Enki was introduced by Norman just as $\overset{\equiv}{\partial}$ was introduced by me, and of course, we have been considering 4 time categories introduced by Mi. Therefore it is 'highly' synchronistic that <u>the square root of all eleven cases is equal to the count for 'Mi'</u>. What would be *your* thoughts about eq.6.46?

At this point I want to take a step backward because very little has been mentioned about *sequential counting* and although there are several issues here, I shall attempt to rectify the situation with just two examples. Firstly my own name count of 182 with a sequential count of 11. The sequential count is tempting in that it might signify 'twin' and one wonders if the 'twin' episode during my school years (as mentioned in the Mi book) might be relevant here. Very well then, let there be two of me: -
6.53a

$$182/11 = 364$$

The missing factor is, of course, 22 – what else could it be! Now take Norman's name count, multiply by 22 and divide by the sequential count: -
6.53b

$$\sqrt{\frac{374 \times 22}{14 \times 224.5}} = \sqrt{\frac{2244\overset{\equiv}{\partial}}{14 \times 224.5}} = 1.617986714$$

In eq.6.53b I have gone a stage further because in this work I have often associated Norman with day 224.5, and here the result is very close to τ. Even ^eC is represented here as 2244 (see page 68).

Finally, in a similar fashion but substituting 'time' for the sequential count: -

6.54

$$\frac{556 \times 22}{47} = 260.2553191 = \left|\overset{s}{\underset{c}{\mathbf{M}}}\right| + 0.2553191,$$

$$\sqrt[4]{\frac{47}{0.2553191}} = 3.683440148$$

Norman's name count plus my name count multiplied by 'Mi', divided by 'time' is equal to $|\mathbf{M}|$ (eq.3.15) plus 0.2553191, but even this fraction is shown as being synchronistic with day 224.

There we shall leave it – well, not quite. Remember the function, $\overset{\equiv}{\partial}$, from page 166, and that it contains the figure of 2.7: this is coincidental to the 2.7 Kelvin of the background radiation thought to have been the remnant of the 'Big Bang', which is important to theorists in both Astronomy and Particle Physics. One wonders about such connotations here. Finding the root of the equation $e^{-x} - x = 0$ (I used the Newton approximation method) also turns up some interesting numbers when combined with $\overset{\equiv}{\partial}$.

It was Norman who made a remark in one of his e-mails to me (given in the Mi book) about the response '...up to twenty four...' Mi stated that Mi life does not use numbers yet Mi actually mentions a number *in* the response. If Mi was aware of the numerical synchronicities that have been found so far in this study, Mi's enigmatic response becomes magnified. For a life form that doesn't use numbers Mi seems to know a lot a number theory!

Mi Mathematics
Epilogue

I frequently ask myself, and I suspect that most people do in one way or another – are 'things' really the way they seem to be? Well, the camera doesn't lie... does it? The various instruments that we use are made to produce what we perceive with our senses, and if a camera takes blurred photographs we send it for repair. How can we be sure that what *we* see is true reality and the short answer is that we can't be sure, but we do the best with what we have. The question is compounded by theories about the macro and micro levels of existence and one can read a 'popular science' book and find from one point of view that there are many micro-dimensions to our existence. These unify and create our macro-dimensions experiences of everyday life. Alternatively, one can read about the 'standard model' that other theorists claim is not satisfied by certain multidimensional theories, and feel that answers are within Quantum theory. *Why we feel* what we feel is somewhere locked away in 'who knows where'. It is all about *connections* and how the Laws of the Universe allow those connections to be made and the question of 'why those particular Laws and not others' is a separate issue.

Bringing the discussion closer to home as it were, I have put before you what I think are the connections between Norman Oliver's researches and my Mi experience, but could there be another alternative. During our researches we, Norman more so than I, met the alleged 'mind control' experiments that were carried out at the Montauk Laboratories, Long Island, USA. These alleged experiments were not just about individuals but seemed more concerned with the populace. I therefore, have to ask of my entity experience, "were 'things' really the way they seemed to me?" Was I subject to, either by design or by accident, some mind control experiment where my reactions to a certain image were being examined? This is not that far from what Norman Oliver suggests in the Mi book, except the suggestion here is that the root cause might be right here on Earth.

Nevertheless, such a suggestion does not fulfil an explanation about the synchronicities themselves – who found

Mi Mathematics
Epilogue

them and how did *they* explain the existence of such numbers. Some may view the synchronicities as obscure and obtuse and, depending on your attitude, they may be so, but in the end we have to bow to the system that we have developed to help us count. It doesn't matter whether we are counting true physical objects such as oranges, cars or people – or imaginary objects such as dragons and unicorns, one plus one equals two and that's the end of it. Regardless of what the entity Mi thinks, our number system worked for the ancients and it works now.

The reason for considering name counts in the first place was due to the various synchronicities, starting with my wife's birthday being the same as my mother's and knowing that my birthday is 23 days to years end. After the entity experience, I then wondered what would correspond to 3×23 and I soon found that 'Thailand' had a count of 69. I had also considered 'Siam' with a count of 42 and although this was the same as 'Odin' (see the Mi book for details) I wasn't sure if this was a legitimate move. Adding them together gives 111, which has connections with the Montauk Laboratory site but at the time, I hadn't yet got to that point. I then multiplied 'Thailand' and 'Siam' together and divided by 23 which gives exactly the same count as 'Thailand' plus 'England', 126. However, although there was no doubting this was a synchronicity, I really was not satisfied and thought that there might be more support contained in the year number when Siam became Thailand. This too, was not clear because Siam was renamed 'Thailand' twice, once in 1939 and again in 1949. I went to live in Thailand 46 years after the second renaming, 2×23, but finally I decided not to include these details in the Mi book. On reflection perhaps I should have done so, at least in passing, so to speak, because 1949 divided by 23 squared gives 3.68431009, a figure synchronistic with day 224, 1943.

The mirror image numbers, (decimal system), also require much more investigation, where certainly at the two and three digit levels there is a connection. For example, with two digit numbers, when subtracting the smaller image from the larger the result is always a number that is devisable by 3. Then multiplying by $^{\overline{\overline{=}}}\partial$ will give a number that is the result of doing the same subtraction on three digit numbers. In other words, the result from the three digit numbers is always devisable by 11. We appear to have two groups calculable with 3, $^{\overline{\overline{=}}}\partial$ and 11.

Ep.1

Dif.	1	11	21	31	41	51	61	71	81	91
10	9	2	3	4	5	6	7	8	9	10
11	2	0								1
12	3		9							
13	4			18						
14	5				27					
15	6					36				
16	7						45			
17	8							54		
18	9								63	
19	10	1								72

The series for 20 starts with 18, for 30 it is 27, and so on for the other series. The numbers in small print are sequential counts. Note also that other than zero the diagonal sequential counts are all 9. The sequential count for the difference of three digit numbers is 18. For example, $\{(78,87), (41,14)\} = 9$, $\{(374,473), (182,281)\} = 99$. More formally, $[Sq.(\text{$\frac{1}{1}$-$\frac{1}{2}$})_n] = 3x$, where x is an whole number. The table does not answer the question of why 9? The reason comes from the (necessary) assumption that the subtraction of one number from another is based upon: -

Ep.2

$$(a \in \mathbb{N} \wedge b \in \mathbb{N} \Rightarrow a * b \in \mathbb{N}), (*) = -,+,\times \div$$

If this were not the case we would have to admit the possibility that 4422-2211 ≠ 8844-6633 and simple counting would be much more complicated. As it is, as long as two numbers are multiplied by the same ratio, the answer will always be in accordance with that ratio.

Mi Mathematics
Epilogue

With $+$ we have the added knowledge that the two numbers contain exactly the same digits. In a two digit number let (a,b) and (b,a) represent $+_2$ then: -

Ep.3

$$\frac{90}{\underset{81}{\overset{09}{}}} = \frac{\max t, \min u}{\underset{\max t - 1, \min u + 1}{\overset{\min t, \max u}{}}}, \quad \frac{81}{\underset{63}{\overset{18}{}}} = \frac{\max t - 1, \min u + 1}{\underset{\max t - 1 - 2, \min u + 1 + 2}{\overset{\min t + 1, \max u - 1}{}}}$$

Since the maximum is always 9, the two digits in the answer are merely set complements and so their addition can only be 9.

With regard to items in this book, could such a system have any relationship between Norman, Mi and me?

$$\frac{(281 - 182) + (473 - 374)}{3^2} = \frac{99 + 99}{9} = \boxed{22}$$

I rest my case.

So numbers have a direct relationship to each mirror image which in turn is related to the sequential count. In Ep.3, the sequential count appears to be *invariant* and with ideas in Part 4 involving a little Set theory, one is perhaps guided towards the Invariant theorems in General Topology. It remains to be seen, however, just how important this group might be in a general way but this is a topic for another occasion.

The final topic is one that I referred in the Mi book Epilogue, the 'Repeatable Relative Function', RFF. I had hoped that I would be able to introduce this topic much earlier but the apparent complexity of the RRF means that I have much more work to do before I can write about it, perhaps another book entirely. Although the synchronicities do play a part, the structure is so complex that the only analogy I can come up with is a type of Time 'DNA'. I have dubbed the issue 'time gene', $\mathring{t}$, and might have some similarity to Mi's Component Time, mentioned in the Mi book. Here is a brief introduction to RRF.

Mi Mathematics
Epilogue

Consider first some simple random numbers, say 9111 and 6391 and the process of $+$.

Ep.4

$+_>$	$+_<$	$+_> - +_<$	$+_>$	$+_<$	$+_> - +_<$
9111	1119	7992	6391	1936	4455
7992	2997	4995	5544	4455	1089
5994	4995	999	9801	1089	8712
999	999	0	8712	2178	6534
			6534	4356	2178
			8712	2178	6534

While the repeated $+$ for 9111 ends at zero it is clear that for 6391 when the numbers reach 6534 the process continues with repetition, never ending in zero. Now, something strange seems to happen because $6391-6534 = 39^{\equiv}\partial$, enter our 'old friend', Enki. Even stranger is that $(6391-2178) \div (8 \times 39^{\equiv}\partial) = 3.682692308$, consistent with figures in the Lists. However, $39^{\equiv}\partial$ does not appear as a factor in the original number 6391, but $(39^{\equiv}\partial$ -22) appears in the subtractions, bar the first, and all of these have a sequential count of 18. The subtractions of $+$ for 9111 have a sequential count of 27.

Now, what is the relationship between 22 and 121? Of course, by division it is $0.1818r$ (r = recurring) but $6391 \div 121 = 52.8181r$, so the conjecture is that any number divided by 121 that gives a result of $x + 0.8181r$ will produce similar results as 6391. Choosing twins 11 to 77 and each time adding $0.8181r$, then multiplying by 121, the answer is yes, except for 66, where the sequence ends at zero. The word 'twin' has a count of 66.

However, there is something a little deeper here. It turns out that simple multiples ($\frac{1}{2}$, 1, $1\frac{1}{2}$ etc.) of $0.1818r$ will also give similar results, and $0.8181r$ is $4.5 \times 0.1818r$. The basic fraction appears to be $\frac{1}{11}$. If this is true then dividing 9111 by 121 and substituting $\frac{i}{11}$ (i =1 to 9) as the fractional part, then multiplying by 121, the sequence should be similar to 6391.

Ep.5 $(75 + \frac{i}{11})$

$75 + \frac{1}{11}$	$\frac{2}{11}$	$\frac{3}{11}$	$\frac{4}{11}$	$\frac{5}{11}$	$\frac{6}{11}$	$\frac{7}{11}$	$\frac{8}{11}$	$\frac{9}{11}$
9086	9097	9108	9119	9130	9141	9152	9163	9174
2277	1188	1089	0	8811	7722	6633	5544	4455
5445	7623	8712		7623	5445	3267	1089	1089
0	4356	6534		4356	0	4356	8712	8712
	2178	2178		2178		2178	6534	6534
	6534	6534		6534		6534	2178	2178

$\frac{10}{11}$, 9185, follows a similar pattern to $\frac{7}{11}$. So the theory only partially works and what does work for 66 does not work for 77. It seems to be that this process might be the result of certain Group Theory interactions. Having said that, it is time to move on.

It would seem that $\overset{\equiv}{\partial}$ is either the, or part of an underlying theory concerning numbers, or functions, that exhibit simple multiples of $0.1818r$. I have claimed that $\overset{\equiv}{\partial}$ is connected to time and 224, so what does the count for 'time', 47, belong to? $\overset{\equiv}{\partial}^2 \times 3^2 \times 47$ belongs to the repeating group (RRG), so does the count for 'Enki', 39, but 22 cancels immediately. 'Enki' + 8 = 47 so we have $\overset{\equiv}{\partial}^2 \times 3^2 \times (39 + 8)$. However, 8 = [$|{}^{e}C|$] 1536 ÷ (3×8^2 ['Eldridge']). In addition, 47 remains in the same repeatable group when: -.

Ep.6

$$\overset{\equiv}{2}\partial \times 3^2 \overset{\equiv}{=} \partial^2 \times (39 + 8) = 7238$$

$$374.18\dot{1}\dot{8} \times 121 = 45276, 182.18\dot{1}\dot{8} \times 121 = 22044$$

$$\frac{45276 + 22044}{222 + 78} = 224.4, \frac{374.18\dot{1}\dot{8} \times 182.18\dot{1}\dot{8}}{7238} = 9.418226577$$

39 behaves differently and changes to the non-repeating group. I

have named the expression $(\overline{\overline{\partial}}^2 \times 3^2 \times 47)\, RRF_{t1} = \mathring{T}_1$ and $\overline{\overline{2}}\partial\, (\overline{\overline{\partial}}^2 \times 3^2 \times 47)\, RRF_{t2} = \mathring{T}_2$. Also in eq.Ep.6 is Norman's name count and mine processed similarly by adding $0.1818r$ to give five digit numbers. When these are added together and divided by 'Lawrencium'+103 and 'Mira Ceti' the result is 224.4. The impact of this is doubled by dividing the name count rational fractions by RRF_{t2} deriving a figure synchronistic with the Sun's R.A. on day 224. If these results are not uncanny then I don't what is.

Now take a slightly different view and say that 121 represents the basic unit of $\mathring{T}$, but instead of the formula on the previous page use $\mathring{T}_1 = 39 + 47 + 35$. The reason for doing this is that 39 comes from 'Enki' a (timeless) God, while 47 represents (endless) 'time' and 35 might then represent some physical aspect of our environment while also being a member to the same group as 39 and 47. 35 is neither synchronistic to items in the Mi book or herein, but it was mentioned on page 154 of the Mi book. My name count minus 147 equals 35 and $147 \div 35 = 4.2$, which just happens to be the mirror image of 2.4 (see Parts 4 & 5). However, I don't think this is enough justification for using 35. There are one or two other ways to incorporate the number 35 (see page 61) but at the moment I personally feel that they lack justification. Perhaps something will turn up in the future, perhaps not.

Ep.7

$$3^2 \diagdown \begin{array}{c} 182 \\ | \\ -\mathring{t}^8- \\ | \\ 374 \end{array} \diagdown \;\overline{\overline{\equiv}}\partial^2 = 6243 = RRG,\; 4\sqrt{\dfrac{121+556}{\overline{\overline{\equiv}}\partial}} = 3.686203521$$

In Ep.7 a $\mathring{T}_1$ unit is constructed using both Norman's name count and mine and $\mathring{t} = 47^{0.125} = 1.618125613 \approx \tau$. The reason behind this idea is that there might something analogous to a chemical valency bonding property in the indices. The number 47 could be connected to four other $\mathring{T}_i$ units or numbers. However, let the index power sequence (2,8,2) be the number 282: -

Mi Mathematics
Epilogue

Ep.8

$$(282 \times 121) - 33920 = 202, 3^2 \times 47^0 \times {}^{\equiv}\partial^2 = 121$$

Converting 202 back to an index sequence the result is the original 'repeatable multiplying factor'. The other equation in Ep.7 indicates that there is no difficulty in finding a synchronicity with day 224. The conclusion is that there is a *theoretical* possibility of forming chains of such T_i units finally ending with something that might be a Complex Time Component.

There are several synchronicities that occur with 121 and 124 (Omicron Ceti) and 222, 374 and 182: -

Ep.9

$$2 \times 121 + (556 + 346) = 1144 = RRG$$

$$\frac{1144}{121} = 9.\dot{4}5, \sin^{-1}(\sin(1144)) = 8^2, 1144 = 39 \times 8 \times {}^{\equiv}\partial$$

$$\frac{1144}{22} = 52, \frac{1144}{2.4} = 473 + {}^{\equiv}\partial, \frac{1144}{2\pi} = 182.0732549$$

The first is synchronistic with the Sun's R.A. for day 224: the second with eight's or 'Eldridge': the third is self-explanatory. In the fourth 52 is the count for 'Earth': the fifth, 473, is the mirror image of Norman's name count. Dividing by 2π the result is a figure synchronistic with my name count. However, what might be more important geometrically is: -

Ep.10

$$\frac{1144}{\pi \sqrt[4]{\dfrac{22^4}{33920}}} = 224.629318$$

In Ep.10 the denominator uses the expression from Part 3, and 33920 arc seconds year 1943 (to the nearest second), the Sun's R.A. for day 224. Again, the coincidence is remarkable. If these figures do really represent some form of realistic sequence then we should be able construct a synchronicity from the figures of day 224 year 1943.

Ep.11

$$\left(\sqrt{33920 - 64}\right) + 121 = 305 \text{ [note that } 47 = 121]$$

In Ep.11 the word count for 'Eldridge', has been subtracted from the arc seconds value resulting in exactly the word count for the full designation of USS Eldridge DE173. The synchronicity is established. Note that $47 + 74 = 121$.

Finally we take an example from Quantum Theory known as the 'Fine Structure Constant' which has the composition: -

$$\frac{e^2}{4\pi\varepsilon_0 \hbar c} \approx \frac{1}{137.036}$$

The synchronicity here is that if 137.036^{-1} were viewed as degrees around a circle we would have: -

Ep.12

$$\frac{1144}{\pi\sqrt{\dfrac{360}{137.036}}} = 224.6685271$$

This result is very close to that of Ep.10.

Therefore, it would seem that the 'time gene' idea of combining units is worthy of further investigation and is part of on going study. However, as mentioned previously, this part of the study is proving difficult, especially when trying to visualize a compact $\overset{\circ}{T}_i$ multiunit. All I can say is 'thank you Mi for giving me something to do with my time, I mean, what else *could* I be doing?'

This has been a journey in to a synchronistic mystery. In this work, I have tried to give some idea of what is the legacy to the encounter with the Mi entity by the elaboration of the Mi book details. There is still much to be studied, certainly from a mathematical physics standpoint, perhaps from both Quantum Theory and Superstring Theory.

You, the reader, having finished this part of the journey with me, will probably be asking questions very similar to those that I think about every day. Even if you cannot accept my entity encounter, I hope the numbers presented herein have sparked a sense of curiosity and you will begin a study of your own.

For example, you might construct a simple 'crossword' table as shown below. Square the number value for each letter, with any numbers contained in a second word (if there is one), in bold type. Some simple sums might show synchronicities, as they do here for 'Lawrencium' and 'Mira'.

	L	A	W	R	E	N	C	I	U	M
L	144									
A		**1**								
W			529							
R				**324**						
E					25					
N						196				
C							9			
I								**81**		
U									441	
M										**169**

Subtracting the total for 'Mira' from the total of 'Lawrencium' gives: -

Ep.13

1. $\dfrac{1919-575}{365} = 3.682191781$, 2. $\dfrac{1919-575}{182 + \,^{\equiv}\partial^{-1}} = 2 \times 3.686783042$

3. $\dfrac{1919-575}{224} = 6$, 4. $\sqrt[6]{1919+575} = 3.68255641$

Mi Mathematics
Epilogue

Originally, I had noticed just the similarity between items 1 and 4 and that they were less than 0.5% greater than $^{\equiv}\partial$. The number 224 was the result of my name count plus 'Odin' (see Mi book) since I hadn't yet got to the point of examining the features of Norman's study. Item 2 shows the synchronicity between the numbers, my name count and the two Tridel factors.

When I began to include the details of Norman's study, I felt that I had already been introduced to it by the 'crossword'. One must be careful, however, and try to 'balance' the words similarly (as far as possible) as in the above example where the part identifying position, 'Ceti' & 103, for both have not been used.

Perhaps you will find answers – perhaps you won't. For me the search continues.

References

The ephemeris program referred to on page 84 has a 'read me' file containing the following information 'plan404 ephemerides The tables of coefficients....to JPL's DE404 ephemerides......The least squares fit to DE404 covers the interval from -3000 to +3000 for the outer planets, and -1350 to +3000 for the inner planets. Steve Moshier, moshier@world.std.com, December1995, December 1996

With reference to the arguments for and against Superstring Theory, I mention just two from among those 'popular' science books that I have read. Both authors enthusiastically express their position and therefore are useful to the layperson for developing an opinion. By author in alphabetical order: -

The Elegant Universe by Brian Greene, Vintage Books, ISBN 0-375-70800-1 (pbk)

Not Even Wrong by Peter Woit, Basic Books. ISBN-13:978-0-465-09275-8 & ISBN-10:0-465-09275-6 (hbk) (Also contains references to Loop Quantum Gravity)

Mi Mathematics
Epilogue Special – <u>Unification Theory</u>

Through much of the book I have maintained, on the basis of the synchronicities, that $\overset{\equiv}{\partial}$ is connected to our Time Continuum. By now you had probably thought that I had yet to 'prove' it and therefore my claims about $\overset{\equiv}{\partial}$ remained within the realm of the synchronicities. Well, that is about to change – that is, up to point.

We all live comfortably in a two-domain universe where Gravity keeps us firmly in position while Electrical Impulses, that keep us breathing, depend on microcosmic uniformity. Theorists say they are the ends of the same 'fundamental rod' and demand that there must be a way to unify them. At the time of writing, the debate is a hot one.

Here, I will present to you some simple equations that I believe provide at least, some justification for my claims about $\overset{\equiv}{\partial}$. However, I have to say that I very nearly abandoned this particular route of inquiry because I realized that it might contain the very mistake that *I* claimed, in the Prologue, others had made in *their* researches. The Gravitational Constant in metric units, Newtons, would not be the same as Imperial Pound units and although I could just use the usual conversion factors this would hardly be consistent with the methods and material herein.

In one of those times when I wasn't intentionally working something out but just doodling, so to speak, my thoughts went something like: -

UT1

$$0.5\left(\frac{182+\overset{\equiv}{\partial}^{-1}}{41}+\frac{182}{41+\overset{\equiv}{\partial}^{-1}}\right)+\frac{1}{182^{\frac{n-1}{n}}}$$

but $\sqrt[4]{182}\cong\overset{\equiv}{\partial}\therefore 182^{\frac{n-1}{n}}=182^{\frac{3}{4}}$

$$0.5\left(\frac{182+\overset{\equiv}{\partial}^{-1}}{41}+\frac{182}{41+\overset{\equiv}{\partial}^{-1}}\right)+$$

$$\frac{1}{\left(182^{\frac{3}{4}}+41^{\frac{4}{3}}\right)}+\frac{\overset{\equiv}{\partial}}{182+41}-\frac{1}{(182+41)^{\overset{\equiv}{\partial}}}\approx 4.448140987$$

232

I then added various other familiar numbers, as decimal fractions, to 182 such as: -

UT2

$$\frac{182.368388917}{41} = 4.448009485, \frac{182.374}{41} = 4.448146341$$

$$\frac{\equiv\partial^4}{41 - \frac{1}{10} \, \equiv\partial} = 4.448394252$$

I suddenly realized what I had found – 4.448 *is* the Force conversion factor for Newton / Pound usually found in textbooks (the accurate figure is 4.4482216). This means that the conversion factor is adequately represented in terms of the synchronicities herein and therefore converting one to the other is a synchronicity in itself. I then used the inverse Fine Structure Constant, divided by G, multiplied by the count for 'Mira' and then divided by my name count plus the day 224 $\equiv\partial$ equivalent, 0.368388917, as the decimal fraction. This meant that the result would be in Imperial units. The next thing to do was to find the same result but in Metric units. The

UT3

$$\text{A} \quad \sqrt{\log_n \sqrt{\frac{137.036}{6.673 * \times 10^{-11}} \times \frac{41}{182.368388917}}} = 3.66457047$$

$$\text{B} \quad \sqrt{\log_n \left(\sqrt{\frac{137.036}{6.673 * \times 10^{-11}}} \times \frac{1}{2} \right)} = 3.671805809$$

$$(3.66457047 + 3.671805809)\tfrac{1}{2} = 3.66818814 =$$

$$1.000414197 \, \equiv\partial$$

two equations of UT3 have a similar structure and illustrates that a figure very close to $\equiv\partial$ can be easily computed. Even the '½' in B might be considered as the inverse of the original $^\text{e}$C.

Equation UT3 clearly demonstrates that regardless of which system of measurement is used, Metric or Imperial, the factor $\equiv\partial$

has a part to play in the fundamental 'building blocks' of our reality. In addition, the two numbers that were the very beginning of the analysis are also present, allowing me to suggest that this book of synchronicities has now been justified. However, allow me to delay that claim for just another paragraph or two, because other numbers important herein also beg inclusion, 22 and 24 for example. Review the satellite equation using day 224.5 as the period T: -

UT4

$$R = \sqrt[3]{\frac{T^2 gr^2}{4\pi^2}}, R^3 = \frac{T^2 gr^2}{4\pi^2}, \frac{R^3 4\pi^2}{T^2} = gr^2 = GM$$

1. $$\frac{R^3 4\pi^2}{T^2 G} = \frac{(22 \times 10^{24})^3 4\pi^2}{6.673 \times 10^{-11} (224.5 \times 86400)^2} = 1.67435 \times 10^{73}$$

2. $$\frac{R^3 4\pi^2}{T^2 G} = \frac{(24 \times 10^{22})^3 4\pi^2}{6.673 \times 10^{-11} (224.5 \times 86400)^2} = 2.173763 \times 10^{67}$$

What I have done in UT4 is to change the position of the numbers 22 and 24 thereby calculating two mass values. Now find the mass ratio kg and then covert to lb.: -

UT5

3. $$\sqrt{\log_n \left(\frac{1.67435 \times 10^{73}}{2.173763 \times 10^{67}} \right)} = 3.681640453$$

4. $$\sqrt[8]{\frac{\left(\frac{1.67435 \times 10^{73}}{2.173763 \times 10^{67}} \right) \times 2.205}{\equiv \partial^3}} = 3.691081014$$

Considering the value of the numbers used in these computations and that the equations contain day 224.5 the results of eq.UT5 are nothing less than an astronomical coincidence. (Computations on MS Excel). Now combine the UT5 3 & 4: -

UT6

$$\sqrt{(3.681640453 \times 3.691081014)} = 3.686357712$$

This result is within the limits of the list on page 130.

Although there is considerably more to add I mention just one more strange synchronicity.

After squaring the addition of the mirror images 4.448 + 844.4, find $\log_n$ and then find the square root. The answer is 3.67256862. This is just 0.002709299 below the average for $\overset{\equiv}{\partial}$ plus $\overset{\equiv}{\partial}$ $_{224.5,\ 1943}$. [Note that '*', 6.673 × 10^{-11}, is the most common value used for G]

If you are still doubtful about $\overset{\equiv}{\partial}$ in this UT then consider the accepted value of the proton-electron mass ratio, 1836 to 1840 (integer values).

UT7

$$\sqrt[8]{\dfrac{\sqrt{\dfrac{1838}{137.036}}}{G}} = \sqrt[8]{\dfrac{3.662312648}{G}} = 22.00033463$$

Not only is the value of the numerator close to $\overset{\equiv}{\partial}$ but the final answer is almost exactly the count for 'Mi' – or does the number 22 refer to something else?

(Using the number 26, twenty-six letters in the English alphabet, another type of 'unification' can be found – but then that's another story.)

The foregoing equations suggest that the fundamental forces of Nature have connection with $\overset{\equiv}{\partial}$ and 3.684 (and therefore the 12th of August). Since both of these are connected to the synchronicities in Mi Mathematics, I make the conjecture that the synchronicities also have a meaning. I hope that some practicing Mathematical Physicist will take up the difficult challenge and search for those meanings. Well, I didn't say it was going to be easy, did I – who knows, a bonus might be a meeting with Mi and if that happens tell Mi to 'give me a call'.

Mi Mathematics
Appendix 1

In Parts 3 to 6 several additional synchronicities could have been cited but there comes a point where one has to decide whether their addition would be useful or not. This is illustrated by the equations of Appendix 1.2 below and the issue about Mi life not using numbers could, again be raised. The count for 'Mi' would appear to be associated with certain mathematical processes and if this interpretation is correct then we can expect to see it in further analysis. Other analyses that have not been considered for various reasons, yet turn out to be synchronistic, are considered in Appendix 1.1. Such ideas, I think, might produce a lively debate in some forum setting.

Appendix 1.3 concerns the Oliver Ratio and is mentioned again in Appendix 1.4 while Appendix 1.5 is concerned with what other situations in my life may be relevant.

Appendix 1.1

Reference has been made to the incident on July 4th 1947 close to the town of Roswell, New Mexico, U.S.A. There was no mention of this in the Mi book for two main reasons. Firstly, compared to other items neither Norman nor I have researched this incident in any depth. Secondly, I recently watched a DVD (for the second time) that I bought a couple of years ago titled 'Roswell', by Jonathan Frakes (of Star trek: The Next Generation). This time, however, I immediately noticed that there are 39 days from July 4th to August 12th, 224-185 = 39, the same as the count for 'Enki'. As one might imagine I instantly reached for pencil and paper and the very first sums I did were: -

Ap.1

$$\sqrt[4]{\frac{104 \times 39}{22}} = 3.684841539, \sqrt{\log_n (104 \times 72 \times 95)} = 3.670822 \cong {}^{\equiv}\partial,$$

$$\frac{(104 \times 72 \times 95)}{365.256} = 1947.565543$$

The first figure is close to the figure given in the list for 1943: secondly, 'Newark' and 'Montauk' multiply 'Roswell' and the result is close to ${}^{\equiv}\partial$. In the third result, although the actual day would be the 25th, the year and month certainly match up with the incident at Roswell.

With my name count, 182-104 = 78, 78 being the count for 'Mira Ceti'. Norman's name count appears on several occasions but here only one is given, plus another that involves our combined name counts, and the count for Cetus: -

Ap.2

$$22^2 - \underset{\equiv \partial}{\frac{22}{}} - 104 = 374, \underset{\equiv \partial}{\frac{22 \times 104}{}} - 68 = 556$$

The military security at the site of the Roswell incident was such that even one of the engineers who constructed the 'experimental balloons', said that there was nothing about the balloons that would warrant such security. So based on this alone it would seem that there was something of extreme importance to the military at the site. The Freedom of Information Act in the U.S.A. does not help because large areas of a document appertaining to the incident are apparently 'blacked out', which supports the idea of high military interest.

However, the concern here is that with other computations the synchronicities above pose a question as to why 'Roswell' should be synchronistic at all. One might suggest on the one hand that this is an example of a single coincidence, or on the other hand did something materialise at Roswell that was related to the 'Eldridge / Montauk' affairs? Obviously, with the synchronicities found so far I tend towards the latter alternative, but this raises a whole series of other questions, none of which will be discussed here.

Appendix 1.2

In Part 1 the reader may have noticed that the equation: -

Ap.3a

$$y = x^4 + x^3 + x^2 + 2, \frac{dy}{dx} = 4x^3 + 3x^2 + 2x = 141$$

was really: -

Mi Mathematics
Appendix 1

Ap.3b
$$f(x) = x^4 + x^3 + x^2 + 2 \text{ about } x = 3$$

and that: -
Ap.3c
$$\frac{dy}{dx} = 4x^3 + 3x^2 + 2x = f'(x)$$

Proceeding in this way, $f^{(0)}(x)....f^{(4)}(x)$ is nothing more than a Taylor expansion of a polynomial, and in this case has a total of 490. In eq.Ad.3d below, again the synchronicity is uncanny and –

Ap.3d
$$\frac{490}{22} = 22 + \frac{1}{\underset{\equiv}{\equiv}\partial}$$

– cannot simply be explained away as just a coincidence. Other polynomials constructed in the same way give synchronicities that also require further investigation.

Appendix1.3

Apart from its derivation and one further use, the Oliver Ratio, $O_{\equiv}$, has not been used. Having said that, the inverse of $O_{\equiv}$ could be legitimately employed in equations on page 133 such as: -

Ap.4

S1 $$1536 \times {}^{\equiv}\partial = 5632 = 22 \times 16^2 = 11 \times 8^3 = 11 \times \left(O_{\equiv}^{-1}\right)^3$$

S2, 7 $$\frac{66 \times 5632}{24 \times 22 \times 8} = \frac{66 \times 5632}{\left(3 \times O_{\equiv}^{-1}\right) \times 22 \times O_{\equiv}^{-1}} = {}^{\equiv}\partial$$

The Oliver Ratio could replace multiples of eight whenever they occur thereafter. However, $O_{\equiv}$ does have another role to play in further theoretical techniques, illustrated in the following example. The number 144 was one of the derivations from the 'reaction chamber' of the Mi book and it is the difference between the counts of 'Mira Ceti' and 'Lawrencium' + 103. I had given both Mira Ceti and Lawrencium fundamental positions so let the number 144 be contained within an equation that *might* be used as three dimensional but containing the idea of the four Mi Time categories. Let the three dimensions be represented by, say, a polynomial in x, $a_0x^2 + a_1x + a_2 = 0$, and let $a_0 \times a_2 = a_1$. Let $a_0 \times a_1 \times a_2 = 144$, and since we are considering four Time categories, let $a_0 = 4$ so that $a_2 = 3$ and therefore $a_1 = 12$. In addition, introduce first and second order derivatives to symbolize our common use of velocity and acceleration, $a_0x^2 y'' + a_1xy' + a_2 = 0$: -

Ap.5a

$$a_0 x^2 y'' + a_1 xy' + a_2 y = 4x^2 y'' + 12xy' + 3y = 0$$

Let $x = 4$ (again representing the four time categories) then: -

Ap.5b

$$4x^2 y'' + 12xy' + 3y = 64y'' + 48y' + 3y = 0$$

$$y(x^u) = y(4^u), -2 < u < 2,$$

$$u = -2, 64(-2)(-3)x^{-4} + 48(-2)x^{-3} + 3x^{-2},$$

$$u = 2, 64 \times 2 + 48 \times 2x + 3x^2$$

The graph of the interval -2<u<2 shows that this differential equation equals zero between $u = -1$ and $u = -2$, so: -

Ap.5c

$$4x^2 y'' + 12xy' + 3y = 64y'' + 48y' + 3y = 0, x = 4$$

$$u = -1.5 = y(x^{-1.5}) \therefore 64y'' + 48y' + 3y =$$

$$64(-1.5)(-2.5)4^{-3.5} + 48(-1.5)4^{-2.5} + 3 \times 4^{-1.5} = 0$$

Therefore a solution to the differential equation appears when x is equal to $4^{-1.5} = \frac{1}{8} = O_=$. Now, given the coincidence of '8' in the Mi book, should Ad.5c be considered as a 'stroke of luck', or something more meaningful in the present context? $e^{2.4}$ and $e^{-2.4}$ suggest the possibility of being solutions to a second order ODE of the form (y''-5.76y) but whether such connect to, say the Fine Structure Constant, remains to be seen and will be studied in the next title. One wonders if Mi has been an influence in 'guiding me towards such equations, but then this raises the question, again, about Mi life not using numbers..

Be that as it may, eq.Ap.5c has been 'assembled' and is not a model representing a given synchronistic situation that may or may not, have use in later studies.

Appendix 1.4

On December 26th last year I received part of a book order I had placed with amazon.com. One book is about [†]Symmetry and I began to read it that same evening. To my surprise I found that the first chapter is devoted to the ancient Babylonian methods adapted from Sumer. Because I have read some texts on Sumerian / Babylonian mathematical methods my surprise was not that these ancient mathematicians had used symmetry in their evaluations, but that the author gives the ancient mathematicians much credit for using methods that are so important in modern times. *"What is most important about the Babylonian mathematicians is that they began to understand how to solve equations"* is a short paragraph from the first chapter. Modern mathematicians have refined and developed such methods that at present have become fundamental to our contemporary ideas on both the Cosmological and Quantum states of our universe. Perhaps I am bias but I believe that this adds further weight to my comments about Norman's introduction of Enki into our analysis.

Symmetry is another topic to be examined in my next title, but is mentioned here because it may add additional importance to the fact that Norman offered the name of 'Enki' (Mi Book page 86). For example, my full name count, 182, and the mirror image number 281. According to the procedure used previously +182 = 463 but because the three digits obey certain 'laws' connecting them, it is reasonable to assume that some pattern might emerge in the construction of other (+) numbers obeying the same 'laws'. Given the number 182 it begins with odd digit, has an even digit in

Mi Mathematics
Appendix 1

the middle and even digit at the end, while 463 has the reverse sequence. We could therefore say ⊣ (o e e) = (e e o) = (o e e)⊢. Next, 'Lawrencium' 119 = 1020, ⊣ (o o o) = (e e e) with '10' interpreted as a single digit. So the particular 'law' that says the digit 1 is an odd digit, zero is defined to be even. If digits are basic then ⊣ 119 = ⊣ (o o o) = (o e e e), but either way from three odd digits the result involves a change that contains three even digits. From here it is not hard to imagine that a particular mirror image number could be defined as a single structure but viewed from different angles.

Finally, what situations in my life have relevance to the synchronicities? As I remember even when I wanted to take a certain path I did, in fact, choose the opposite and I now wonder if I really had the 'freedom' to choose. I suppose this could be said of many people but it does seem that I was 'destined' to be in Thailand at some point. The question of what is or is not significant is very difficult and is probably best left to history to answer, yet the date that I left England to go and live in Thailand was surely important. It is exactly the same date as my first marriage, 8th April, and if the number of days between these two events is considered: -

Ap.6

$$((1995 \times 365.256) + 98) - ((1961 \times 365.256) + 98) = 12418.704$$

$$\log_n (728685.72 - 716267.016) = 9.426959002$$

Although the result has the dimension of days, the figure is synchronistic with R.A. on day 224. However, other items of less importance to me remain vague in memory and I am certainly not able to give exact dates.

However, certain names that I am able to recall can be counted with accuracy, such as 'Church Lads Brigade' as mentioned in the Mi book (page 3). The count for this is 143, equal to the count for 'Victoria Park' (referred to as the 'local park' on page 1 of the Mi book) where 143 is also equal to 'Enki'$\times^{\overline{\overline{=}}}\partial$, but are they important herein? The other park referred to on page 4 of the Mi book, Grove Hall Park, was closer to my home than Victoria Park and was my destination when I had my 'twin' experience, but the count for 'Grove Hall Park' is 145, a figure not mentioned among the synchronicities. As far as my Mi entity experience is concerned, one might expect Grove Hall Park to be more synchronistic than Victoria Park, but apparently not. Having said that the average of 143 and 145 is 144, which *is* synchronistic.

The question is – to what extent have the lives of Norman and I been influenced by the entity Mi and will this continue? Broader still, How many other people have suffered similarly?

[†] *Why Beauty Is Truth*: *A History of Symmetry by Ian Stewart. Basic Books 2007 ISBN 10*: *0-465-08236-X*

Mi Mathematics
Appendix 2 – Equation Reference

In this reference section the equation number with the page number in square brackets is followed by a brief description of the equation. Example: 1.1[16] Simple harmonic equation. 'syn.'= synchronicity or synchronicities

1.1[16] simple harmonic equation

1.2[16-17] 'Earth', 'Moon' and 'Sun': '8 and 3 syndrome': Tridel 1, $\frac{11}{3}(\overline{\overline{\partial}})$, or Tridel 2, $1 + \frac{3}{11} (\overline{\overline{2\partial}})$,

1.3[17] Sidereal motion with $\frac{4}{\pi}$

1.4[18] Parent name counts

1.5[18-19] Fibonacci recursion sequence

1.6[19] Combined name counts & 'time' $\cong \tau$

1.7[19] τ & $\frac{4}{\pi} \approx \overline{\overline{2\partial}}$

1.8[20] $(\overline{\overline{\partial}}/\pi) \approx$ Name counts

1.9[20] Name count of 81

1.10[20] Name counts & $\overline{\overline{\partial}}$

1.11[20] Name counts Including 'Mi' and 'Enki'

1.12[21] Combined name counts $\cong \overline{\overline{\partial}}^{-1}$

1.13[21] Polynomial about 3 & $\frac{dy}{dx}$

1.14[22] Ditto

1.15[22] Ditto

1.16[22] Polynomial about 3

1.17[23] $\int y dx$

1.18[23] Ditto

1.19[23] Area of ellipse

1.20[24] $\frac{4}{\pi}$ & $\overline{\overline{\partial}}^{-1}$

1.21[24] $\frac{4}{\pi}$

1.22[24] Ditto

1.23[25] Proof of $\frac{4}{\pi}$

1.24[25] 22 & $\overline{\overline{\partial}}$ syn. from ellipse

1.25[26] From SETI 1679

245

Mi Mathematics
Appendix 2 – Equation Reference

Mi Mathematics
Appendix 2 – Equation Reference

2.10[53] Mid-bar designation for twin digits

2.11[53] Fibonacci sequences defined with mid-bar designation

2.12[54] Fibonacci sequence exmple

2.13[54] Area of ellipse plus mirror image (⊕)

2.14[54] Norman's full name count & mirror image

2.14b[55] Ditto with Mira Ceti count

2.15{55} Norman & Chimes count +

2.16[55] Norman's full name counts +

2.17[56] Counts for Lead (the metal)

2.18[56] Author's name count with Lawrecium and Mira Ceti

2.19[57] Norman's and the author's individual name counts +

2.20[57] Norman's and the author's name counts +

2.21[57] Mirror Image theory for $\bar{t}_3$

2.22[57] A proof

2.23[58] Mirror Image theory for $\bar{t}_4$

2.24[58] Ditto

2.25a[58] Synthetic division of a generating-function

2.25b[59] Ditto

(–)[59] Chio's method on + matrix 1, 2 & 3

(–)[60] Ditto 4, 5, 6, & 7

(–)[62] Chimes matrix 1 & 2

(–)[62] Tetrad 1

(–)[63] Tetrad 2

(–)[63] Tetrad 3 with Chimes expression, ^eC

2.26[64] tetrad rotation

2.27[64] proof of eq.2.26

2.28[65] Minimum tetrad matrix

2.29[65] Synthetic division for generating-function alternatives for $+^eC$

2.30[66] Ditto

2.31[67] Root substitution for eq.2.30

2.32[68] $^eCS_i = 22$

2.33[68] $^eCS_i = 2$

2.34[68] $^{\overline{\overline{=}}}\partial\ ^eCS_i = 22$

2.35[68] Sequential addition, Sq_iS_i

2.36[69] Last term in ^eCS_i as sequential

2.37[69] Ditto

2.38[69] ^eC as a diagonal matrix

2.39[69] $|^eC_s|$ & $\int(Ex)$

2.40[70] $|eq.2.33|$

2.41[70] $|\int(Ex)|$

2.42[70] Ditto with $+$ and name counts

2.43[71] $\sqrt[8]{}$ 'time' $\approx \tau$

2.44[71] Fibonacci sequence for twinned seeds, $+ \approx \tau$ & $^4\!/\pi$

2.45[72] Counts for 'E. Cameron' & 'A.Bielek' $\approx\ ^{\overline{\overline{=}}}\partial$

2.46[74] Counts for 'Carl Meredith Allen' and 'USS Eldridge' $=\ ^{\overline{\overline{=}}}\partial$

2.47[74] Counts for 'Carl Meredith Allen' & 'Morris Ketchum Jessup' $\approx\ ^4\!/\pi$

2.48[74] Sixteen number matrix

2.49[75] Total counts $= 1959$

2.50[75] Name counts 'merry go round' with $+$

2.51[76] 'Newark' and 'Norfolk' counts with $|\int(Ex)|$

2.52[76] 365 day with Counts for 'Carl Meredith Allen' & 'Morris Ketchum Jessup'

2.53[77] Time periods and $e^{\overline{\overline{=}}\partial}$

Mi Mathematics
Appendix 2 – Equation Reference

2.54[78] Planet names in binary code = ½$\overset{=}{\partial}$

(–)[79] Christian counts

(–)[81] Eigenvalue and Eigenvector values for basic tetrad matrix

3.1[82] Norman's researches and Chimes = $\overset{=}{\partial}$

3.2[82] Day 224 and Mira ≈ 9.442

3.3[83] Degrees/ days ≈ 9.271

3.4[83] Sun's Right Ascension formula

3.5[83] Sun's Right Ascension calculation for day 224

3.6[84] Corrected Sun's Right Ascension calculation for day 224

(-)[84] Short year/R.A. list

3.7[84] Sun's R.A.– eighth root of arc seconds

3.8[85] Synchronicity of arc seconds derived from 22^4

3.9[85] Ditto

3.10[86] Sun's R.A. on March 3rd 2002

3.11[86] Ditto

3.12[86] From eq.3.12 but using 22 days

3.13[87] Norman's name count and det. ^{e}C

3.14[87] Why 2002?

3.15[88] Synchronicities with ^eCS_i, [^eCS_i], items 1a and 8 = $C_{J}1$

Name count[89]

(–)[89] Sixteen numbers

3.16[89] Mi Ratio

3.17[90] Ditto

3.18[90] Ditto-generalized

3.19-3.22[91-92] Root 4 of 22^4 ÷ (arc seconds 12th of August)

3.23[92] (^{4}⁄π)^2 or τ

3.24[92] Eq.3.23 synchronistic with τ

3.25[93] $^eCS_i = 24$

3.26[93] ^eCS_i using Mi Ratio

3.27[94] Eq.3.26 synchronistic with 3.68…

3.28,d1 & d2 [94] Frequency and wavelength

3.29[95] Name count matrix using S_i

3.30[96] $^eCS_i = 0$

3.31[96] Ditto

3.32[97] Coulomb's Law

3.33[97] Coulomb's Law plus Gravitational Inverse Square Law

3.34[98] Frequency and period function

3.35[99] Ditto

3.36[99] Ditto with first harmonic

3.37[99] Ditto

3.38[100] Velocity of Sound, 343 m/s, converted with name counts

3.39[100] 343 with $(^{\overline{=}}\partial \div 4)$ and Planck length

3.40[101] 16th root of eq.3.39

3.41[101] 64th root $\approx{}^{\overline{=}}\partial$

3.42[101] Exp. value of item 5 in eq.3.15 $\approx$ det. ^eC

3.43[101-102] Exp. $^eCS_i \div{}^{\overline{=}}\partial \approx \tau$

3.44[102] 365.256, Exp. ^eCS_i & $^{\overline{=}}\partial$

3.45[103] Exp. $^eCS_i \cong{}^{\overline{=}}\partial$

3.46[103] $\sqrt{(\text{Exp. }{}^eCS_i)}$

(–)[105] Speed of sound

(–)[105] Meters to inches $\approx{}^{\overline{=}}\partial$

(–)[106] Weibull model

(–)[106] Bessel function power series $J_1(x)$

3.47[107] Factorials- name counts, items 1-7

3.48[107] Ditto

(–)[108] Gamma function Γ - definition

3.49[109] ^eCS_i Gamma function evaluations

Table 1[109] $\Gamma(x)$ table

Table 2[111] Exponential and Power models

3.50[111] From Table 2- model constants with $^{\equiv}\partial$

3.51[112] Ditto

3.52[113] Model constant, 2.7, with $^{\equiv}\partial$ in correction formula

3.53[114] Model constant, 2.7 with 224.5 & 365 days

(–)[117] $z = x + iy$

3.54[117] $Cos(x) + iSin(x)$ ^eCS_i evaluations

3.55[118] Graph constants with π, τ & $^{\equiv}\partial$

3.56[118] Graph constants with name counts

3.57[118] ^eC constants as radii

3.58[119] eq.3.57 with 365

3.59[119] Ditto with 22 & $^{\equiv}\partial$

3.60[119] Circumference syn.

3.61[120] Equation 3.60 generalized & Oliver Ratio defined

3.62[120] Fourth roots of -16

1a[122] Exp. $^eCS_i = \cup T$

1b[122] Standard height /velocity calculation $s + v = 16t^2$

1c[123] $\prod e^i = 1$

1d[123] $\frac{d}{dx} e^i = -1$

1e[123] $e^i \div 22$

C_s4[124]

3.63[124-125] Various $\sqrt{(e^i)}$ & $\sqrt{(^eCS_i)}$ syn.

3.64[125-126] Ditto with 365

3.65[126] Ditto with $^{\equiv}\partial$

3.66[127] Day 118 and 224

3.67[127] Circle $\tau \approx$ arc seconds Sun's R.A. day 224

3.68[128] A proof – inscribed circle

S1[133] Det. $^e\mathrm{C}^{\equiv}\partial$

S2(1-4)[133] Ditto with name counts and $+$

S2(5-13)[133-134] Ditto

S3[134] Det. $^e\mathrm{C}^{\equiv}\partial \times 365 \div 224$

S4[135] Log_n(Det. $^e\mathrm{C}^{\equiv}\partial$)

S5[135] (Det. $^e\mathrm{C}^{\equiv}\partial$) plus numbers from Norman's researches

S6[135] (Det. $^e\mathrm{C}^{\equiv}\partial$) Ditto

S7[136] (Det. $^e\mathrm{C}^{\equiv}\partial$) with $8^{\equiv}\partial$

S8[136] (Det. $^e\mathrm{C}^{\equiv}\partial$) with various counts $\approx {}^{\equiv}\partial$

4.1a[137] Magnetic force on a particle

4.1b[137] Ditto-vector diagram

4.2[138] Differential equation of eq.4.0

4.3a-d[138-140] Matrix computations of eq.4.2

(1-6)[140-142] Various syn. with results from eq.4.3

4.4a-b[142-143] vector projection

4.5a[144] 4×4 matrices- name counts and $^{\equiv}\partial$

4.5b[144] Trace of eq.4.5a $\approx$ $+182$

4.6[145] More 4×4 matrices- name counts and $^{\equiv}\partial$

4.7a-d[146-148] Linear combinations

4.8a-c[148-150] evaluation of e^{M1}

4.9a-b[150] Synchronicities using trace of e^{M1} - (Roswell)

4.10-12[151-152] evaluation of e^{M3}

4.13[152] Synchronicities from trace e^{M1} & e^{M3} combinations

Mi Mathematics
Appendix 2 – Equation Reference

Appendix 2 – Equation Reference

Mi Mathematics
Appendix 2 – Equation Reference

6.11[198] Substituting counts in gravitational expression

6.12-6.13[198] Ditto

6.14-6.16[199-200] 2-D metric & arc length

6.17-6.21[200-201] Ditto using day 224 & Earth's orbit parameters = τ interval

6.22[201] 365, 2.4 & $e^{2.4}$

6.23[202] Earth-Sun radius × 2.4

6.24-6.25[203-204] Relativistic velocity

6.26-6.30[204-206] Galilean & Lorentz coordinate transformations

6.31[206] Relativistic velocity,τ^{-1}

6.32[208] An interpretation of a velocity 'jump'

6.33[208] 3-D (x, y, z) with day 224 syn.

6.34[208] Ditto = ct

6.35[209] 4-D time

6.36[209] Eq.6.35 & day 224 connection

6.37-6.39[209-210] 'Glimpse beyond'-Geometrical possibilities

6.40-6.41[210-211] String Theory

6.42a-6.42b[213] Quaternion multiplication

Sp.1-3[214] Spinorial object syn.

6.43[215] Silver mean

6.44-645[215-216] A little number theory-syn.

In conclusion [216-219], Eq.6.46 syn. in combinations equal to 22
Eq.6.47-6.49 Norman's recent contactee study
Eq.6.50 66 & twin ideas
Eq.6.51-6.52 Interpretation of eq.3.15

6.53a-6.54[219-220] Sequential counts

Epilogue
Ep.1-3[223-224] Mirror image numbers

Mi Mathematics
Appendix 2 – Equation Reference

Ep.4-11[225-229] Repeatable
numbers and 'time gene'

Ep.12[229] 'Fine Structure
Constant'

Ep.13[230] 'Crossword' syn.

Epilogue Special
Unification Theory
UT1-UT7[232-235]

Appendix 1
Ap.1-2[237-238] Further
reference to Roswell

Ap.3a-d[238-239] Taylor
expansion

Ap.4[239] Oliver Ratio

Ap.5a-c[240] Oliver Ratio as
solution to Differential
equation

Ap.6[242] 8th of April 1961-
1995

Mi Mathematics
Appendix 3-Spinorial object

1. Hold the piece of cardboard at full belt length.

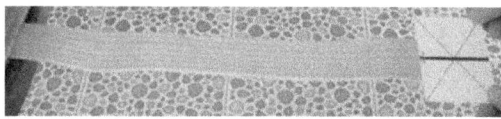

2. Rotate the piece of cardboard a 180°

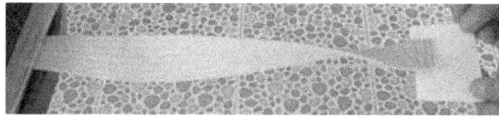

3. Rotate the piece of cardboard another 180° to complete full 360° turn

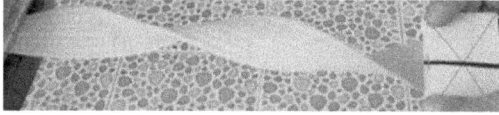

4a. Now repeat the 180° rotation –

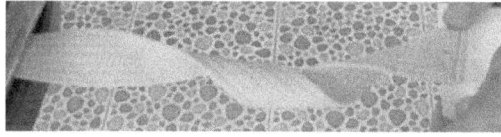

4b. – and again to complete the second the full 360°

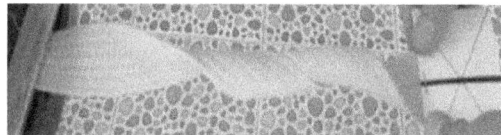

5a. Move the cardboard slightly to your right, then inward towards the fixed end until the cardboard and fixed end are side by side

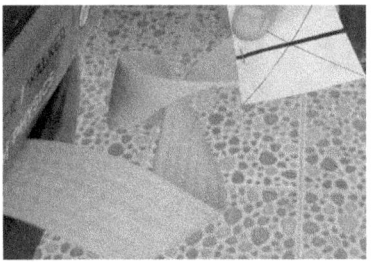

5b. Now move the cardboard beyond (behind) the fixed end

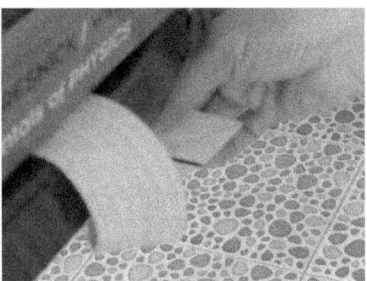

6. Without changing the orientation of cardboard take the cardboard in the left hand and move it to your left (anti clockwise)

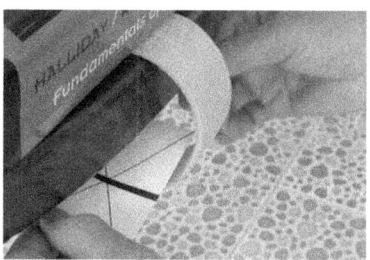

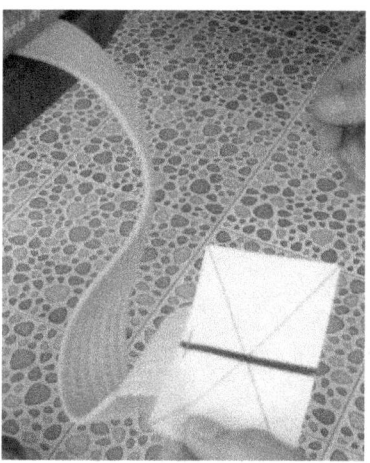

7. Completing the move return the belt out to full length so that the cardboard is now in the original place that you started from

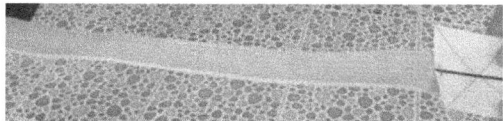

Index

Index

Index

Index